Healing Spirits

TRUE STORIES FROM 14 SPIRITUAL HEALERS

Healing Spirits

True Stories from 14 Spiritual Healers

Judith Joslow-Rodewald and
Patricia West-Barker

Photographs by Susan Mills

THE CROSSING PRESS
FREEDOM, CALIFORNIA

For information on bulk purchases or group discounts for this and other Crossing Press titles, please contact our Special Sales Manager at 800/777-1048.

Visit our Web site: **www.crossingpress.com**

Library of Congress Cataloging-in-Publication Data

Healing spirits : true stories from 14 spiritual healers / [edited by] Patricia West-Barker, Judith Joslow, and Susan Mills.
    p. cm.
  Includes bibliographical references.
  ISBN 1-58091-064-5 (pbk.)
    1. Spiritual healing. 2. Parapsychology and medicine. I. West-Barker, Patricia. II. Joslow, Judith. III. Mills, Susan.

BF1045.M44 H43 2001
615.8'52'0922--dc21

00-064432

Acknowledgments

It truly "takes a village" to complete a book! We would like to take this opportunity to thank the following people for their contributions: Pamela Cady, Jane Clavin, Nadine Koenig, and Steve Rodewald transcribed endless reels of interviews. Bless you all. It was not an easy job.

Sharon Wolmouth, Larry Teacher, and Ellen Levine provided encouragement in the early days. Without their support, we may never have gotten this book off the ground. When we began to lose heart, Nadine Cobb and Cynthia Black stepped in to provide new momentum. Without their encouragement, we may never have completed the interviews. Our gratitude, too, to Elaine Gill, publisher of The Crossing Press and our editors, Caryle Hirshberg and Sharon Cadwallader, who understood immediately what it was we hoped to accomplish with this book. They helped us bring this four-year journey to a happy completion.

We interviewed a number of healers whose stories, for various reasons, are not included in this volume. Since many wish to remain anonymous, we won't name those people here. We will simply thank them all for the good work they have done, and continue to do, to make the world a saner, safer, healthier place for us all.

Many people read and commented on drafts of various chapters—David Barker, Richard Cady, Kris Estes, Judy Fratus, BJ Harris, Katherine Kenney, Jean Sousa Makalou, Terry Mason, Lucille Minuto, Frea Rosen, Susi Steiner, Louise Thomas, Joan Vann, and Jesse West-Barker—we thank you all for your time, your interest, and your sharp eyes. Your insights helped us refine the book's format and clarify its message. Steve Rodewald deserves an especially large thank-you for reviewing the final drafts of all the chapters. His editorial suggestions helped polish our prose and bring out the best in each chapter.

Finally, a big round of gratitude to the friends and family who offered ongoing encouragement and support: Susan thanks Bob and Nicola Anderson, Karen and Casey Bancroft, Martha Blowan, Felice Boucher, Ron Bouffard, Valerie Chelseth, Doreen Closson-Mahoney, Camille Davidson, Jane Donelon, Susie Drucker,

Tereann Greenwood, Ann Hurley, Charlie J. Lemay, Mee, Charles and Connie Mills, Wendy Morgan, Jane Page-Conway, Winter and Michael Robinson, The Secret Women, Tony, The Women's Artist Tribe, Sylvia Wyler, Gale Yohe, and Gert Zimmerman.

Judith acknowledges, with love, her three children—Zachary, Aaron, and Maya; Gary, who cared for them during her many weeks of travel; Bronco, her dog, for being a ready companion, journeying into nature at all hours of the day and night; Hugh Kent, for the many hours walking in the woods, weaving talks with spirit; Chris Raywood, for his spiritual support, integrity, and humor; and Jane Larsen, for the gift of a writing retreat. She also wants to thank a Higher Being for bringing Steve Rodewald back into her life, and Steve for walking in love beside her.

Pat thanks Richard Cady for never questioning the value of the work and never complaining about the travel expenses, even as he was undertaking a healing journey of his own; Susan Capuano for clearing the clutter and keeping us afloat; Barbara McClellan for time and more time; Barbara Walzer and Sally Hayden von Conta for holding the sign for the finish line; Nancy Weston for good food and a kind heart; Kris Estes for the yak-buttered box that allowed the last few chapters to slip out with greater ease; and David and Ted Barker, Jesse West-Barker, and Florence West for their ongoing support and understanding.

May the love and support you all gave us return to you one hundred-fold!

This book is dedicated to Frea Rosen,

weaver of webs of relationship and light,

whose constancy, love, and belief in our efforts

held the space for this book to take form.

Contents

There are three things our culture has forgotten:
basic health, healing and holiness.
All three words have the same linguistic root,
and the concepts have the same goal:
sanity, integrity, completeness,
salvation, happiness, liberation, magic.

—Holger Kalweit
Shamans, Healers and Medicine Men (1992)

Introductions

Patricia West-Barker

Like many healing journeys, this one started with an illness. One morning, I woke up tired. The next morning, I was even more tired. Within a week, my life—at least the way I was accustomed to living it—had completely unraveled.

I knew I had been overworking and was on the edge of burnout, but this was beyond any exhaustion I had ever known. I—who had always been able to dig in and find the resources to work one more hour or churn out one more chapter—no longer had the energy to even sit at my computer, much less the clarity of mind to do my work. I had been a freelance writer for a number of years, accustomed to sixty-hour work weeks, juggling multiple projects for corporate clients and writing hundreds of pages of complex material off the top of my head.

Suddenly, I hadn't the brain power to complete a simple paragraph. A full page was beyond question. For the first time in my professional life, I had to send a project back to a client, undone.

The fatigue and befuddlement lingered and I began the rounds of doctor visits and lab work. But allopathic medicine had no answers for me. Many hours, x-rays, blood tests, and dollars later, I was still undiagnosed, still barely able to drag myself around the house. Work was no longer an issue. Getting through the day was my major concern. If I had had more energy, I probably would have been terrified. As it was, the days passed in a gray blur, one running into another, days turning into weeks, weeks becoming months.

After a while, stomach and chest pain joined the fatigue as my constant companions, and my fear as well as my discomfort increased. It felt as though my life were slipping away, and I didn't know how to stop it.

About a year into this process, Judith—a close friend for more than twenty years—suggested I consult with a medical intuitive. She had taken a weekend workshop several years earlier with Winter Robinson, an intuitive who lived in Maine, and was impressed with her abilities. Better yet, she still had Winter's card!

With nothing to lose, I picked up the phone and called Winter. She agreed to do a reading for me and asked me to send her a letter outlining my symptoms and concerns. When Winter received the material, she would go into a trance state, record her responses, and mail me a tape.

Winter's tape was fascinating. She reviewed a number of body systems, pointing out strengths and weaknesses, prenatal and birth traumas, and body memories that she felt were affecting my health now. Her recommendations were simple: yoga, breathing exercises, dietary changes, acupuncture, and practice using my own hands and mind to move energy through my body. I followed her instructions and slowly—very slowly—I began to feel better.

At the time I spoke with her, Winter also told me that she was going to be giving a lecture as part of an in-service nursing training program at a hospital near me, and invited me to sit in on the portion of her presentation open to the public.

I attended the program and was most impressed with Winter's personality and delivery style, as well as her professionalism and ability to discuss intuition not as a magic act but as an everyday phenomenon. Perhaps, I thought, I could write again if I were really interested in the topic. I debated asking Winter for an interview, something that could be the basis of an article in a mainstream women's magazine.

As I returned from a break in the program debating the pros and cons of speaking to Winter, I looked up and there she was. Here was the opportunity I had been fantasizing about just a moment earlier. It felt as if a door was swinging open in front of me. I took a deep breath and stepped forward...

When I returned home, I called Judith immediately to tell her about the appointment. For some reason, Judith insisted that she had to come with me. She didn't know why, but she felt that she had to be there. She offered to drive me to Maine so she could sit in on the interview and I accepted.

Needless to say, the article for the women's magazine was never written. On the trip back to Boston, after a fascinating afternoon talking with Winter, Judith and I had another fantasy: Wouldn't it be wonderful, we thought, if we could spend more time like this—meeting people whose work we admired, hearing the stories of their lives, learning more about how unseen forces could affect not only our health but our everyday lives. Another fantasy—and the seeds for this book were sown.

We thought we could complete the work for this book in a year. We had a protocol, a list of questions, and a game plan: We would locate and work with twenty healers in ten geographic regions, people who represented all the major ethnic and racial groups in our country. That was what we thought—but that was not how this book chose to be born.

By the third interview, we had discarded our protocol and our list of questions. By the end of the first year, our racial, ethnic, and geographic distribution wish-list fell by the wayside. Rather than a rigid work plan, what we found was required of us was the ability to surrender to a process beyond our control.

Writing this book was like picking up a ball of yarn and watching it unwind. One interview would lead to another, each in its own time and place, and the questions appropriate to each person would arise naturally as we sat together. As we became more and more willing to trust the process that was unfolding in front of us, all the people and the pieces came together.

They say it takes three points to define a plane, to bring something into being in the physical world, and when Susan Mills joined the team as our photographer, our work really began to take off.

The three of us did things together that none of us would ever have contemplated doing alone. Although none of us had much money at the time we began this project, whenever an appointment with an interesting new healer beckoned, we always found the funds to buy one more plane ticket, rent one more car.

Every trip was worthwhile even if the healer we visited chose not to participate or we decided we were uncomfortable about including the person for one reason or another. Our travels through the American countryside fed our souls as well as our eyes. They gave us an opportunity to know and bond with each other and turn our fantasy into a reality.

Time passed and one year turned into three. No matter how hard we pushed, we couldn't seem to make this book move any faster. With a nudge from Denise Linn, whom we interviewed in the second year of this process, we slowly got the message: We could not investigate spiritual healing from a distance. The forces we had been learning about, the forces that shifted and healed other people's lives, were also moving through our lives.

Some parts of this process were great fun. Holger Kalweit, in his book *Shamans, Healers and Medicine Men*, notes that the universe is synchronistic, synergistic, and symbiotic—and we certainly found that to be true. We were often amazed, and always entertained, by the many synchronistic events that guided us from the start to the completion of this book. When we were willing to note and follow the signs that appeared before us, things went well. When we attempted to work our will, we ran into delays and difficulties.

Other parts of our personal healing journeys were more painful. When you are in a healing process, we learned, anything that runs counter to your well-being becomes impossible to maintain. Things that are hidden away, tucked into dark corners of minds and bodies, surface. In the process of working on this book, health crises came and went, friendships ended, long-term marriages dissolved, career paths changed.

None of us is the same person we were when this journey began. Susan, who could barely describe herself as a photographer when we first met, is now an impassioned and well-respected mixed media artist. Judith, who had a more or less traditional private psychotherapy practice, has rediscovered and reconnected with her own psychic and hands-on healing abilities. And I have finally fulfilled my twenty-five-year heart's desire of moving from the East Coast to the high desert southwest.

And the journey has not stopped with us. As we shared what we learned and passed information and phone numbers to friends and family members, the benefits of the work we did with the healers we met spread, like ripples in a pond, first to the people we loved and then, through them, to people we have never met and never will meet.

As Peggy Huddleston, the last healer we interviewed, has noted, learning how to activate our own self-healing powers has become as essential to us as aspirin and band-aids. Not only our approach to healing, but the way we look at life has shifted—and we can no longer imagine living any other way.

Edgar Mitchell, Apollo 14 astronaut and founder of the Institute of Noetic Sciences, once said that "There are no unnatural or supernatural phenomena, only very large gaps in our knowledge of what is natural...."

The way the healers in this book look at and talk about life—and the unseen energies they work with to facilitate healing—are certainly no longer something we would consider "supernatural." Rather, they seem to be the most normal thing in the world, the natural heritage of thousands of years of human healing experience.

It was never our intent to offer proof of the existence or the effectiveness of spiritual, or energy-based, healing in this volume. We only wanted to share our experiences and impressions, and let the healers speak for themselves. Our hope was that this book would provide readers with an opening, a window into the amazing possibilities for healing available to all of us—not in some future society but right now, right here, on this planet.

We do believe that, in time, the split between the seen and the unseen, between science and nature, allopathic medicine and spiritual healing, will be resolved—probably by investigations now being conducted on the fringes of science itself. For those who wish to look into the data, Larry Dossey's book *Reinventing Medicine: Beyond Mind-Body to a New Era of Healing* pulls that research together quite convincingly.

We have arranged the chapters in the order in which we first met the healers. Each chapter opens with our impressions of the person being interviewed. The stories that follow are in the healers' own words, extracted from transcriptions of taped interviews. When, for clarity, it was necessary to insert a word or two, we enclosed those words in brackets. If there are words or concepts in these chapters that you don't understand, we apologize. To keep the storytelling format clear and flowing, we decided against footnotes or insertions into the text. We hoped that by intruding as little as possible into the text, you would have a more direct and intimate experience of each healer, getting a true sense of who each person is and how he or she works.

Every healer profiled here is different. Like the spokes on a wheel, each offers a different insight into a process that is difficult to define—at least in the terms we currently have available to us. Once you begin to question the possibilities for healing, we learned, you must also begin to question the nature of time, energy, and space—the very fabric of what we call reality. One thing all the healers would agree upon, though, is that the key to healing is within each of us—and the point of a healing practice is, ultimately, to empower clients to seize that key and unlock their own self-healing power.

We hope that this book will open doors for readers as it has opened doors for us, bringing new hope to those who suffer and new visions to those who seek to expand their definition of what it means to be a human being and live fully, healthfully, joyfully in the world.

Judith Joslow-Rodewald

I have always believed that there were larger forces guiding me. I feel this most strongly when I step outside the drama of "me." There are unseen beings, presences, that dwell in the air around me and ride on the currents of the ocean.

As a child, I would sit for hours on the rocks, mesmerized by the sea. These were peaceful and sacred times. There were no boundaries—just a deep connection with everything that surrounded me. It was as natural to be a rock, shell, or droplet of water as it was to be a person.

Since childhood, I have been magnetized by "daydreams" so powerful that they became, at times, my reality. It always felt so natural and easy for me to step into an inner world of visions or "pictures." The adults around me often became angry when I disappeared into these other realms, for at those times I no longer saw nor heard what was going on around me.

"What are you doing? Why are you doing that?" they would ask. When I answered that I did not know, they usually thought that I was either being rude or wasting time or both. How quickly and insidiously creativity, possibilities, dreams are squashed in children! But within every person is the ability to connect with the Divine, and it is from this energetic resonance that the soul is fed, that one's own creative and healing abilities open.

About four years ago, Pat—a friend for more than a quarter of a century—called to tell me about an interview she was going to do with a medical intuitive in Maine. Although I did not have a clue as to why, I knew with my whole being that I was to go with her.

As Pat conducted the interview, I drifted in and out of a dreamlike state—an exquisite blend of two realities: the present and another dimension that wove like ribbons of silk throughout the afternoon—and I learned why I had come to Maine with Pat.

Pat and I—two mothers—had conceived a dream with its gestation and birthing time unknown. The universe had beautifully orchestrated the conception of this book. Now it was time for us to be introduced to another woman, one who would complete our triad—our photographer, Susan.

In the time it took to complete our work, Pat, Susan, and I were separately and collectively challenged with life events that might have been devastating if we'd had to face them alone. Together though, we transcended all obstacles. Our relationship was created out of love, respect, and a shared dream. The silver threads that bind us together are strong and flexible and infused with light.

I often think about that magical afternoon in Maine, about the flow, the light, the enormous energy and love I carried within me that day. Although I did not know it at the time, it was that inner faith in the universe that was to carry me, to be my guide, through the book's completion.

I want to thank both Pat and Susan for all they have given me. We have all grown over the years of our shared journey, and they have helped to fertilize my soul, my being. I will walk with them in love and friendship into eternity.

Susan Mills

Working on this book has affected my life, my work, and the way I think about myself.

When I started to photograph the healers we met on our travels, I quickly learned that I couldn't work with them the way I worked with other clients. This project was not about me staging and orchestrating the shots, using reams of film, shooting until I was sure I had something I could use.

On this project it was the healers—not the photographer—who called the shots. I had to learn to get out of the way, bearing witness to what was happening instead of orchestrating it. And I had to learn to work within the window of opportunity each person afforded me. Some people were very comfortable with the camera and allowed me to shoot and re-shoot until we achieved an image we all liked. At other times, the window was very small. One of our healers would stay for only three shots!

Much of what I learned while I was working on this book has revolved around learning how to let go. First, I learned to let go of trying to cover all the bases when I was working. I discovered that I could take just a few shots and trust that the photographs I had were the ones I should have.

Then I had to let go of my fantasies about healers. I half-expected, half-hoped to meet superhuman men and women who could materialize from rocks. Instead, I met generous, insightful people who knew the value of a good laugh—no more or less human for their great gifts. I realized that by trying to make the healers I had the honor to work with *more* than human, I was actually de-humanizing them. So I learned not to put the individuals I was working with on pedestals, but to *be* with them as they presented themselves to us and to the camera.

As my approach to photography was changing, my identity as an artist also began to change, to grow stronger and more clearly defined. When I met Judith and Pat in 1995, I still thought of myself as a medical technician who happened to do photography—even though I had been showing my work in galleries in Maine since 1982.

Less than four years after I began work on this book, I was a recognized mixed media artist. Most importantly, I recognized myself as an artist. In the past few years, I have been invited to participate in gallery and museum-based shows in Maine, New Hampshire, and New Mexico; had my work featured in two books on healing and the arts; designed two well-reviewed theater sets; and served as sculptor in residence at a small New England college.

My mixed media artwork—which grew from my need to create props for some of my personal photography—is inspired by nature and by myth, by the physical world and the world of spirit. When I am working in my studio, I feel the same energy that I experience when I visit ancient stone circles and touch a more sacred space.

The objects and the photographs I create are my way of recording my inner journey. They embody my search for a metaphor that pierces the illusion of separation, honoring and illuminating both the visible and invisible realms. We are all individuals, yet we are all connected. When one of us takes a journey, it affects us all. It is my dearest wish that these photographs and stories help those who see them reconnect with the oneness we all share.

Winter Robinson

Bar Mills, Maine

I want to bring people back to the woods and to the meaning of winter on the planet. Winter is a quiet time—it's when the Earth is at its most creative, rejuvenating itself under a blanket of snow.

*T*he first time we pulled into the driveway of Winter Robinson's home, we were confronted by two large white geese. Honking and flapping, they surrounded our car, daring us to open the door and step into their domain. City-bred women that we are, we huddled behind closed doors until Winter appeared to casually shoo them away.

We had come to interview Winter for an article about women and intuition. Sitting on her back porch, however, looking over the lake and the garden of bird feeders hanging from the trees, we began exploring many more issues than we had originally intended: spirits and spirituality; nature and the supernatural; the roots of illness and the essence of healing.

It was as if we had suddenly stepped from a dark room into the light; had suddenly remembered how interested we both were in alternative healing practices; had suddenly gotten back in touch with another way of living in the world, where the unknown and unseen were as alive, as real, and as important as the known and the seen.

We consider Winter Robinson the "fairy godmother" of this book. When we realized we needed a photographer to capture the full essence of the healers we were meeting, it was Winter who introduced us to Susan Mills—and to the power and magic of working in threes.

Born in North Carolina, Winter Robinson studied music at the University of Tennessee and received her master's degree in psychology from the University of Virginia. At the time she discovered her psychic capacities, she was employed by the Department of Mental Health of the Commonwealth of Virginia.

After several years of intensive training to develop her abilities, Winter began practicing as a medical intuitive—a person who "reads" the body to see how healing may be facilitated. In the mid '80s, she moved to Providence, Rhode Island, to expand her work with physicians and students at the Brown University School of Medicine. Winter now lives and works in a secluded cove in Bar Mills, Maine, with her husband and partner, Michael, two dogs, a cat, and a pair of geese.

Together, Winter and Michael travel the world conducting seminars on intuition, paradigms, and creativity. To balance their inner work with physical activity, Winter and Michael lead a few workshops each year in the Abacos Islands, swimming and communicating with dolphins.

Winter spends a large portion of her time writing and working with physicians, nurses, and others in the healing professions. Writing, she says, is her meditation. It *nurtures her and connects her to her source. Winter has recently completed her first novel (science fiction, of course!) and produces a periodic newsletter called "Morning Coffee." To round out her endeavors, she has helped found a futuristic business consulting service known as THinc.*

Although she is spending more time teaching and "training trainers" these days, with Michael's assistance Winter continues to do individual intuitive readings for people who visit or write to her with questions about their health and well-being.

To me, healing is the body coming into its natural balance. When I'm doing my work, it's mainly helping the individual hear his or her body. Slow down, hear the body, bring it into a space that allows the body to do what it does naturally on its own.

If we cut ourselves, we don't know the exact moment the body heals itself. Suddenly it's healed; suddenly it's well. The body knows how to heal. We often get in the way of our own healing.

When I'm working with clients, I take them away from their world, their active world, into a space where they can go "inside." I'm like a travel agent. What I do is listen and see, psychically, where they're "traveling," what they're doing, and add suggestions or thoughts to help them expand their awareness of the whole concept of healing—pulling in energy, using energy in healing.

Chinese medicine believes that when an energy current (called chi) flows through the body with no blockage the body is well. When there's a blockage of that energy, problems develop. So we focus on the chi, moving it back into balance.

When I do medical readings, I don't even try to see what the people I'm reading look like. I'm more interested in their energy and how the energy moves through their body than in their physical appearance.

The Cellist

One of the first people I ever worked with was a woman, a cellist, who had temporal lobe epilepsy. I had done a medical intuitive reading for her. She thought she had a brain tumor, and I knew she didn't. From the medicines and her disorder, her hands had twisted and contorted and she had very slurred speech. She wanted to meet with me, but I kept saying, "I have nothing else to say."

But her therapist encouraged me to meet with her, so I did. I met with her, the physician from Brown University who did the initial reading with me, and her neuropsychologist.

I remember sitting on the sofa, looking at her and saying, "I've told you everything that I can say," and this voice in my head said, "Heal her!" I said to the voice, "You've got it wrong; I don't do healings." And the voice said, "Heal her!"

I argued with it: "I don't do healings. I scan the body. I don't do healings." It came back again, "Heal her!" So I looked at her and said, "Couldn't you give me somebody easy? I mean, she's really hard."

Then I remember turning to the client and saying, "This is what I see: your energy is turning in on you. I can feel it turning in. You need to turn it out. If you want to get better, it's got to go out."

And I immediately saw this picture in my mind of her in a previous life in Japan, where she'd let her nails grow so long that they pierced her hands. I told her that, too, and she turned white and said, "Oh my God, I saw that when I underwent hypnosis."

I think she may have completed the ending to the story herself and we ended the session. She thanked me, but she still had slurred speech and her hands were still twisted.

About two weeks later, the physician I worked with called and asked if I had heard what happened to her. I said, "No." My thought was, "Oh God, she died." He said, "She got well!"

One night she forgot to put on the splints that she used on her hands...and when she woke up, her hands were normal. She spent four days going around, seeing that her hands and her speech were normal, before she called her doctor. She went to see the doctor (with the therapist who had been present at the reading), played the tape I made, and told the doctor, "This is what happened."

The Power of Threes

My belief is that there were three of us there with a lot of focused energy, and I was able to see something the cellist had already seen. Somehow, in that process, she literally believed it, took the ball, and ran with it. And she healed.

I'm always working in threes; I believe that there is power in threes. I really do. If you want something to happen, you want three people working together with the mind-set to do it. Sometimes I work with my husband, Michael, to do a reading, and sometimes I work with a physician. That makes two of us. The patient, or a friend or relative of the person being read, is usually the third party.

There was a time when I was in Arizona and a physician I worked with in Rhode Island called me because the son of a mutual friend had been diagnosed with some type of lymphoma—very serious—and he said, "What can you do? Let's do a reading." I remember taking time just to settle in, and I remember that just as soon as I read the body, I said, "It's serious, but he'll get well; he doesn't have lymphoma."

Sure enough, he went for more tests. When they came back, it wasn't with the original diagnosis. Now, whether it changed as we looked at it or whether it was a misdiagnosis, I don't know.

Healings aren't always dramatic. A reading I did for an elderly woman in Rhode Island is a good example of a simple but effective remedy. She had suffered from shingles for years, and none of her medications could relieve her symptoms. The reading suggested that she needed to bathe in peppermint, and included instructions on how to do it. She took one bath and was immediately relieved of her pain. But even when a healing appears to be simple, I'm not sure how it works, or where the information comes from.

"The Help Knows"

I've read people in Australia as easily as I've read someone right down the street. I believe it's turning all of my awareness, all of my focus to that person. I believe I have a lot of help and the help knows. Maybe they get the information and just tell me. I definitely believe it's a team doing it, not just me. If we really knew how it worked, we'd be Nobel Prize winners!

I had some good teachers who taught me it's not you doing the healing, it's the higher source, whatever you want to call it. You're just the medium for it; you focus in and help the person pull in the information. You have to have the self-confidence, the knowledge to know the healing power is there. To believe in yourself, to believe in what you're doing or what's taking place. And at the same time, there's the paradox to know it's not you, you're just in touch with it.

There's a voice that speaks to me when I do medical readings. The voice always says "We have the body." Whoever "we" is. Or, it will say, "We are here and ready to begin." And when I'm finished, the voice says, "We're ready to leave the body now," and I let go of the body.

My belief is that when I look at a body, I take it on. I mean, I just feel it. It's like stepping into the body. I start at the head and I go all the way down, feeling it. It's in that process that I think something sometimes happens on the other end. I believe you can't look at something, enter its field, without changing it.

I believe a good intuitive just tells what is, and the individual discerns. I cannot legally do an evaluation or recommend treatment. I'm not a physician. I will never go against a doctor's opinion, for a lot of reasons. I may suggest a second opinion, or a third. I know a lot of people, and sometimes I say, "Go to this person, see what he or she says." It may be another physician, or someone in an alternative healing practice.

Animals Can Be Healed, Too

Once, when Michael and I were working in Australia, our house sitter called to tell me that our dog, Gisela, had a bulging disk in her spine and needed emergency surgery. The vet wanted us to give our consent over the phone. The operation might be able to cure Gisela, but it could also paralyze her.

We were coming home in a few days, so I refused to give permission for the surgery. Instead, I asked the sitter to keep her quiet. And I asked several of the people we were with to sit and help us visualize the dog bathed in white light, running around with a strong back.

That's just what she was doing when we arrived home: running around with totally healed disk. Gisela ultimately lived to be sixteen and a half years old—and never needed surgery.

Encounters with Spirit

My father, when he died, had come to me, had been with me—and that did not seem unusual to me. Never did I think, "Ooh, this is strange," it's just the way it was.

I was fifteen, away at school, when I woke up at 12:23 A.M. I remember sitting up in bed, and my father was there in the room. He told me he had had a heart attack and died; he was fifty-six. I got up, packed my suitcase, and waited for the call to come. While I was waiting, I decided I had not packed anything for a funeral, so I took everything out and repacked. Then the call came. They said, "Your father is very ill; we're sending someone to get you." But I knew he was dead.

The next thing I remember—when things are traumatic, you remember these incredible details—is walking in the front door of my home. It was the day after Easter. It was early in the morning, and I remember the sun coming up. I remember the curtains and the sun coming into the living room, and it was so beautiful. Everything was filled with white light and my father was right there.

My mother had been sedated, and all these people were telling me I would have to plan the funeral. I had really never been to a funeral. I remember standing there and him telling me, "I'll help you." And I remember being in the funeral home and looking at all these caskets and thinking, "I don't have a clue." "That's a beautiful rosewood," he said, "that one."

People argued with me because I wouldn't go see him in the casket. He wasn't there. I said, "That's not him, I'm not going to the funeral home, I'm not looking at his body."

The night of the funeral, I was sleeping with my mother and he told me to come out and sit at the top of the staircase. As I sat there, he said, "I have to go on, I have business to do. You and your mother will be fine. There's an insurance policy. I want you to check it." And I felt him leave. I always wondered where he was going, what he was doing.

The next day, I called about the policy; they told me he had taken out a life insurance policy but had not signed it. I had to argue with them to get them to take another look. The policy was signed. That policy paid for my education and took care of us.

At the time, I never thought any of this was strange. I just took it for granted.

The "Wrong" Numbers

I was working as a forensic psychologist, building defenses for litigation against the Commonwealth of Virginia, when I first had a precognitive experience that involved knowing something in detail. I was working on a two billion dollar lawsuit. For three years I had worked to put together the case for the state by interviewing everyone who was even remotely involved in the case, which included two governors and every major agency head.

One morning my secretary came into the office and said that my boss wanted certain exhibits for next week. Exhibits are documents that you use for your defense. I wrote down the numbers of the exhibits my boss requested and handed the list back to my secretary. She came back in ten minutes and said, "These are not the exhibits we need; these are random documents. They were packed in boxes that are going to the state archives this afternoon."

I had worked on this case for three years. That's all I did; it was my life. I knew the case and the exhibits better than anyone. I couldn't believe that I could mix up the numbers like that. It was like doing a dissertation and suddenly writing something that had nothing to do with the topic you were working on for so long.

So I wrote down the correct exhibit numbers, gave them to her and went to lunch. When I came back, somebody ran to me and said, "We have a new lawsuit....You're probably going to be here forever." I looked at the new case and saw the plaintiffs' names and suddenly I knew what had happened earlier that morning.

This new lawsuit literally came out of the blue; we were not expecting it. But the exhibit numbers I had written down earlier were related to these two plaintiffs. Not only had I kept the relevant exhibits from going to the archives, but six months later I discovered that I had written them down in exactly the order they ended up being labeled for the trial.

I knew there was magic, and somewhere in this period of my life, I'd forgotten about it. I had really gone the traditional route: marriage, job, climb-the-career-ladder. I was working my way up to be Commissioner of Mental Health for the Commonwealth of Virginia. That was my goal, and on that day it changed.

Changing Direction

Not long after my psychic experience in the Attorney General's office, an inner voice told me to look around Charlottesville. Being true to form, I decided that a bookstore was where I could find answers. So I went to the bookstore.

I asked the owner of the bookstore a question and another woman, a customer, just turned around and answered my question. I knew she was coming from a place of knowledge that I wanted to come from. I didn't want to be her; I wanted to come from that place. Whatever she'd done to get there, I wanted to do it.

She had been a trainer at the Monroe Institute, an educational and research center in Farber, Virginia. I called the Institute, and they told me they didn't allow

you to come visit when they were doing programs; there was nothing to see when they weren't doing programs, and it was very difficult to explain over the telephone what they did! And, not only that, it was expensive.

But I asked them to send me a form and I sent in an application. I was in the middle of a major trial. Logically I thought, "This will never work." I didn't have the money, and they didn't have any openings anyway.

What happened was they had several cancellations and I got in. The trial in which I was involved ended abruptly, and I got a tax refund I wasn't expecting for the exact amount I needed. So I went.

Monroe was getting ready to reopen their lab with the second set of what they called "explorers," and my trainer encouraged me to become a research subject there.

Part of the criteria for being a research subject was that you had to have the ability to go into a deeply altered state, talk, and not be emotional about what was going on. It was very important that no matter what you saw you had to be removed enough to tell it clearly. It turned out that I was very good at that. I spent two to four hours a day, every weekend, for probably two to three years, in that lab.

Monroe used sound to help you relax, to help you move into an inner state. This is how I was trained and this is how I work now. I use music to help people move into the right hemisphere of the brain so they can enter what we call an "altered" state.

In the Monroe Institute lab, I was in an isolation room, a sensory deprivation booth, a room within a room. They would talk to me over the headphones and ask me questions, and I'd answer. This is the basis of the work I do now. Ask me a question, I'll give you an answer.

And along with that I did psychic readings on everybody I could. I didn't charge for the readings; I just did them. I was really exhausting myself, but I needed to do it to see how I got information. I still book days in certain cities where I do nothing but readings because it tunes me up, it keeps me on edge. I'm just amazed at how much information is there if you just ask the questions.

It's important for the person who asks the question, because the answer is within the question. If you ask the question, if the question's bubbling up, you already have the answer. So in readings I'm really reflecting back to people their internal dreams, pictures, whatever is going on.

Taking Control

A therapist once brought me a college student with a multitude of medical problems, including temporal lobe epilepsy. One of her main issues was that she kept falling asleep, even when she was running. She not only had to stop running, she was in imminent danger of flunking out of school. As soon as I walked into the room, I could see that she had an enormous amount of energy and it was all turning in on her.

The young woman argued with everything I said, until I reached behind the couch and started playing with a pair of toy cars. For some reason, that quieted her and she started listening.

I told her that her intuition was frozen, and that if she wanted to cure herself of epilepsy she would have to learn to turn her energy outward, away from herself. She was very frustrated because I kept telling her that all she had to do was take control of her body and she would be able to heal herself.

"Sure, lady," she said. "I'll just take control of my body and then I'll be better."

One month later the student showed up on my doorstep with a big bunch of tulips. She had decided to pay attention to the reading and take charge of her body. She stayed in school and she started running again. She has since earned both an M.D. and a Ph.D.

Fran Farrelly

Another of my teachers was a woman named Fran Farrelly. I can't say enough about Fran. She's a Ph.D. biochemist, and a very down-to-earth, normal lady who can do these amazing things. Fran could flip a coin and it would always come up the way she wanted it to come up. She could affect physical matter. None of us can hold a candle to Fran.

I'd heard about her through Monroe. I knew the minute I heard her name that I wanted to meet her, so I wrote to her. Didn't hear. Wrote to her again; didn't hear. Okay, I thought, she's too busy. I'm obviously not meant to connect with this woman.

Then, out of the blue, this phone call came, and Fran said, "I'm teaching a class. I didn't write to you because I was not going to do any more classes." At the time she was in her seventies; she's probably in her late eighties now. "I was not going to do any more classes, but now I have to." When she said that it meant that some spirit was saying, "You've got to do at least one more class." She said, "I don't know why you're supposed to be here, but I just know you are." And, would you believe, the week she was doing the class, I had nothing booked. The rest of the month my calendar was full. So I went to Florida, where she lived, and it was work, it really was. We worked from eight or nine in the morning until six at night, nonstop.

Fran's expertise was in radionics. Radionics is a very old way of reading the body and diagnosing illness. In the radionics system, every known disease and every body part has a number. You use the fingers of one hand to dowse the body with the list of ailments, while the fingers of the other hand go back and forth between "yes" and "no."

When I first started using my psychic intuition, I thought that I should not use a tool. I believed that I had to walk into a room and know exactly what was going on with a person just by focusing my awareness. So, when Fran told me to use my fingers to get information, I'd already set myself up; I couldn't do that. It literally took me eight days to catch on. What happened was I just got exhausted, and that's the whole point. Give the left brain something to do and your intuition will talk to you.

Putting Radionics to the Test

Shortly after I finished studying with Fran, I got a phone call from a colonel in the military whose daughter's boyfriend was dying. He was twenty. The colonel said, "I want you to do what you do. Tell us what's wrong. He's in the hospital."

The colonel was in Ohio and I was in Virginia. I couldn't call the doctor I often worked with in Rhode Island because he had just gone on vacation. The only thing I could do at that moment was radionics.

They overnighted me a picture, and I put it on the little radionics box I got from Fran. I did the process. What I learned was that they were giving the young man too many antibiotics. They were giving him four, and they were canceling each other out. I knew he only needed two antibiotics.

I called the boy's girlfriend. She said, "What will we do with this? I know the doctor won't accept it." I said, "Tell the doctor you had a dream and this is your dream." I knew the doctor would listen to a dream. The girl did just that, and the doctor changed the medication. I didn't hear anything more for seven months. Then I learned that the boy was released from the hospital two days after they changed the medication.

Was it the reading that helped cure him? Or was it because the three of us—the colonel, the boy's girlfriend, and myself—were all involved, wanting it? I don't know.

An Angel in the Corner

At the time I do a reading, I am not usually aware of what the person I'm reading is experiencing. In one case, though, the daughter of the man I was working with was in his hospital room in Nevada at the same time as I was doing the reading in Rhode Island. She transcribed the tape I sent her and correlated it to what she had witnessed at the time. This is what she told me:

Her father had been hospitalized with an air bubble in his intestinal tract. As the days went by, his condition worsened. His speech became slurred, he had trouble swallowing, and he became increasingly vague and disoriented. Doctors began to suspect a mild stroke. The family was feeling very discouraged and asked the doctor I worked with in Rhode Island to arrange a reading. He said we would do one in the next few days.

The next morning, the woman's mother called and said that something very strange was happening. Her father was doing better. She hurried to the hospital and sat with him for several hours, watching his speech, breathing, and orientation steadily improve.

When he was able to speak clearly, he pointed to a corner of the room and asked, "Who's that over there?" She asked him what he saw and he said, "A person in white—but I can't see the person very clearly without my contact lenses." The daughter saw nothing, but assured her father that whoever was in the room was there to help him get well. He mentioned the person in white several more times that morning, trying to figure out who it was.

Within a matter of hours, the man was sitting up in a chair, and his daughter felt that she had witnessed a miraculous turnaround.

Later that day, the daughter called to find out when we would be doing the reading. She was told that the reading had been completed that day, at 12:00 P.M. Eastern Standard Time. She was also told that one of the first things I saw was an angel, dressed in white, standing in the corner of her father's hospital room. The angel had told me, "Don't worry, we're here to take care of him. He'll be fine."

The daughter pointed out that when I did the reading it was 9:00 A.M. Pacific Standard Time—the same time her father began to ask her about the person in white in the corner of his room. Apparently, he and I saw the same angel. His daughter saw only his recovery.

"This Is It!"

Sometimes I get letters from people who want me to fix them. But if they don't realize they have their own power, it's not going to work. They won't be fixed.

In fact, in a reading I just did for someone, the issue was not his pain: it was that pain was the only thing he was feeling, and how much he was covering up. People often don't want to see that; they don't want to go back and look at what might be lying behind their illness.

But I'll tell them right up front that if they don't take a deeper look, it's a lose/lose situation. I can't heal them; I can't even put them in a healing space if they're giving me all the power. Even if they had some miraculous healing, it would fade away and they'd be back where they started. At least that's what I believe.

I suggest to people that they look to see what they could let go of with their illness. How is this illness serving them? Because it does serve them. It always does. It serves us all. If I get a cold, for example, Michael waits on me. I get to lie there and not do anything but nurture my cold.

Once I literally stopped a cold before it fully developed. I was tired, and all I wanted to do was climb into bed and read a book. I said, "Uh uh, I don't need a cold to do this. I'm going to sequester myself for two days and read because I need the time." So I did just that—and I never got the cold. Every once in a while an illness will catch up with me because I haven't been taking time to just be quiet.

I think illness is being out of balance. I don't know that we necessarily get sick on purpose. We can say, "There's learning here," but more important than the disease itself is what was going on in our lives to cause us to get out of balance. What were we not in touch with? I think sometimes people create illness because they're bored, or they want to escape something.

I would suggest that we can make a change without doing it so drastically.

I think illness always calls to us to change something that we're doing, one way or another. We can step back, see what's going on, what we're doing, and really take time to smell the flowers, or play with the dog, or hear the children, the elderly, because this is it.

This is it. We're not preparing for life; this is life, even the illness. This is it. Healing occurs in the moment; it doesn't occur in the future. It occurs in the moment. Everything takes place now because this is all we have.

Often I'll see clients who say, "I've been working on healing for the last year." To me, that says you're never going to be well because it's always out there. You're always doing one more thing to get well instead of saying, "This is it. I'm going to bring the body back into balance."

Nature Is a Key to Healing

I believe that nature is our true balancing, and that we have separated ourselves from nature. That's the key.

Nature has its own intuition, its own equilibrium. We get in there and we disrupt the natural balance, like the clear-cutting we do here in Maine. Yes, we plant trees, but we can't plant old growth, so we don't have the birds or the wildlife that we had with the old growth. I think it's time to get back in touch with the old growth, with the trees, because they have a real energy.

I always said that if I ran a healing center, it would be out in the woods and I'd just send people out to be with the trees: to watch nature and be with the trees; to be present; to be fully in the now; to take time to be with nature, let nature be with you; to just live, and love, and laugh, and play.

One of the reasons that we're ill is because we're so emotionally stressed, we're not in touch. We're not in touch with what we're doing to the planet and, thus, to ourselves. It's not the dolphins, the sharks, or what have you, out there dying; it's us. If they're dying, we're dying. What we're doing to them, we're doing to ourselves.

In order for all of us to survive, we have to reconnect with nature.

Remembering

I think it goes back to remembering that we all know who we are, what we can do, our abilities to heal, to be present, to be spiritual, to be a spirit. We just have to remember.

We've gotten away from nature, from our children and our elderly, who have things to share with us. We don't have time for them. So it's all lessons, it's all about connecting with nature, with water, trees, life. And that's healing. That's healing!

I believe there's magic out there. The writer, Robert McCammon, says "We're born in a magic time, in a magic place; we are all magicians." I believe that. We all need to remember it before it's too late.

Peter Roth

New York, New York

My hands are my "power tools";
they're an extension of my mind and intention.
When I move my hands in healing,
they're actually moving in prayer.
I read bodies and speak
with my hands and I use them
to feel and move energy.

There is a nature preserve near Judith's home that we think of as a cornucopia of consciousness, a storehouse of life-enhancing experiences. Out of these woods have come friends, clients, dog-walking companions. mystical encounters, and many conversations about healing and healers. On one afternoon stroll, Judith heard stories about a man in New York who was hard to define, a man who worked with his hands in unusual ways and "pulled files" from the universe. We didn't know what any of that meant, but we knew that we wanted to meet this man—so off we went to Manhattan.

Peter Roth was the second person we sought out for inclusion in this book. At the time we met, he was just getting started in his full-time practice and we had just begun our search for healers. Interestingly enough, Peter was also the second-to-last person we talked with as we brought our travels and interviews to a close.

Somehow, his book-end position in this process seems intuitively right and meaningful. In the three years between the first and second interview, the first and second photo shoot, we have collectively been through multiple changes of residence, separations, divorce, unexpected losses of old and new friends, changes in fortune, of occupation, and several serious illnesses—and Peter has been there for us through it all.

His intuitive healing abilities have helped us, and many of the people close to us, rid ourselves of such ailments as chronic skin rashes, back problems, food allergies, high blood pressure, high blood cholesterol, and acute pancreatitis. He has helped us dispel the fear that can accompany sudden hospitalization and minimize the negative impact of aggressive chemotherapy. His profound integrity has allowed us to build up the trust needed to move through and heal harmful life patterns and deep personal wounds. We are grateful to Peter Roth for all the contributions he has made to our lives and to the lives of our friends and family members. He has become, in many ways, our "family healer."

Over time, we have watched Peter's practice grow and mature; witnessed the birth of his school; and celebrated his ability to maintain both his uniqueness and his balance as life, change, clients, and students continually swirl around him. Peter continues to work on and heal himself, and it shows. He looks ten years younger now than he did when we first met him.

A runner since high school, Peter Roth began studying physiology, biochemistry, and biomechanics in his mid-thirties, primarily so he could keep himself injury-free.

Before long, however, his desire to share his knowledge with others led him to volunteer more and more of his time as a teacher, coach, and healer.

Peter taught exercise courses at New York City's West Side YMCA for eleven years and was the "fitness expert" on Gary Null's daily call-in radio show for almost fifteen years. He became adept at applied kinesiology (the science which uses muscle testing to ask questions of the body), and later studied at energy healing schools in Arizona and New York, ultimately breaking away from his teachers to develop his own unique approach to healing.

As a healer, Peter works intensively with adults and children, face to face and over the telephone. Much of his healing work involves sensing, moving, and channeling energy. Looking at a range of influences from past lives to present eating habits, Peter uses direct touch or a variety of remote healing techniques to find and remove energy blocks in the body, mind, and spirit.

Peter recently established the Heart River Healing School in Manhattan to help others become more familiar with the life energy patterns that block or inhibit wholeness in mind, body, and/or spirit. Because he believes that true healers are "originals" who only need to be helped onto their paths, Peter does not teach any one method of healing to his students. Instead, he offers them a wide variety of information, modalities, and empowerments designed to help them uncover and maximize their innate abilities.

To balance his practice (and keep himself grounded), Peter stays in touch with the world of sports. He is an active runner, and still serves as an officer and director of the New York Road Runners' Club—the organization which sponsors the New York City Marathon—a position he has held for more than 20 years. For the last eight years, he was also Chief Coach of the West Side Soccer League, overseeing 250 soccer teams and more than 2,700 kids and coaches.

Born in New York City and raised in suburban Westchester, Peter currently lives and works on the west side of Manhattan with his wife, Deborah, and his sons, Ben and Chris.

To me, healing is an empowering process rather than an end result. It's not what the issues are—it's who we are and how we face them that's important.

We have so many layers of issues, of lessons, of opportunities in life that all we can really do is move along from one challenge to the next. You could think of an illness or an issue that needs healing as a mountain to conquer. Well, let's say you get to the top of the mountain. On the other side could be another mountain, an even bigger one! So healing is not just a matter of getting over the mountain. It's a matter of developing your climbing skills, so that mountains are no longer ominous forms that block your path but opportunities for you to experience your strength.

Life is full of opportunities to discover our strengths. The illnesses or issues that need healing are really there to test us. We put them there so we can grow and learn about our own power. Part of power is being resourceful. It's knowing that you can create answers; that you can create strength; that you can reach in and find that deep place inside yourself that will move you along no matter what obstacles you meet.

Adversity is there so we are forced to dig deeper into ourselves to find out what we're made of, who we are. The ultimate is to find out that we are one with the universe, one with God, and one with everyone else. We're a community. We're here to help each other work through our lessons.

A Healing Partnership

Healing is also about getting in touch with feelings, knowing that your feelings are okay, allowing yourself to feel a pain so that you can heal it.

I've been doing that with my students. My advanced students have shown such abilities that I said, "Why don't I just work with my students and let them heal me?" And I've been able to go deeper into my own psyche and my own life than I ever could before, because you cannot do this kind of work alone. We need to find people we can trust, and I have found that in my students. I am as willing to put myself in their hands as they are willing to be in my hands. There's something about that kind of a partnership that is so beautiful and so rich.

It's not the kind of thing you can do with a life partner, even though life partners are meant to heal each other and often do so as a life process. With a healer, you work more directly and with more focus on getting through particular blocks, putting yourself at risk by going into feelings, by going into places in the body or in the psyche that you wouldn't go into unless you were in a safe space.

So I'm very lucky to be doing a shared work with my students. We have gone to the deepest places in our souls in our healing sessions. One on one and then back and forth, me on them, them on me, on the table and off the table.

Every Body Is Different...

On the table we use our hands to open up energy blocks we can't get to any other way. It's amazing how powerful that is. When I put a student on the table, all the other students stand around and we analyze the person's energy field. Each student does it separately and then we talk about it. After that, we look at what needs to be done.

Occasionally, students will balk because they want the solution to be structured, they want a box. You know, a cookie-cutter approach to healing: "If you find this, then you do that." But I said. "No, no. If you have this, then you have to ask the universe what to do." "No, no, no," they said. "That's too vague."

"Well," I said, "How will you know which of the thousands and thousands of healing techniques that you could use is the correct one for this situation?"

"What do you mean thousands...? Just give me five techniques—and write them down so I'll know what to do!"

My answer is that every body is different, every session is different, every moment is different. And each different experience calls for a different healing technique. So you need a huge tool box to draw from, plus the communication with the universe that makes every class, every session, every person on the table a brand new experience.

So we stand around after we analyze the energy field and we start asking the universe what to do. Sometimes I get that two or three students in the class have the answer, so I'll say, "You have the answer!" and they'll say, "Who me?" And I'll say, "Yeah, you! What is it?" When they respond, I'll say "That's it! That's what you're supposed to do."

Or it might just be that I hear what has to be done and then either I'll do it as a demonstration or I'll assign different students to it. Very often these are solutions that no one's ever heard of before—but if that is what the universe is saying to do, we do it.

Once we use these techniques, I have everybody re-analyze the energy field. Lo and behold, it's shifted. They can't find the same problem anymore; it's just not there. I won't let that student off the table until everybody in the class is satisfied that there is nothing left to do at this time. I do not mean forever—I mean there is nothing left to do at this time for this person.

Developing My Healing Abilities

I began by working with running injuries—feet, legs, hips, backs. I was seeing these bodies as complete entities, so if there was something wrong with a person's feet, for example, there could also be associated breakdowns or deficiencies in organs and glands. I became adept at identifying these imbalances and recommending changes. I wasn't diagnosing diseases; I was just balancing bodies—and that's all it took to make many people better.

I once worked with a doctor who had a cardiac arrhythmia. He was a runner, a veteran of many marathons, but at this time he could only run a mile or two without uncomfortable heart palpitations. Within thirty seconds, I was able to identify the exact location of the problem. He told me it took four cardiologists a month to come up with the same information. Then I said, "But they didn't have a solution for you, did they?" And he said, "No."

I tracked the problem back to an energy block in his neck, where I found there was a vertebra out of place. Then I noticed that the neck was out of alignment because his feet were out of balance, so we fixed his feet by having him put some padding in certain places in his shoes. I then moved some energy in his neck and energized the nerve to his heart.

I didn't know if I had helped him until I saw him in the park a few days later. He was excited and told me he had been able to run twenty-five miles over the weekend!

Developing Confidence in My Inner Hearing

Early in my career, a middle-aged woman from Connecticut came to see me. She didn't say a word or bat an eye for at least half an hour. She just sat in her chair and stared at me as I looked into her energy field and gave her an overview of all her major life issues, including her parents, childhood, career, and relationship patterns.

After about forty minutes, she just stood up and said, "I've had enough. This has been a total waste of my time. I'm leaving!"

I was shocked. Could I have been mistaken? I had thought I could trust my inner hearing and my ability to sense the life patterns embedded in the energy field, but now I had to wonder if my confidence was misplaced. So I asked her which parts of my reading she thought were inaccurate.

"Look!" she said, "I've been in therapy all my life! I don't want to hear it all again! Just heal me so I can leave!"

I breathed a sigh of relief as I realized that I could trust my inner knowing after all. Then I explained to this woman that we couldn't work on healing until we knew what kinds of patterns and life lessons we were dealing with.

She said, "Okay..." and sat back down.

It doesn't always work that way, you know. Sometimes people aren't ready to hear about or deal with a life lesson.

Using the Energy Field to Fine-Tune Diet

For some people, foods are the key to better health. I'll feel the energy of certain foods and the energy of the person I'm working with; if they're the same, that's fine. But sometimes I see that there are certain foods the person needs that are not being taken, so those foods need to be added to the diet. I may also see that the energy of certain foods doesn't work with the person's energy field; those are foods that the person really should avoid.

For example, I'll take the energy of a particular food, and I'll take that food out of the diet. I'll say, "Okay, we're removing corn from this person's diet." Then I'll look at the energy of the body, organ, or gland again. If it shifts after the change is implemented, I'll know it is the correct thing to do. I can get extremely fine-tuned with any food, any ingredient in a food, any supplement. I can even get to the right brand and quantity of a food or supplement just by feeling how the energy of the product aligns with the energy of the body.

I had a session recently with a woman who had two lists of supplements she was taking—about sixty different products, recommended to her by two different practitioners. When we were finished, we found that there were only about fifteen or twenty that were actually worth taking. We were able to edit that list down to the products that she really needed.

There are a lot of products that are good for you, but you don't *need* them. And there are a lot of products that sound good, but they are not good for *you*. Using the energy field is one way to find out what works, including what people are either allergic or sensitive to.

I'm always careful not to generalize in this area, because no one food or nutrient is good for everyone. For example, when I was young I made myself a health drink every morning. It consisted of orange juice, a banana, an egg, some brewer's yeast, and a few other nutrients. While I was taking this drink, I didn't really feel all that good—and I couldn't understand why.

At one point, I stopped making the drinks. Soon I started feeling better. When I went through some testing a few months later, I discovered I had a strong allergy to brewer's yeast. So much for my "health drink!"

Recently, a client who has leukemia came to see me and told me he had started having vitamin C dripped directly into his veins—a technique that had proven useful to some people. When I asked how he was feeling, he said, "Well, my blood count is terrible—worse than it's ever been." I suggested he discontinue the vitamin C for a while. Sure enough, a few weeks later he called to report that his blood count had improved.

When we think we're doing something good for ourselves, but we're not getting good results, we need to pay attention. Most of us doubt ourselves rather than question the tool we're using. Maybe we shouldn't be eating that food or taking that supplement, even though other people are getting better from it. We need to trust ourselves—and the feedback we're getting from our bodies—more.

You Can't Get Attached to the Outcome

I have no preconceptions about what people should eat or not eat; everybody is different. There are bumper stickers that say, "Friends don't let friends eat meat." I find that extremely arrogant. Some people need to eat meat. I know that will outrage purists, yet we're talking about healing, we're talking about making people whole—and you can't force people to be whole!

There are people walking around who have been intimidated into being vegetarians, but their bodies need the protein and other nutrients that come from meat. I have a client who is a vegan—and her body needed fish. But she said, "I never want to hurt those fish." So I reminded her that Jesus was a fisherman.

I'm sure that no animal wants to die, but at some point the universe needs its balance—the whole animal kingdom is based on this balance. On a higher level, the animals we eat are offering themselves as gifts. We need to bless them and thank them and honor that sacred gift.

We should make it a sacred activity, taking life from animals for food. It shouldn't be done without heart. We need to become experts at that, so there is a higher purpose to eating meat. We don't have to carry guilt around this; we just need to do it right. It can only enhance us if we do it right.

Of course, not everybody needs to eat meat. Part of healing is knowing and holding onto your boundaries, knowing what's right for you and not allowing others to bully or intimidate you.

It is much easier to know and espouse the party line. It is much harder to stand by your own principles and be vulnerable. But that's what healing is about—knowing yourself as whole. Because when you know yourself as whole, you are part of the wholeness of the universe, feeling your oneness regardless of the circumstances. You can't always change the circumstances, but you can change how you hold them.

Healers shouldn't think that they can always change the circumstances, either. All we can do is offer our healing and then get out of the way. And what will be will be.

Of course, we'd like the healing to be the way we picture it. And often that happens. But I never say something will definitely turn out a certain way. What I say is that this is what it looks like might happen from where we stand now. People will often come back and say, "You hit it right on the nose; it was exactly what you said."

But I can't get attached to that because if I get attached to an outcome I'll want the same result the next time. And that might not happen. So I have to get out of the way and let people heal as they're supposed to heal. It's nice if I can play a role, but they have to take the credit for it themselves.

Healing into Death

Here's a situation in which I healed a man, but I didn't save his life. At the time I met him, this man only had about ten days left to live. I knew that he had chosen to go, but he needed a completion.

I normally don't like to go out to see clients, but I went to see him in the hospital. The whole family was standing around. He was in his mid-seventies and he had lung cancer. I looked in the lungs. When I couldn't find the cancer in his physical body, I went into his emotional body. The cancer was in the lungs of his emotional body. So I went back in time and I found that his father hadn't loved him. This was a very traumatic experience; it dominated his life. So I told him that when he was a child his father didn't love him. That had been an unresolved block in his life and that was why this cancer was there.

And he said, "This is the first time I've talked about it; I've never told anybody that my father didn't love me. You're right. I've lived my whole life to not be like my father, to give my children the love that my father didn't give me."

All his children were crying, and he was crying; it was an incredible release for him. When I left, I knew that I helped him find his completion.

For the next ten days, until he departed, he kept asking his family if that guy, Peter, could come back: "I feel so good since he came to see me." And he died in peace.

There Are No Victims...

I'm doing a lot of work now with yin and yang, going into chakras with my hands. Yin energy is soft fingers; yang energy is a fist. If you put a yang energy into something that is too yang to begin with, then yang and yang blow each other out and the energy field weakens. That's because yang doesn't balance yang; yang overwhelms yang. So I look for yang energy or yin energy because it will show me if the energy field in any particular gland or organ or chakra or part of the body is stable. And, if anything is out of balance, I'll feel it.

When I go into the chakra system and look for imbalances, I also look for the chakras that hold chief life issues. When I see what the chief life issues are, I'll go back into the person's childhood to look at the chief life issues of his or her parents. All this information can be found in the chakras.

You can see, for example, if people were loved or not loved as children. You can tell if they lacked nurturing or if they were abused, abandoned, or rejected. Then you can see how they may be trying to heal their childhood by the way they are living now. We have to stir things up to heal an old wound—and the way we do that is by attracting obstacles. Nobody is a victim: we're all attracting our challenges. We choose them without even realizing it.

People come to me saying they are engaged or they're getting into a new relationship. And I look at the chakra structure of their parents and of the person they are getting into a relationship with, and I can see that the same problems are there. But they can't see them. They don't want to know about it; they're in love.

"I looked into this person's eyes and I knew this was my partner for life," they tell me. The reason they know this is because the partner they chose has issues they themselves need to heal. So I say to them things like, "You know your father wasn't around much for you and you are trying to heal that, so you've found a new partner who is very destructive, who doesn't really give you as much attention as you would like...."

And my client will tell me, "Oh, I know that. He says he loves me but he is very busy...and I need to give him room. Occasionally, he'll show up at my door when I don't expect him to because when I do expect him to do something, he lets me down. But I love him and he loves me and we're going to get married. And I'm sure that after we get married he'll be around a lot more...."

Well, guess what? This is going to be a tough marriage. This woman is marrying this man to heal her inner child, a child whose father wasn't there. To do that, she's found a guy who is also not going to be there for her. She'll think that this is love and fool herself with that until she reaches the point of breaking. Then she will have to either heal herself or heal him or get out of the marriage.

Healing at a Distance

When I first started working with people, I healed by touching them physically. If they were in pain, I would rebalance them and quickly move them out of pain. Later, I learned that I could move energy and heal people without touching them. The first time it happened, I was on the phone with a woman from Long Island. She asked me to check out her back and tell her what was wrong with it.

I cradled the phone on my shoulder and felt the energy of her spine. The spine was fine, but her pelvis was unbalanced. Holding the energy of her pelvis off to the left, I said to myself, "What if I just move this energy to the right?" I silently pushed it to the right.

Immediately, the woman said, "Wait a minute. What did you do?" And I said, "What do you mean? I'm just checking your back." She said, "You did something to me, didn't you? I felt my hip being pushed to the right."

And I thought, "What am I into here? This is really amazing." I realized at that point that I could move things around in the body energetically, even over the telephone.

As a healer, I can often help clients learn their life lessons by going back and looking not only at their parents, but at the parents' childhood. Describing what I feel as it comes through can help people understand the patterning they have been born into and now need to rise above.

For example, I was in a session on the phone with a woman in California, and I saw that in her early childhood she had been sexually abused by her mother. This was something I could feel, but not physically. I could picture the emotions of it. I could picture her mother and her together, and her mother being in a great rage and doing these things without being able to control herself. And I could picture my client being terrorized and shouting for help, but not knowing how to protect herself.

I was trying to see how I could introduce this information so that it wouldn't put this woman into a traumatic state. At one point, it became clear that she was prepared to hear what I had to say. When I shared what I saw, she said, "I'm so glad you told me; my father recently told me about this and now you've confirmed it."

I think the work I do at a distance empowers people to do their own work. Often, people who are in trauma call me, and over the phone I can bring them out of trauma. The energy I can transmit is so deep it gets to the root of the trauma so people can relax and start to feel better right away.

"Thank You for Sharing Life with Me..."

There's a very divine energy touching the earth; I bring it up through my hands. I use my hands to heal people with that energy. I really send it from my heart, but I guide it with my hands. My hands are almost like transformers of that heart energy.

I like doing work with my hands. I get energy with them; I feel life with them. It's hard to describe how deep our relationship is with our hands. Our hands are communicators; they not only send information out, they receive information. They are our antennae.

When we touch people, shake hands with people, we're not only downloading, we're also uploading. Not only are we receiving everything about that person's life, body, and feelings, but touching people is a healing in itself.

People touching each other. When you make contact with people, you're giving energy and you feel energy moving into you. It's a beautiful experience of sharing on a much deeper level than we realize. By touching people, we're saying, "Thank you for sharing life with me."

Working "Hands On"

Since I started teaching, I've been doing more "hands-on" work. When I work with a client on the table, I have something of a ritual. Generally, I'll start by moving light into the body by holding the feet—just to put some light on the subject so I can see better.

Then I'll work structurally. I'll go up the body on both sides, gently rocking the body to see if it can stay strong. There are times when just a gentle rocking will upset the energy field because the body is structurally out of balance. Then I'll just put different pressures on different parts of the skeletal system to see where it's weak, and do some gentle manipulation of the skeletal system to realign it. It's not like a chiropractic manipulation; it's more like an instruction to the body than an adjustment. The body can then manipulate itself.

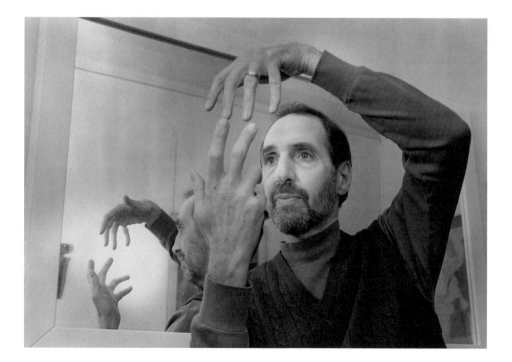

I work a lot on the sacrum because often the coccyx is involved. The coccyx is our tail bone. You know how dogs are when they're afraid? You know where their tails go? They draw their tails underneath them—and we do the same thing. So the coccyx can get stuck withdrawing, and a lot of our energy flow will be blocked. The idea, then, is to gently push the coccyx and energize it in a way that opens that flow.

The sacrum is similar in that it's an important bone in the body, so it also usually needs to be energized. I usually do that with breathing patterns, too. I'll wander around the spine looking for imbalances, and I'll use breathing patterns to release the energy in the spine.

Then I'll have the person roll over and I'll do the same thing, the same gentle rocking, and look at the pubic bone and the belly button. The belly button is like a computer center, a gateway. When the belly button is out of alignment, the energy's not going to go straight through it, so that has to be realigned and opened, too.

I work with the ribs, with the sternum, and the breast bones, right up to the jaw, facial bones, cranium. Just getting everything lined up. Then I'll look at the energy of the organs and glands and energize those.

After that, I'll start doing chakra integrations; I'll put my hands on different chakras and work directly on the body. I can actually feel it in my head. My head does involuntary movements when energy needs to be adjusted. When my head stops moving, I'll know the energy in that chakra is coherent.

Then I work in the auric bodies; I'll do yin and yang and wiggle my fingers to find unstable energy. Once I get the whole energy field coherent—when I can't find any more disturbance in it—I'll do an empowerment and align the sacred geometry (the energetic patterns of life forms) of the body. Then I'm usually done.

It's a very deep work and the more I work on the same person, the deeper I can go—especially in the chakras and the central core and soul levels of the body.

Often, when I'm done, I'll find that I've healed issues from other lifetimes, or from childhood. I'll see that the energy that I was working with radiated back into other lifetimes, and that the healing was a complete healing because it actually went back to the source.

An Example of Healing a Pattern from a Past Life

One time I was working with someone who had a breathing problem, a problem he'd had for decades. Medicine had no answer for him, so he came to me.

I felt the energy of his lungs. Then I took the energy back in time, feeling his lungs back through his life. At birth his lungs were weak, so I followed the energy back into the fetus. I saw that his lungs were weak then, too.

I said to myself, "Obviously, this problem comes from something earlier than the fetus," so I went back into his conception and his lungs were still weak. You might say, "Well, it's genetic," but I wasn't getting that. I was getting that the breathing problem came from a past life.

So I flipped back and saw right away that in his last life this man was in a fire in Tibet and that he was suffocating. As I told him this, he became very emotional because he really didn't want to accept that death. But I saw that I could heal his lungs if he would just let go of that life. Letting go wouldn't change the fact that he died in that life, but it would keep his damaged lungs from radiating into this life.

When we completed the session and came back into this life, my client's breathing problem was completely resolved.

Intention Is the Key to Healing

Healing tools—such as our hands, voice, a visualization or ritual—are only the handles of intention; we use them to create better clarity for the results we intend.

Because you can't focus without language, if you want to do a healing you will need a language for it. Your language of intention can be anything you choose, any ritual that allows you to recognize that you are holding a particular intention.

Healing utilizes the language of its tools. For example, if you had past lives in the Native American world, you might come into this lifetime familiar with Native American healing tools. So, when you call yourself a healer and need to draw on some language to describe what you do, you go to what you know best from your history. In this case, it might be Native American rituals and instruments, special kinds of sticks, or certain herbs or stones. Or, it could have less to do with the particular instruments than it has to do with the clarity that working with them gives you and your language. The important thing is that you know if you have these instruments and you use them this way, you're going to heal somebody. The language of these tools gives you clarity of intention.

But, as much as you can receive healing from just the clarity of intention, you can do an even better job when you go back to the source of your problem and look at why you have it to begin with. And that in turn actually creates more intention, more clarity.

Healers Help Lighten the Load...

Here's an image for you: As we go through life, we accumulate a lot of baggage from our disappointments, from our rejections, from our confusion, from our fear and our anger.

Let's picture all this baggage that we are walking around with as suitcases, backpacks, shoulder bags. They makes us big, cumbersome. Now let's say the opportunities in life are like doorways that we have to pass through. And they are not very large doorways.

If you're trying to get through one of these doorways while you're carrying all of these suitcases and backpacks and shoulder bags, you're not going to fit so easily. As you're trying to squeeze everything through the doorway, suitcases will land on your toes and you'll cut yourself on the door jam. In other words, you'll get hurt trying to move through the opportunities of your life because your baggage won't let you get through without pain.

What happens if you can heal yourself and unload a suitcase or two, a few backpacks and some shoulder bags? All of a sudden these doorways are a lot more accessible! You may still bump a little bit as you go through a doorway, but you don't get blocked. And you don't get swollen toes.

Moving through the opportunities in life is a lot easier when we've reduced our baggage. It's not that we don't have issues. It's not that we don't bump into doorways. What matters is that we are in good shape when we do it: "Oh, I bumped into a doorway. Okay. That doesn't feel so bad. I just need to move this suitcase a little to the left and I'll get through easily."

We can all make those kinds of adjustments. A healer's job is to help you lighten your load.

...And Heal Themselves in the Process

When I have an ongoing relationship with people, I can be more sensitive toward the way they carry their baggage, the way it needs to be lifted off of them. Somehow, I feel as if the people who came to me in the past came more to *hear* about their baggage than to get rid of it. And then they took off, saying, "Okay. Good. Now I know what I'm carrying around in life."

But I want to help them get the baggage off, so I love it when people come back and say, "Remember this suitcase you identified? I'm ready to let it go now. Let's work on it." Then the next time they come we work on a few other items they are carrying around. After several sessions, we are really able to work with much more light and to go deeper and deeper into those places that create a greater expression of wholeness.

There's a difference in the way people appear when they are not loaded down. There's a lightness, a wholeness you can see. What I love is that you can see a difference in me, too. My life is so much richer working with people at deeper levels. When I can go deeper, I can fly into the energy field with more power—and moving with that kind of power heals me, too.

Carl R. Hewitt & Sidney Schwartz

Gifts of the Spirit Church, Chesterfield, Connecticut

The Bible is...filled with people who heard voices, saw visions, prophesied, had prophetic dreams, healed, wrote inspired messages, heard voices from the void and dowsed for water. Jesus of Nazareth was the most gifted medium in the Bible. He was the only person in history to demonstrate all the Gifts of the Spirit.

Carl Hewitt told us many fascinating stories about his encounters with electromagnetic elements and devices.

When he was an infant, lightning struck his mother as he nursed. She was seriously injured by the hit; he, strangely enough, was unharmed. Throughout his life, he said, electrical appliances would behave oddly in his presence; credit cards would be stripped of their data; light bulbs would explode or leap from their sockets; movie marquees would brighten when he stood nearby.

We knew that many spiritual healers worked with "energy," however that force may be defined, so it seemed logical that they might also have an ability to affect magnetic fields and electrical currents. A variety of events that followed our initial meeting with Carl confirmed that hunch, and gave further credence to his stories.

When Susan arrived to photograph Carl and Sidney, her strobe lights refused to work in their presence—although they functioned perfectly well when checked in the sockets of another room. A few days later, when she entered the darkroom to develop the film from that photo session, Susan found that—even without the extra lighting—all the shots of Carl and Sidney were overexposed, necessitating much work in the darkroom to salvage the images. She also noticed that the edges of the film looked as though they had been burned. Susan felt that this was especially odd because, on the same roll of film, the frames shot before and after the session with Carl and Sidney were perfectly normal—neither overexposed nor burned.

Without knowing any of this history, the woman who was typing Carl's interview tapes called to report that she was running behind because her computer was acting up; the transcribing machine kept breaking down; and, for some reason, the light bulbs in her home kept blowing out.

But perhaps the oddest event associated with our work with Carl and Sidney occurred on the ride home from our first meeting with them.

Under normal travel conditions, the trip from Carl's office in Connecticut to Pat's home in Rhode Island took just over an hour. Because we had lingered much longer than planned, we stopped to call home just before we got onto the highway so our families would know when to expect us.

It was a rainy night and we paid little attention to the traffic or the landscape as we drove slowly along, rehashing the stories we had heard from Carl and Sidney. Suddenly, Pat noticed the "Welcome to Rhode Island" sign on the side of the road, and started spluttering and stuttering: "But where were the bridges? Do you remember driving over the bridges?"

Not familiar with the highway, Judith laughed and replied, "No. What are you so upset about? We just haven't gotten to the bridges yet. They must be up ahead!"

What Judith didn't realize was that to reach that particular point on the road, we would have had to cross several wide, brightly lit bridges, including the one that passes over the New London submarine base. The road, as we recalled it, had been very dark and quiet, and neither of us had seen so much as a dim light, much less a large, multi-lane bridge.

We assumed that we had been so preoccupied by our conversation that we failed to notice our surroundings. This explanation faded away, however, when we arrived at Pat's home and her husband said, "How did you get here so fast? You must have been flying!"

Somehow, we managed to arrive only 30 minutes from the time we called—a half hour earlier than would be expected. Interestingly enough, that was just about the amount of time it would have taken us to traverse the section of road we had somehow "missed."

Later, when we asked Carl what he thought happened on that trip, he just laughed. He suggested that we had somehow wandered into a time and space "warp" designed to teach us that what we then considered "physical reality" was a lot more fluid than we ever imagined.

Carl Hewitt was born in Shallotte, North Carolina, the eleventh and youngest child of a rural farming family. His psychic abilities, apparent from a very early age, were a source of fear for his family and embarrassment for him. It wasn't until he was introduced to Spiritualism, in adulthood, that he was able to see the gifts he was born with as a blessing rather than a curse.

Spiritualism is a system of religious beliefs, dating back to the mid-19th century, based on the presumption that communication with the dead is possible. Spiritualists believe that departed spirits communicate with the living through a medium in a trance state, or by means of other physical phenomena. From the Spiritualists, Carl learned that his abilities identified him as a natural medium, a person who can attune himself to receive the words, thoughts, and visions that emanate from the Spirit World. It is this mediumship that enables Carl to give psychic readings and do hands-on healing.

Carl believes that the Bible is a record of psychic history and that Jesus of Nazareth was the most gifted medium that ever lived. When he established his independent ministry in Chesterfield, Connecticut, Carl named it the "Gifts of the Spirit Church and Psychic Research Center." The Bible explains the "gifts of the spirit" in 1 Corinthians 12:1-11 as including (among other phenomena) clairvoyance, clairaudience, prophecy, automatic writing, trance, and healing.

Sidney Schwartz came to Carl for a reading in 1975. He was so impressed with Carl's abilities that he made the weekly drive from New Jersey to Connecticut to participate in his psychic development classes. In time, Sidney was certified as a healer. Now, student and teacher have joined forces to develop educational seminars.

For the last few years, Reverend Hewitt has been in contact with AWAN, an entity who speaks to him and, through him, to Mr. Schwartz. Three books have been compiled to share both Sidney's detailed biblical research and the teachings that AWAN has channeled to Sidney through Carl.

Carl currently sees clients privately by appointment for "hands-on" healings and psychic readings. He also holds public healing services at his church.

A s a healer, I'm only a channel, an instrument. It's like the wires that come in here to illuminate this room; the energy is coming from a dynamo somewhere else. When I go into an altered state to do a healing, the healing doesn't come from me, it comes through me.

When people ask for a healing, I tell them that I don't know whether I can do anything for them, but I'll do my best. Then I ask the Lord God of my own being to come forward, and to activate the person's self-healing mechanism. After a healing, when the energy has come through me, I'm wiped out. That's why I only see two people a day.

A Healing Heritage

My grandmother, my mother's mother, was a healer, too. The nights that I stayed at my grandmother's house, I would always hear people outside. Sometimes I could hear low whispering, but most often people were sobbing and crying.

It was only fifteen years ago that I found out that people came to my grandmother's house for healing at night. Because we lived in the heart of the Baptist Bible belt, no one openly discussed the healings my grandmother performed. The Christians considered it the work of the Devil. But my grandmother had extensive knowledge of herbs and often mixed up her own "home remedies." Since these were the depression years, people would leave something in lieu of money. When I got up early in the morning, there would always be a bushel basket of fresh vegetables, eggs, or a container of milk on the front porch.

Early Signs of the Gift

A few months before I was born, my father bought one of the first models of phonograph. In those days, phonographs played cylinders rather than records, and the sound was amplified by a big horn instead of a speaker. One day, as he was walking by the phonograph, my father heard a voice coming out of the horn. This greatly frightened him, since he wasn't using the machine at the time.

The voice was telling my father that his son, who would soon be born, would grow up to be a special person, a light of knowledge to the world. Because of his Baptist teachings, my father thought that this must be the voice of the Devil. He packed the phonograph into the crawl space of the attic and never let anyone touch it again.

Today, I have a better understanding of this incident because I understand psychic science: the spirit people used the horn of the phonograph as a trumpet and spoke through it. This was quite common in the early days of Spiritualism. In the Bible, the Ten Commandments were given to Moses through the use of trumpet mediumship. Exodus 19:19 states, "And when the voice of the trumpet sounded long, and waxed louder and louder, Moses spake, and God answered him by a voice."

When I was about four years old, a stranger came to the house driving a pickup truck. I was not tall enough to see what was up in there, but I heard the man tell my father he was selling fish. Then I heard a voice, as clear as you are hearing my voice right now. It said, "Ask him how many jars of white lightning (bootleg liquor) he has under the ice."

I tugged on the stranger's pants leg and said, "How many jars of white lightning you got under that ice, Mister?" The man jumped into that truck and took off, as if someone was holding a gun to his head. My father was furious with me. He thought I was making up stories and began chasing me around the house to spank me. (He didn't catch me!)

Some time later that afternoon, a neighbor came to the house and asked my father if "so-and-so" had stopped here. Daddy said, "Yes," and the neighbor said, "He's in jail! He had a few fish under that canvas but all of the rest of it was white lightning." My father looked at me. He didn't say a word, but every time I looked up he was staring at me. How did I know?

The way people thought down there in the Carolinas was that if you can't touch it and you can't see it, it doesn't exist. Or it's the Devil's work. Those beliefs affected me greatly. As a child, I was convinced that something was wrong with me. I was thrown out of all the churches I went to as soon as I mentioned that I heard voices and saw visions. I was ashamed of the things that happened to me when I was a child, and for years I would never talk about them.

Opening the Door to Spiritualism

One morning, when I was forty-one years old, I got a strange phone call at the beauty salon I owned and operated in Gales Ferry, Connecticut. This voice said, "You are to go to Willimantic to a class dealing with psychic phenomena at seven o'clock tonight." The caller didn't give any other information.

I always worked late on Thursdays, but, at about one o'clock that afternoon, my receptionist came in and said, "Four people have cancelled their appointments. Now you don't have a thing booked after five o'clock."

When I finished work, I remembered that phone call. I got in the car and drove toward Willimantic. An inner voice told me to go to Valley Street. When I got there, I saw a light over a doorway. It was a little church.

I opened the church door slowly because I felt very funny. I saw a large group of people sitting in a circle with one empty chair. An old man was sitting with his back to the door, talking to the group. The minute I opened the door, he said, "You're Carl Hewitt; I've been expecting you." I said, "What makes you so sure?" But I walked in and I sat down. That class was my introduction to Spiritualism.

I felt so good with those people that I thought, "This is great." But I suddenly felt so tired, I didn't know if I would fall asleep or not. I must have slipped right into a trance. (Now, when you go into a trance state, you lose consciousness. You don't know or remember what you do or say.) At the end of the meeting, I said, "Well, people, I'm sorry I went to sleep on you," and everybody laughed. In the meantime, a woman was rewinding a tape recorder. She turned it on, and there was my voice. That was the first time I heard what I said when I was in a trance state.

Because of what happened that first night, I became the new leader of the group when the old man died. On June 2, 1974, I was ordained a minister by the National Spiritual Alliance of Churches—where ministers must also be certified mediums and healers. A few years later, I left that organization and—following the directions of my spirit guide—established my own, independent healing and teaching ministry.

Spiritualism and Healing

The energy that I use for psychic readings is the same energy I use for healings. It feels different only in that healing takes much more energy than reading.

Sometimes, when I'm in a deep trance, many spirits in the other dimension use my body and my chemistry to heal the people who come to me. A good example is a psychic development class I once held at the church. That night, I was teaching different techniques of healing. At the end of class, I was tired and ready to go home. But the voice of Spirit said, "Now we have to demonstrate healing." (Before, we were just discussing it.)

Nine different people came up to the chair, one at a time, to be healed. And for every person that came to the chair, a different entity superimposed its features over me.

The people in the class were standing back there with their mouths open. They could not believe it. At one point, they told me, a black man, very tall in build, took over my body. They said that I looked almost a foot taller.

My understanding is that these entities were healers in the other dimension; on this occasion, a different one came forward to heal each person.

Recently, a woman came in for a psychic reading. About three-quarters of the way into the session, when I asked her if she had any questions, she pulled a surprise on me. She put her hand out and said, "I want you to heal my hand!" This woman had been a nurse at a hospital in Norwich. She hadn't worked for a year and a half because her right hand was paralyzed.

I was already in the altered state of consciousness, so I put my hand on top of hers. I felt a tremendous amount of energy coming from my body. We just sat there for a few moments in silence as I put my absolute focus on healing this hand.

She called me the very next morning and said, "I have some wonderful news; last night when I got home, I sat down and wrote a whole letter with my right hand." She told me she was no longer having any problem with her hand.

This woman is a good example of a person who has faith that she will be healed—and that helps a great deal. If a person who comes to me (or my associate, Sidney) is skeptical or fearful, these feelings could prevent healing from taking place. The nurse knew she could be healed. That knowingness activated the healing mechanism in her own body.

Healing Vision

I once worked with a five- or six-year-old girl whose eyesight was so bad that she couldn't see at all unless she wore glasses with thick lenses. Doctors gave her no hope for improvement. She started coming to our healing services with her family every week. Then, one day, her mother noticed that the child hadn't put on her glasses. The mother watched the child run around, doing everything that she normally did with her glasses on. The mother said, "Honey, don't you want your glasses?" And the child said, "No, I don't need them."

The girl's vision continued to improve. After a checkup, the family's doctor wrote me a letter. He said that he didn't believe in miracles, but there was no other word to describe what he had seen. The child's eyes were getting better. Today, that girl is twenty-six years old. She's married and has a child—and she doesn't wear glasses at all.

A Laying on of Hands

I feel that we healers are instruments, like batteries. All we need to do to help activate healing is use our hands as jumper cables.

When I owned the beauty salon, my manager's neighbor had an eighteen-year-old son. The boy was born with no lining in his stomach; he could only eat baby food and was nothing but skin and bones. He had finished high school and worked at Pratt-Whitney Aircraft. But now he was out on sick leave.

One morning the boy's mother brought him to the salon. I think Dorothy, my manager, had something to do with that because she wanted to see this boy healed.

We went into my office, and I moved the chairs back because the boy said he felt so weak he wanted to lie on the floor.

When he was lying on the floor, I sat down in a lotus fashion. I sat there for quite some time before I ever touched his body, putting myself in an altered state of consciousness, and asking to be used as the instrument of healing. Then I asked him to tell me what it was that bothered him. He said, "Right here; my stomach."

I said, "I want you to close your eyes, listen to me, and follow all my instructions. I'm going to slowly place my hands on your stomach. If you feel heat, then I want you to understand that you are feeling the healing energy coming from the unseen."

I placed my hands, palms down, over his stomach. After about seven or eight minutes, he said, "Please remove your hands; you're burning my flesh." I said, "Please allow me to continue this way; picture that you're being healed."

I don't know how long it took, but eventually I felt the energy change and then I slowly removed my hands. My hand prints were on his stomach. It was as if my hands had turned into heating elements and burned my prints into his flesh.

I said, "This is what I want you to do: Go home and go right to bed; lay on your back, close your eyes and visualize what happened here today. Let your body relax and go to sleep. He said, 'I will do it, Mr. Hewitt, I will do it.'"

He went home and laid on his bed, just as I told him. Later, as his mother was putting dinner on the table, the boy came bouncing down the stairs. He sat at the table and began eating dinner. He had a voracious appetite. (Remember, he had only been eating baby food until then.) He ate spaghetti, meatballs, sausage, everything that was in sight. His parents sat there in shock.

When I came to work the next morning, there was a Sunoco tanker truck parked in front of this building. The trucker headed toward me. He said, "Mr. Hewitt, I want to thank you for helping my son. He was here yesterday morning and you won't believe what happened. I still don't believe it; I'm in absolute shock." He then proceeded to tell me of his son's appetite.

About six months or seven months later, we were having a service and a kid with a beard came in. He said, "Don't you remember when my mother brought me here? And Daddy came down the next morning driving the Sunoco truck?" I said, "Oh, my God, you gained weight; you look fantastic."

Closing a Hole

Another couple who attended the services here had a daughter named Jean. One winter, as she was driving in her jeep, she hit a patch of ice. Her car skidded, flipped over, and came to rest on an enormous pile of rocks.

Jean had a hole jabbed in her back so deep that you could actually see her spine. The doctors could not decide how to treat her because they were afraid that she could become totally paralyzed. Immediately, her family called me and I went down to the hospital.

When I saw the problem, I said, "Oh, God. I need more help now than I've ever needed in my entire life." Then I went back to the waiting room, and told her father that I wanted him to come and help me. I asked the rest of the family to stay in the waiting room and concentrate on Jean. "No talking," I said. "Concentrate on what she looks like, and visualize that you are directing healing energy from yourself to her."

Then her father and I went into the room. I had her father sit on one side of her while I sat on the other. I held one of her hands and put my other hand on her side. I asked her father to do exactly the same thing. The energy was coming through both of us. It was as if it were coming down, splitting, and moving through both of us.

It was about that time that he and I saw the light. I remember him looking up to see where it came from. And I remember saying to him, "You won't find it up there."

The light was like a pendulum. You could see it swinging back and forth over her body, from her head to her toes. As the light expanded, it got softer and softer until it was covering her whole body, just swinging back and forth, back and forth. Then it stopped in the middle and faded out.

I released my hands, and motioned to the father to do the same thing. When he got up from Jean's bedside, he was a little bit wobbly himself. I said, "Your daughter's going to be fine. She's going to be fine. Just let her rest. The healing will continue to take place even after I leave."

They never had to do a bit of surgery on that girl. Her wound healed, and there's not one thing wrong with her. Talk about miracles. To this day, I don't really understand it. I've seen wonderful things happen, but it's not me who does it. I'm only the instrument.

A Message from Spirit

I think one of the most powerful experiences I've ever had in my life is when my half-brother (who died a number of years before) was trying to get through to me. I kept seeing a vision. I kept seeing "Etna Maine."

So I went to the telephone book to call everybody by the name of Maine, but I couldn't find anybody named Etna. Then a medium from Norwich called me. She told me of a little community in Maine named Etna where there was a Spiritualist camp, one of the oldest in the country.

When I arrived there, I found that they were having the last service of the season that evening. The medium bowed his head and went into trance. I saw this soft light coming down, and as soon as the light touched him he started speaking.

He didn't look out at the audience; his eyes were closed. I felt the presence of my father and my brother around me. Then, the medium's voice spoke and said, "I want to come to my son, Carl Hewitt." It was my father using the medium's vocal cords to speak to me.

My father said, "Son, I never realized that you were a gifted person; I could not tie it in with my own beliefs. They taught me that you were possessed by an evil being. I had to come over here to find out the truth about you." Then he said, "There's somebody else here who is pleading to talk with you." The next voice that was heard was that of my half-brother. My half-brother had been very jealous of my position as the "baby" of the family and had tormented me throughout our youth. And the first thing he said was, "Please forgive me; please forgive me."

Tears were running down the medium's face. He continued, "You have to forgive me so I can get on with my life over here. I was wrong to treat you the way I did. Please forgive me; I didn't even know you until I came to this side." This happened on the last Saturday of August, 1976; I will never forget it as long as I live.

Sidney Schwartz on Meeting Carl

I drove up from New Jersey for a reading with Carl twenty-four years ago, and it totally blew my mind. I knew there were many charlatans in this work. Therefore, I deliberately phrased my questions to give Carl as little information as possible. In every case, Carl would not only answer my question but fill in all the information I had deliberately withheld. This proved to me, beyond a shadow of a doubt, that Carl was legitimate.

After my third reading, Carl said to me, "It's too bad that you live so far away in New Jersey." I asked him why, and he said, "Because I would invite you to be in my psychic development class." I said, "Well, don't let that stop you." He looked at me kind of strangely. But I did join the class. I'd drive from New Jersey to Connecticut to attend a class; after class I'd drive home to New Jersey.

Every once in a while, at the end of Carl's classes, we would do healings. For me, going into the healing state is like throwing a switch. I am able to put my mind in a certain place, a blank space, and the energy starts flowing. I would feel my hands go from warm to hot, and have an inner sense of where in the body the healing was needed. By attending Carl's class, I developed the gift and was certified as a healer along with several other people from the church.

Carl's Work Enters a New Phase

Years ago, one of my spirit guides told me that a great teacher would appear to me later in life because of another phase of the work that I would have to do.

One night, following a friend's funeral, I came back to my office and sat down. I didn't even turn the lights on; I guess I was feeling sorry for myself. It was at that moment that the room filled with light, and suddenly, standing there in front of me was an entity. He was so tall that he reached all the way to the ceiling.

Because of my Southern Baptist background, I really thought that entity was Jesus. He had long hair that looked like polished silver. His eyes were like giant topaz stones. His whole face smiled, and he didn't say a word. I had never experienced anything like this in my life. When I was finally able to untie my tongue, I said, "Please tell me who you are."

His expression didn't change; he didn't make a sound. Finally, he broke the silence by saying, "I cannot and I will not tell you who I am or who I was, but I am not who you think I am. In the past, people have made gods and religions from their conversations with people in my dimension. You already have too many religions on your planet; therefore, I will not reveal my name. I have come to use you as my messenger. I'm going to teach you where God is and how you can communicate directly with God."

Just as Moses insisted that he needed to know the name of the spirit who spoke to him, I kept badgering this entity for a name. The second time he appeared, the entity relented and said, "Visualize the words, 'Angel Without A Name,' and remember me as AWAN."

For the last three years, AWAN has been speaking through me to my associate, Sidney Schwartz, when I am in a deep trance state. Sidney has written three books about AWAN's predictions and teachings. The first book in the series, *My First Encounter with an Angel: Revelations of Ancient Wisdom*, describes Sidney's experiences with mediumship, especially as he has experienced them through me and the classes he took with me. The second volume, *My Second Encounter with an Angel*, features Sidney and AWAN's dialogues about metaphysical topics and the psychic roots of religious rituals.

Activating the Self-Healing Mechanism

AWAN says you can turn on the healing mechanism in your own body by sitting down, every day, and putting your focus on your aura, the egg-shaped light that surrounds your body. (AWAN calls the light on the outside of the body the "Lord of your being"; he calls the source inside the body that produces the light the "God of your being.")

When you can clearly visualize the light outside your body, close your eyes and say:

Lord, God of my being, unto the Father within, come forward this moment, this hour, and release the enzymes from my brain into my bloodstream, that my body, your temple, be healed. So be it.

When you say these words, the light of your soul expands, as if you were turning up a rheostat. When you say, "So be it," it's like pressing the "enter" button on a computer keyboard: the soul registers your request and complies with it.

AWAN taught us some other prayers, too. If you need guidance, you can sit down for a few moments and visualize yourself in an egg-shaped container of light, with the narrow, pointed end on the bottom. Then you can say:

Lord, God of my being, unto the Father within, come forward this moment, this hour, and walk in front of me, and help me do the right thing, help me say the right thing, in all that I do this day. So be it.

When you put this prayer in your soul, it radiates out through the life field; it becomes magnetic, and draws to you that which you're supposed to do.

Knowledge Is the Key to Healing

The Bible says, "Physician, heal thyself." But most of us on this planet have been taught that whatever it is that does the healing is out there, outside of ourselves. The problem is that when we concentrate on "out there," we are ignoring and rejecting what's in here, inside ourselves.

Jesus taught that the kingdom of God lies within. That's why, as much as this is a healing ministry, it is also a teaching ministry—because if you can teach people the truth, then they can learn how to turn on their own healing mechanisms. I love when it happens that way.

Kay Cordell Whitaker

Eldorado, New Mexico

*This work is my Path. This is what
I came here to do, to participate in helping
the world, my community, my people. To do that,
I had to first find out about me, help me, heal me,
learn who and what I am, and how I connect
to the whole world. Once I was able to do that,
I had the tools to help someone else.*

*T*here we were, on a cold and rainy autumn night, soaked through and splattered with mud, searching the overflowing banks of the Amazon Creek and nearby yards and driveways for "stone people." We had arrived in Eugene, Oregon, earlier that day to interview Kay Cordell Whitaker. After a brief introduction and a demonstration of her healing process, she bundled us off to search for cornmeal, tobacco, and stones—tools we would need to build sacred altars so she could lead us through the "Dance of the Earth Fire Serpent," an energy-raising ceremony she teaches at her Level One workshops.

It was the perfect introduction to Kay, who teaches more by creating experiences for her students than by talking with them. As we stumbled through the darkness, each sure we were the only one who could not find any stones, we discovered more about ourselves and each other than we ever could have learned sitting in Kay's living room. Convinced that there wasn't a single stone to be found in all of Oregon, we whined a bit and kept looking. When we returned to Kay's home hours later with our mission accomplished, we were warmly welcomed but not coddled. Instead of tea, cookies, and sympathy for our bedraggled state, we were led immediately into the ritual—an experience that left us warm, energized, and glowing by the end of the evening.

We have, in the years that have followed that first meeting, always found Kay to be highly focused and totally committed to her work; the quality of her attention is, in fact, one of the things about her that we find most striking.

A three-day workshop we took with Kay a year later was structured in much the same way as our first meeting. As a group, we spent at least 90 percent of our time engaged in the process of shamanic journeying; we spent very little time talking about our experiences, no time at all analyzing them.

We have always felt totally safe exploring unknown territories with Kay. A reserved and private person by nature, we find Kay to be both strong and feminine, the way the earth is strong and feminine. To us, she epitomizes the word "grounded."

In 1974, Kay Cordell Whitaker began a highly unorthodox and somewhat "reluctant" apprenticeship with Chea and Domano Hetaka, two Andean shamans from the border country between western Brazil and eastern Peru.

Kay first met Domano Hetaka when he approached her during a violent thunderstorm on the beach in Santa Cruz, California. Soaking wet and barefooted, Domano started yelling at Kay in broken English, telling her that he had been waiting *for her all day, that it was about time she showed up. Kay, thinking Domano was a crazy vagrant, ran for her car.*

Several weeks later, Domano approached Kay again, this time in a coffee shop on her college campus. Domano was smiling joyfully. He looked so innocent and child-like that Kay, although she was still frightened by his unusual appearance and manner, decided to sit and listen to what he had to say.

Domano told Kay that he had been led to her by a number of signs, and that he and his wife, Chea, wanted to train her to be a "teller of medicine stories" to fulfill a tribal prophecy. Kay, in turn, would be required to bring their culture's teachings to a world that was desperately out of balance. And so the apprenticeship, described in detail in Kay's first book, The Reluctant Shaman: A Woman's First Encounters with the Unseen Spirits of the Earth, *began.*

Secretly meeting and working with the Hetakas for more than thirteen years, Kay Cordell Whitaker was slowly transformed from an "ordinary" housewife and art stu-dent to a "kala keh nah seh," a traditional storyteller, seer, healer, and "builder of webs of balance."

Domano and Chea always encouraged Kay to study as much as she could about different ways of being in the world, and to learn through direct experience rather than through her intellect. So, in addition to training with the Hetakas, Kay spent five intense years studying the Kahuna and Egyptian mystery school traditions and lived for a number of years with and among many different Northern American Indians, primarily those following the Lakota Sundance tradition, learning much about their ways of praying and thinking. The Hetakas saw this additional training as another way of fulfilling their tribe's ancient prophecies about bringing all of the many dif-ferent and diverse knowledges and traditions together so that we might come to see the bigger picture that they make—a picture so grand that we can't even imagine it right now.

Kay now spends her time consulting with individuals, training apprentices, lec-turing, and leading intensive workshops across the United States and in Europe. She has completed a second book, Sacred Link: Joining Fortunes with the Unknown, *about her training with the Hetakas, and has produced five CDs that help listeners experience some of the major ceremonies of the tradition in which she was trained. Her writing and teaching are a fulfillment of her teachers' request that she share the traditional knowledge she learned from them with the Western world, and that she heal and teach all those who ask for her assistance.*

Although we first met her in Oregon, Kay currently lives outside of Santa Fe, New Mexico, with her husband, Helmut Wahrmann.

We are a culture that is based on the idea that we are separated from everything: from our Creator, from our Garden of Eden, from nature, from the animals, the plants, the people. We're even separated from ourselves. This separateness creates a hierarchy in which we place ourselves on a ladder, somewhere between very good and very bad.

Here we are—we've been kicked out of the Garden and we're stuck way down at the bottom of the ladder. This doesn't do very much for our self-esteem. It also creates a social condition where, in order to get up the ladder, you have to yank off someone who is above you. So we end up judging and creating an environment of "shoulds" and "better than" or "less than." We're constantly scrambling, trying to get up the ladder to be in a "better than" place, yet we're always somehow still separated, still not good enough. We don't know who we really are—we don't know our own Song, what the Hetakas called the vastness and joy of our own essence. We are riddled with fear and uneasiness.

The world view of my adopted grandparents, the Hetakas, on the other hand, is one of connectedness, of being connected to all things, of being a part of Creator and Creation.

In this paradigm, everything is wondrously unique, yet also a part of everything else. When one thing is benefited, it is never at the expense of something else. Thus, in this tradition, we don't heal the patient at the expense of the disease, because everything has the right to live, to express itself, to be happy, to be in its fullness in a communicative environment that it truly enjoys.

A disease inside a body does not really enjoy being there: it's out of place, a stranger in a strange land. It's usually very willing to leave. But, if you try to force it out without any consideration for it or its purpose for being there—the message that it has to deliver—it fights back, because its job isn't done.

In the tradition in which I was trained, healing is a win/win situation. It's finding the elements inside a system that cause dysfunction and imbalance and communicating with them, developing a conversation between the healer, the body parts, the disorder, and the spirit helpers that are present.

Healing is balancing, so all the elements must be honored. You approach the disease with an attitude of gratefulness, of wanting to pass on its message. A disorder always has an inherent message, a reason why it's there in the first place. If that message can be passed on, the disorder is usually willing to leave.

The Two Major Healing Traditions

There are two major indigenous traditions for psychic, hands-on healing around the world: there is the win/win type and there is the warrior type. Warrior-type healers literally go to war with the disorder. They go into the patient's system, confront the disease, wrestle it, overpower it, and force it out of the person's body. Usually the way they force it out is to take at least some of the condition into themselves; they then wrestle it within themselves and expel it. This is not an easy way to do healing and warrior healers typically don't have long lives.

The other tradition is the one in which I was trained. Based on a win/win philosophy, its approach is one of peace. I learned to approach a disorder with respect and gratitude, providing some element of gain and win for everything involved in the process of the healing. The organs win something; the disease wins something; your patient wins something; you win something. Everyone is happy.

In a win/win scenario, the disease willingly gives its message, its information, to the healer and the client and leaves the body. Sometimes it just downright rushes out of the body. No one has to use an excessive amount of energy, so there's no danger and no harming.

As healers in the win/win tradition work, the energy that flows through them is coming from an ultimate, endless source, the Creator; it's coming through the heart-center of the Mother Earth; it's coming from the heart-center of the Sun; it's coming from the heart-center of our Galaxy.

Access to this extraordinary volume of complete life energy is through a special initiatory ceremony or spontaneous energy system opening granted by the spirits. This energy pours through the healer's body, like a conduit, and out through the heart and hands—so you're not taking energy from your own being and giving it to someone else. You're utilizing an extremely large energy source and directing it. This particular method is much healthier for the healer.

Meeting My Spirit Helpers

There's a process in an apprenticeship with the masters, the medicine people, that's common to indigenous peoples around the planet: somewhere in your apprenticeship you are taken on very specific quests and journeys to find your spirit helpers. The helper that stays with you and becomes very much a full-time partner and buddy is termed your power animal. The finding of your power animal is a vision quest all of itself, and that ritual was given to me very early on when I met the Hetakas.

To quest for your power animal in this tradition, you must go on a specific spirit journey to another world—the world of the animal spirits. This is a very real place that is talked about in traditions all over the planet. In the Hetakas' way, one must go to this place for oneself, by oneself.

When I undertook my journey, the ancient traditional location to access this world provided me with a hair-raising adventure through an excruciatingly long and dark cave. But I refused to let fear take over: I kept the awareness and feeling of who I really am, holding onto the feeling of my Song, my uniqueness, as I stepped forward. I persisted and the shaft opened out into an incredible, beautiful, vibrant, passion-filled landscape populated with thousands upon thousands of different life forms with all their smells and sounds and colors and textures—thousands upon thousands of different Songs.

I wandered out into the environment looking, touching, sniffing, listening, talking to everything I passed, taking in everything I could as I followed the instructions that had been given to me by Chea and Domano to locate my power animal. Every sort of animal that I knew of (and many that I didn't know) showed themselves until finally my power animal, my companion, arrived.

There was an instant familiarity—I knew this being. Others of the species came and together they showed me how to shapeshift my spirit into their form. Time was very different in that place. We played, hunted, hung out, went to ancient ruins, performed ceremony, slept. They taught me more than I could ever express. Ever since that journey I have been aware of my power animal and its communications with me.

My other spirit helpers came of their own accord over a period of years. Some I sought out purposely by doing vision quests, seeking their attention and their alliance, their knowledge and their help. When you seek helpers that way, sometimes they agree to work with you and sometimes they do not. Very often, one or two helpers will come of their own accord when you're not expecting it. They just plop themselves right there in your path and say, "I'm here to help you." The vulture, one of the two primary healing helpers that I work with most often, came to me in that way.

When I'm working with a client, both animal spirits are right there with me, observing and telling me to look here, look there. "This is what's wrong; this is where you go; this is how it's done." And I ask them many questions: "Show me the history of this. Is there something else in the body or the energy field that needs to be worked on?"

Anything that I would ask the body parts, or the disease itself, I would also ask the power animals, the helpers. Sometimes it's a three-, four-, five-way conversation going on.

Healing with Energy and Spirit

In the eastern Peruvian tradition in which I was taught, there are three basic levels of hands-on healing. The first level is just giving out energy; the receiving body system does whatever it wants with it. The next level is actually examining the energy field and the body, identifying and negotiating with the disorder. The condition may decide to leave at that point; sometimes it works that way. The third stage of healing is psychic surgery, where the whole energy system literally has to be cut open because that's the only way you're going to get to the disorder that's deep down inside the body.

I was taught the different stages of healing many months apart, and I had to work with one stage at a time to really learn it.

When I examine a body, I use all of the senses of my spirit. I let the energy pour out as I move my hands up and down the body, scanning all of its levels, looking for anything that is out of balance. It helps me to move my hands and to utilize the chakra centers of the hands as a sensory organ, but it's not necessary. I could sit there with my hands at my sides and just observe with my spirit and see the same thing. But using my hands facilitates a faster, bigger picture.

As I'm working on people, I'm flooding their whole being with more and more of the life energy. The more energy you flood them with, the easier it becomes to observe the body system. That's when I start moving in; I move my consciousness, my awareness, into the body.

An Aztec healer I once knew said, "I make myself very, very tiny and go walk around inside the body." And that's exactly what it's like. You take your awareness and shrink it down very small and walk around inside the body. That's when you talk to the body parts; that's when you talk to the disorder, and the three-, four-, five-way conversations begin.

So I move my hands up and down, anywhere from three to ten inches away from the physical part of the body, from the toes all the way up to the top of the head, up and down both sides, front, and back. With the senses of my spirit, I'm looking for visual pictures, I'm listening to anything that sounds wrong and I'm also listening to any information that might be coming from the body itself, or the disorder, or my spirit helpers.

In the tradition in which I was taught, it's very, very important to use your spirit guides to help you with healing. That's what they are there for. You don't have to depend on your own inner library of anatomical, medical resources. The spirits will definitely tell you what's wrong, and they'll give you as much detail as you need. What has always amazed me is that later I'll look in the medical books that I've collected and sure enough, it's all right there—exactly as the spirits described it, just as I saw it.

Not all healers see the body that way. Some of them see it as very abstract imagery; some see what looks more like car parts, because they understand cars. The image that comes through is the one that makes sense to them. For me, it's the anatomy. I see the anatomy. And as I'm looking at the anatomy, I'm also seeing the energy fields, the energy counterparts of our physical bodies.

If the physical body is sick, those spiritual images are sick; they're distorted. There's discoloration, and the energy that is surrounding them or moving in and out of them has the wrong vibrations. It's the wrong color, it's the wrong smell. Sometimes, the energy is not moving—it's stagnant. So I'm looking at all those different things at the same time.

Very often, the longer a disorder has been there, the more serious it is and the less the energy in that area has moved. The life energy itself has become stagnant. When it does that, it changes its vibratory frequencies, its color, its ability to give off light. It usually becomes darker or dimmer, even to the point of being kind of black. When a disorder is really, really bad, it's sort of like a "black hole." You literally can see the surrounding life energy gravitating toward it and just being sucked in.

Basically, what healers do is offer a person an input of new, fresh life energy. Sometimes, that by itself is enough to generate the healing. A person's body takes that energy and utilizes it to bring about a balance, to bring about healing. As I scan the whole body, this energy is just flowing out of my hands—very large volumes of it. And, as I do this, the field of the person I'm working on begins to take on more light; it gets brighter and brighter and starts to fill up with this energy.

If the person has got something like a "black hole," some problem that's very long-lived, very dense, very much out of order, then all this energy sort of gravitates toward it and disappears. And I can't do anything about it. Nothing lights up, nothing gets refreshed from that input of energy; it's all being sucked into that place. In that case, I know I have to find the "black hole" and deal with that first.

Working with Women

Women in our culture are taught to give and give and give. It's like they are pouring themselves into a "black hole" of their own.

Many women have experienced a great deal of pain, a great deal of disappointment. And all of that pain and disappointment gets shoved away—stashed in the breast tissue, in the lymph glands, the mammary glands, the uterus. These are the places where women give nourishment to other people. This is where they give life. But they're not able to give in the ways they really want to give, so they injure the very organs that they wish to use the most. These women end up with breast tumors, breast cancer; they end up with uterine tumors, endometriosis, cervical cancer.

When I work with women with tumors developing into cancer, I don't have to try to think it out for myself. I'm always instructed by the spirits on each individual case. I'm directed to go to different places where there's a great deal of disorder, and that would be the place where I would work first, where there's something like a tumor. That tumor is very much like a "black hole": it's sucking in the energy and it requires psychic surgery.

In the Philippines, psychic surgeons are famous for literally separating molecules of physical tissue and yanking out tumors. There are a lot of charlatans pretending to work in that tradition; they've had a lot of bad press. There's some of that old tradition in Peru, but mostly it's what they call "bloodless psychic surgery."

You can utilize this Peruvian technique to cut through the auric layers of a body or condition. The entire auric field has to be surgically opened up—the mental body, the spiritual body, the emotional body, right down into the physical body. That tumor has to be removed and it has to be done as a win/win operation. This is nothing to play around with; it can be dangerous if you don't know what you are doing. You must have a great deal of training to do this.

In the healing, I interact with the whole disorder and the tumor. I explain that there's a much better place for the disease than here, that this tumor has a world it can go to where it can be happy, that it doesn't have to stay in this place where it doesn't belong and is not loved and wanted.

And all of the messages, all of the stored pain this woman has ignored, tried to shove away, tried to pretend didn't exist—all of this has to be looked at by the patient. She has to acknowledge the pain. She doesn't have to go through the terror of it: she just has to acknowledge its existence, without judgment. Often, the person does not want to believe the pain is there. She doesn't want to confront it.

When you're doing this kind of healing, you are working on all the levels at once—on the physical, mental, emotional, and spiritual bodies. And, as you're scanning and observing, you are looking through all the levels at once. A problem has to be cleaned up all the way, through all the bodies and levels.

If you try to clean up just the physical manifestation of the problem and you don't address the emotional or the mental or the spiritual bodies, people will recreate the condition in their physical bodies at an alarming rate. That's what happens when people go into surgery to have a cancerous tumor removed. The doctors look around and they don't see any more cancer cells in there. They think everything is okay, sew the patient back up, and send her on her way.

But, if everything stays as it was in the person's emotional and spiritual and mental bodies—if she hasn't changed her way of doing things—that tumor, that cancer, is going to manifest itself again. It may not be in exactly the same spot, but it'll be back, and very rapidly.

Success in Healing

One thing that is impressed upon an apprentice is that success rate means absolutely nothing. Individual patients are going to be healed or not, according to what *they* want to do—how badly they really want to find health and balance. Sometimes people choose to have a particular disorder long before they were ever born. It's part of the life experience they came here to have. In that case, it doesn't matter what kind of healing you do. You aren't going to affect them, or make any change in their condition; their agenda has been fixed.

So, the very first step, the very first rule, when you approach people to heal them is to have your spirit helpers ask their spirit, "Can this be done? Is this an allowable thing?"

Sometimes the spirit says, "No, don't bother. Don't go in. It's none of your business." Sometimes you can do some band-aid stuff, give people a little extra boost of energy, and they'll feel better for a while. That's all you can do.

Sometimes, the individuals kind of know that already. Sometimes they've decided that they want to check out and this is the way they have decided to go. One part of them, in their conscious daily life, is saying, "Oh, heal me, heal me." But the rest of them has already made the decision to die. Some people are sort of straddling the fence; they haven't really decided yet whether they want to live or die. Sometimes you can encourage them to stay and work on healing themselves and sometimes you cannot.

There isn't a healer alive who can heal anyone. You can ignite change in other people's bodies and systems; you can ignite change in their emotional selves; you can ignite change in their total belief system—and that always reverberates out into the physical—but you can't heal someone else. You can provide a boost to bring them over the hump. You can remind the system how it's supposed to work. You can intercede with spirit. But it's the same story: you can take the horse to water, and then it's the horse's decision. Will it drink or won't it? You can't force it.

So you have to give up any attachment that you might have to succeeding, because you just do what you're shown, what you're instructed. You give as much as you can and that's all you can do. You pray for them. The people themselves have to do the rest. They're the only ones that can truly finish the process of healing themselves.

Healer, Heal Thyself?

A lot of healers are taught not to try to heal themselves. There's a reason for that: We get in our own way!

In the tradition in which I was trained, however, I was told that everything we do for someone else, we can do for ourselves. Yes, you probably will get in your own way to a certain degree, but if you work hard enough, you can facilitate some good results.

A good example is when I broke a bone in the middle of my foot. I was wearing high-heeled clogs, walking down a slanted driveway. My foot turned and I heard this terrible cracking sound. It was Saturday night, about midnight, and I was all by myself. So I hobbled into the house, kicked off the shoe, and looked at the injury. There was a triangular piece of bone pushing the skin outward on the side of my foot.

I knew that I had to get all the jagged edges lined up so that the healing, the knitting, could start. I'd been taught that you can move bones and align somebody's spine just by using energy, not touching anything with your physical hands. I hadn't had a chance to work on a broken bone yet, so this was my big test. With my hand about twelve inches out from my physical foot, I used energy to lift and push the bone back in place. I couldn't just push it sideways and have it go in; it had to be lifted up to have that triangular piece fit back into the slot.

Using psychic surgery, I cut open and went down into the foot to put different drainage devices in place so that the edema that usually happens around a break could drain away. As the pain started to come around, I would take the pockets of pain and just remove them, so that I was somewhat uncomfortable but not in severe pain. The thing that I had the most difficulty with was the pain.

The next morning, I called a friend who was also a healer and very good with bones and asked her to come over. The triangular piece was back in its proper place—all the little jagged edges had lined up completely, just where they were supposed to be. There was no swelling and no bruising. So my friend worked on getting the bone to weave, to begin the process of building tissue between the cracks. She got the rest of the pain out, too, and took me to see a doctor.

He was a cocky young man, the type who would like everybody to think that he had seen everything. I had to do a lot of talking to convince him that I had a broken bone in my foot and needed an x-ray!

Sure enough, you could see it on the x-ray: there was the break, and there was the ligament that had been yanked out of place. My friend and I had set it back down where it belonged and the end of the ligament was starting to re-root. You could see that it was not like it was supposed to be, that obviously this piece of bone had been way out of line, otherwise the ligament wouldn't have been torn off. And this doctor is looking at it as if he knew exactly what had happened...

When he left the room, his assistant said, "How did you do that? I have to know!" So I explained it to him and he was really excited. I did get a kind of strap-on cast for my own feeling of precaution, but I didn't need it and I didn't have to go through all the other medical procedures.

It can take several years for a ligament that gets ripped off the bone to reattach itself. Sometimes, they never heal at all. Yet the ligaments on my foot grew back exactly the way they were supposed to within months. The energy moved the bone back in place and reattached the fibers, literally sewing them back down into the bone. Then it stimulated the cells to do the things they're supposed to do. This is a great example of hands-on healing, of giving the body the things it needs to re-build and to heal.

The Backward-Turning Wheel

Ours is a culture the Hetakas described as a wheel that's turning backward. When a wheel turns backward, turns counterclockwise, it destroys itself. This is the energy that takes things apart. It's a natural force.

If you build a culture on this force, on this concept, the culture tears itself—and everything else in its path—apart. The Hetakas used to say that our backward-spinning wheel is an energy that is addicted to power over others and gain for the self at any cost. That is our culture, and we are in the place where our wheel has just about disintegrated.

The Hetakas described us as "the walking dead." They said that we are asleep and that we don't have any idea who or what we truly are. We are running around in this backward-turning wheel controlled by our own psychological addictions, our own dysfunctional patterns, and we're blind to it. In our fog, we identify ourselves with these patterns and addictions.

Our culture cannot sustain itself. Our materialism cannot maintain itself. The social interaction we have, the social structures of "power over" and personal gain at the expense of others, cannot maintain itself. This goes for individuals, groups, the entire culture. The environment is falling apart. It cannot maintain itself.

Our economic system is fragile, and becoming more and more fragile every year. It will topple. It can't continue the way it is. The way we do things socially, on a mass level—some people with a great deal of wealth and resources, others with no resources, starving to death—there's no need for it. The planet can support all the people who are on it.

Things just have to be done a little differently. Our whole cultural construct has to be different; our priorities have to be shifted. When we're hooked on that backward-turning wheel, our priority is fulfilling our addictions, no matter what the expense to others or the expense to the environment.

Another kind of a culture is one that the Hetakas described as a wheel turning clockwise, an energy that creates and manifests. This kind of culture is based on connectedness. It is based on a diversity and acceptance and joy and is committed to the generations yet to come. It creates an entirely different world.

When you're in a culture where the wheel turns clockwise, where everything is connected, you're aware of how precious and unique everything is. You're aware of how you are connected to other human beings, to the animals, the plants and the land, the soil, the rocks, the oceans, the rivers, the winds. They are all alive and conscious, each with a unique Song that radiates out into the universe. When you are consciously aware of the connection, you can't possibly continue to take power over or damage others or the environment.

As we build and live, as individuals, within the positive-turning wheel—the one that turns clockwise, the one that is consciously aware of its connectedness to all things, that is consciously aware of the generations yet to come—the decisions we make are entirely different. The priorities are entirely different. If it's not good for the babies five generations from now, you don't do it. If it's not good for the animal nations, or the plant nations, or some little creek, then you just don't do it. It's a very obvious choice; it's a very obvious decision.

As the backward-turning wheel disintegrates, we have to make our own individual wheels—our own beingness—turn in a clockwise direction. We have to wake up and take responsibility for living the truth of our Song, our own unique piece of Creator. This is the only way to build a culture in which the entire community turns clockwise.

One Person Can Change the World

The Hetakas, my adopted grandparents, always said that one person can change the world. One person. That's all it takes to change the world. We each have the power and the ability to create that forward-turning wheel within ourselves, living it, radiating it out. As we do that, we influence everything around us. We become an example, imprinting with our energy that pattern, that growth, that understanding, on everyone and everything. We imprint that energy and that knowledge in the spaces we've been in: in the rooms, the buildings, the furniture—so that anyone who comes into that space, even years later—is imprinted with that energy, that knowledge, that understanding. And that facilitates growth, learning, change.

Our thoughts and emotions are far more powerful than we've ever believed them to be. In this modern culture, we're taught that they don't mean anything, that they don't amount to anything, that they don't affect anybody else. But they have an extraordinary effect on everything. Our thoughts and emotions affect people that we have never met and never will meet, people on the other side of the planet, people who aren't even born yet. We are affecting them by what we think and what we feel and what we do, by the actions we take. And how we affect everything and everyone is our choice.

One person can change the world.

It has to start inside the self. We each have to change ourselves first. A drowning person cannot save another drowning person. We have to take the responsibility to heal ourselves, as individuals, first. As we do that, and learn and grow, then we have something we can offer. We will have the growth pattern in our own energy field that will radiate out and people will learn from that pattern. Just by being in contact with that energy, they will learn from it. One person's thoughts, emotions, and prayers, set in the right direction, the right context, can imprint on the tone of human consciousness, on the entire energy field of the planet.

One person.

Denise Linn

Seattle, Washington

Heaven isn't 10 miles up in the sky; it's a dimension
that coexists with this one, here and now.
Synchronicity is a good way to tell when you're close
to that dimension: You need something and it appears;
you think about something and it happens;
you're walking in the forest and the person who has
the key to the next step in your life appears...

*S*ynchronicity and a rainbow led us to Denise Linn's Seattle home. When we started thinking about the people we wanted to interview for this book, Denise Linn came immediately to mind. We had read her book, Sacred Space, and were impressed with her multicultural, multidimensional approach to working with and healing the physical environment. We were also intrigued by our brief glimpses of the woman behind the book. So we wrote to the address in the back of her book. When we received no immediate response, we assumed that Denise was unavailable to meet with us, let go of the idea of interviewing her, and went on with our work.

Months later, we made plans to meet with Kay Cordell Whitaker, who was at that time living in Eugene, Oregon. The same day that we booked our flights, a postcard arrived from Denise. She said that she had been working abroad and had only just received our letter, but would be delighted to meet with us when she returned to the States; she promised to contact us a few weeks later to set a definite date.

Carl Jung coined the word synchronicity to describe simultaneous events that are both too unlikely and too meaningful to be mere coincidence. As "luck" would have it, the week Denise planned to return to the U.S. was the same week we had already scheduled a trip to the Northwest coast. We felt that the synchronicity of Denise's card arriving the day we had booked a flight to a city a four-hour drive away from her was so strong that we would trust the universe and add a few days to the end of our trip—even though we knew we wouldn't actually be able to confirm the dates with Denise until long after we paid for the tickets.

The signs were right: A few days before we left Boston, we got a call from Seattle confirming that Denise would, indeed, be able to meet with us on the exact date we had set aside!

Fortune stayed with us. Heavy rains and severe flooding had plagued the Pacific Northwest for weeks. But, as we drove from Oregon to Washington, the rain stopped and the sun came out. As our eyes adjusted to the light, we noticed a perfectly formed rainbow arched in front of our rental car.

Normally, a rainbow stretches across the sky, reaching from one distant plane to another. This rainbow was different: it was only about four feet in front of us, and it stretched from the left to the right bumper of our car. As we drove, the rainbow kept pace with us—escorting us to Seattle, and to our meeting with Denise.

In her book, The Secret Language of Signs, Denise Linn says that a rainbow is "a message from spirit...that you are going in the right direction and that your path is *blessed and guided." Some synchronistic events, like rainbows, are easy to see and easy to recognize as blessings. Other events may be more painful or difficult to experience, but contain the seeds of blessings nonetheless.*

Denise herself may have been so blessed when, at age seventeen, she was shot by a stranger and left for dead by the side of a country road. When she reached the hospital, Denise was not expected to survive. When she beat the odds and lived, her doctors predicted that she would be incapacitated for life. Today, Denise is not only well and fully functioning, she is an internationally acclaimed teacher and author. And she says it was the near-death experience resulting from that fateful attack that started her on her spiritual path—and changed the course of her life forever.

Following her near-death experience, Denise was drawn to study many ancient traditions. She lived for two years in a Zen Buddhist monastery, and then began a series of apprenticeships that helped her develop both her spiritual life and her healing abilities: she studied with a traditional Hawaiian kahuna (or shaman); a Shiatsu master; and the woman who introduced Reiki (a Japanese system for channeling energy) to the West.

In time, Denise also delved into the teachings of her own Cherokee heritage and worked with healers in a variety of traditional, earth-based cultures, including a Pueblo Indian, an Australian Aboriginal tribe, the Zulu in Africa, and the Taranaki people of New Zealand, who recognized her as a "tohunga" and made her an honorary member of their Maori tribe.

Her study of native cultures around the world—as well as her own near-death experience—led Denise to acknowledge and honor the living spirit within all things. Central to all of her work is the idea that we are not separate—neither from each other nor from the animals, rocks, trees, and energy fields that surround us.

After twenty-eight years as a "hands-on" healer, Denise no longer sees clients one-on-one. Instead, she devotes her time to writing and leading seminars, working with an average of 2,000 people a month worldwide. When she is not on the road, Denise lives quietly in Seattle, Washington, with her husband, David, and her daughter, Meadow.

I believe that you only teach what you need to learn and, if you are a healer, the energy you put out always returns to heal you as well. I certainly find this to be true in my healing practice. Each person who comes to me represents an aspect of myself that needs healing. As my clients heal, I heal. My healing, in turn, enhances their healing. It's a remarkable phenomenon.

Sometimes it is very obvious. For example, one day I had a sore shoulder in the morning and, "coincidentally," that day four people in a row came to see me with sore shoulders. When things were "eating away" at me, people with cancer would schedule appointments. I would heal as my clients healed and vice versa.

My first teacher taught me that when people come to me for healing, the honor is not theirs to be with me; the honor is mine to be with them. I believe the most profound healing can occur when you recognize that you are not separate from the person with whom you are working.

The Near-Death Experience That Changed My Life

It is often the traumatic and difficult times in life that give us a new definition of ourselves, a new sense of purpose. For me, it was an experience I had when I was seventeen that catapulted me into a whole new way of perceiving the reality in the world around me. It was a sunny summer afternoon and I was riding on a country road, through the cornfields, on my motor bike. I didn't realize that a man I had never met was following me in a car. Suddenly, he plowed his car into my motor-bike, throwing me onto the dirt.

I couldn't understand why he had done this, because I had never done anything to him. As I was trying to get up, I looked up and saw him aiming a gun at me. Sometimes, when you're in a traumatic situation, everything seems to happen in slow motion. I can remember looking at the barrel of the gun and noticing how big the hole looked. Suddenly, I felt like I had been hit by a train. There was the loud noise of the gunshot followed by incredible pain, and I was left on the side of the road.

That was the sequence I remembered: I was shot and left on the side of the road. But I always wondered why the man who shot me didn't shoot again, especially when I learned that he had killed several other people. Years later, in a very deep meditation, I went back to the shooting to see if there were any details I had missed, anything that would explain why I was the only person to survive his attack. What I remembered during the meditation was amazing...

I remembered lying there on the side of the road after he had shot me; my eyes were closed and everything was magnified. I heard the sound of a gun being cocked again. Then I remembered opening my eyes and looking at this man. For some reason, unknown to me at the time, all I felt for him in that moment was compassion. Maybe it was because I was out of my body anyway—but I just felt love and compassion.

As he aimed the gun and looked at me, I could feel a struggle going on inside of him. He had already wounded me, and now he really wanted to kill me—but he couldn't shoot while I was looking at him like that. I wasn't afraid; I wasn't angry. I just looked at him with love. All of a sudden, it was as if his great internal struggle reached an apex. All the energy went out of him. He turned around, got in his car, and drove off.

A farmer found me on the road and I was taken to a nearby hospital. I was in a lot of pain, but I was still conscious. I remember being in the ambulance, looking out at the trees and thinking about how beautiful everything was, how precious life was...I'll never forget that experience.

A Place with No Separation

When we got to the hospital, I remember people yelling, "She's been shot..." I remember how bright the light was and how intense the pain was. Then, all of a sudden, everything became dark. It was as if I were in this black, soft bubble. Suddenly, the bubble seemed to burst.

A radiant light surrounded me. Everything in the entire universe, the entire cosmos, was a part of this light....I didn't seem to be observing the light, I seemed to *be* the light. There was wonderful music, too, and the music and the light weren't separate from each other. I know this sounds strange, but the light and the sound were the same thing...and I *was* the light and the sound.

There was also a deep sense of love. It was different from the way we usually experience love. Usually, our sense of love includes a sense of separation: I love you...I love this object...this person loves me...But this love was not separate. There was nothing that was not love. And I *was* that love.

I remember trying to think about the past, and the past didn't exist. I could not conceive of the past. Everything was *now*—no past or future. It seemed physically impossible to try to think about the past or the future. I couldn't do it because everything was occurring simultaneously.

Everybody who has ever been and everybody who will ever be was there, but we were not separate from each other. It wasn't as if we were all squeezed together. We were all the same thing. This all seems so strange now, but at the time it was the most normal, natural experience. It was so comfortable that I knew I was home.

There was a river of light, and I knew that if I could cross that river I would not return to this body. I really wanted to stay in that beautiful place. However, as I got about half-way across the river, the golden light parted on either side of me; I felt something, like a rope, tug at my middle.

As I was yanked back into my body—and this is common to people who have near-death experiences—I remember saying, "No, I don't want to go back." But a voice said, "It's not your time; there's something you need to do…" It has occurred to me over the years that coming back didn't necessarily mean I was special. Mostly, I think, my near-death experience meant that I was so far off my path that it took a huge cosmic kick to get me back on it again.

Seeing the World in a Different Way

When I got back into my body, it was very damaged. I'd lost my spleen and an adrenal gland; I had damage to my intestines, my left lung, my stomach, and my spine. Eventually, I also lost a kidney and had a tube inserted to replace my aorta. However, something was also ignited in me: it was a different way of perceiving the world around me.

I began to sense and experience things that other people did not. One night, while I was in the hospital, I felt someone hold my hand. I opened my eyes to see who was holding my hand, but I couldn't see anybody—even though I could feel the fingers and the warmth of the hands. Every night my hand was held. One night, it felt like a child's hand was holding mine. I now believe that these were the hands of angels.

I talked to a minister in town about the hands, and he said, "Oh, that must have been the drugs they were giving you…" There wasn't anyone to talk with about the things that were happening to me, anyone who could help me understand why I could hear music that other people couldn't hear, or why I could sense things other people couldn't sense.

I believe my view of the world changed because my identity shifted during my near-death experience. Before that event, I identified with my body. I am Cherokee on my mother's side, but she was a scientist, as was my father. They both had a very traditional, scientific view of the world. They said, "This is it...When you die, you're dead; there's nothing else. Unless something is scientifically provable, it doesn't exist." But after I was shot, I knew that I was more than a physical body; I knew I had a soul that was infinite.

Searching for the Source of My Experience

In subsequent years, I wanted to find out more about that place I had gone to during those moments when I was thought to be dead. I lived in a Zen Buddhist monastery in Hawaii for over two years because I'd heard about Zen enlightenment experiences. People said that when you reach enlightenment, you merge with the light, you become one with all people and all things and have a sense of infinite "now-ness."

I thought that sounded similar to my near-death experience, so I moved into a Zendo and sat in meditation, sometimes for up to sixteen hours a day. It was a good time in my life; it was also difficult to meditate for that many hours a day. But even though I meditated for long periods of time, I didn't reach the place for which I was searching.

I also trained with Morna Simeona, a Hawaiian kahuna (medicine woman). She was the first person to teach me about healing and energy. From her, I gained an understanding of healing in accordance with the ancient ways. She taught me to listen to the clouds, to hear what they have to say, and to listen to the trees. She said that everything is communicating to you at every moment.

Later, I trained with a woman named Hawayo Takata, who brought something called Reiki from the East to the West. I organized her first courses for Westerners and she taught me how to move energy through my hands for healing. I also trained with a Shiatsu master, who taught me how to use the energy points in the body for healing.

When I gave a Shiatsu treatment and pushed a body point, I could sense how that point was connected to a corresponding point on the planet and a point in the universe. This led me to understand that the body is a microcosm of the macrocosm. The sensations I experienced during my Shiatsu sessions were the closest to those I felt in that wonderful place of light during my near-death experience.

One of the things I realized as a result of my experience in the hospital is that heaven isn't ten miles up in the sky; it's a dimension that coexists with this one, here and now. Synchronicity is a good way to tell when you're close to that dimension: You need something and it appears; you think about something and it happens; you're walking in the forest and the person who has the key to the next step in your life appears.

The Healing Touch

After I left the Zendo, I became a very successful healer. I found that I could touch people and take their pain away, literally take their illnesses away. This was really exciting. I thought, "I've been given a gift of healing and I want to help as many people as I can."

Many people came to me for healing. I placed my hands on the area of their body which needed healing, and their discomfort would seem to travel through my hands into my body. Then I would feel a small twinge of whatever was troubling them inside myself. Immediately, their pain or disease would be gone.

During this time, I experienced a dangerous health emergency myself. I have a six-inch plastic tube replacing my aorta near my heart. One morning I woke up and discovered long lines of bruises resulting from blood clots in the veins of my arms and legs. The tube had begun to separate from my aorta. It was very serious.

While I was recovering, I began to wonder why this had happened to me. I thought, "Wait a minute. I'm helping as many people as I can. I'm working from early in the morning until late at night. I'm doing good work. Why did this happen?"

I searched my soul for answers until I came to the realization that something was wrong in my healing practice. It may sound strange, but what I realized was that I was taking opportunities away from people.

I came to understand that almost every physical problem has its source in some area of unresolved emotional difficulty within us. When you take away a symptom—without healing the source of the problem—something else will occur, some other problem will manifest. For instance, if I took the pain away from a client's sore shoulder—and if that sore shoulder had been caused by her carrying more burdens than she felt that she could handle and the underlying problem was never addressed—then something else might happen to her. She might, for example, develop stomach difficulties.

So I began to change the way I worked with people. I also changed where the healing came from within myself. Originally, I believed: "I am the healer and you are the one being healed." I saw myself as separate from my client. When I began working in a different way, it wasn't only that I would say, "Okay. Let's find out what the cause of this problem is...." The change was deeper than that.

I began working with people in such a way that the boundaries between us simply disappeared. I would place my hands on my clients and become very still and quiet. Then I would imagine that I was sinking beneath the surface of their body to find a place of unity, a place where we were not separate. It was as if we merged for a moment. It wasn't a merging of personalities; it was a merging of spirit. I didn't think about their problem—all that I experienced was being. It seemed to me that this "being-ness" ignited the source of remembering inside people, and, when that place of remembrance in the Self was ignited, a powerful opportunity for healing was created.

I discovered that this new kind of healing was more profound, more lasting. It wasn't symptom-oriented; it was human being-oriented. It wasn't as dramatic as when I would touch someone and take the pain or disease away. But this healing felt—and continues to feel—much deeper because it comes from a place that is real, a place of truth. With this kind of healing, one symptom didn't replace another: the healing lasted.

Eventually, I found that same method of healing could also work for whole groups of people. In my seminars in Europe, Australia, Africa, Asia, South America, and the United States, I work with groups of 200 to 400 people in a way that allows them to get to the primal source of their limitations, so they can be healed. I also train people in feng shui techniques that can transform ordinary home and work environments into places of sanctuary, beauty, and spiritual retreat.

I give verbal information in my seminars, but I think growth and transformation really occur during the times of silence—so I also do guided visualizations and meditations. When someone takes the opportunity to still the mind and enter into that quiet place (which happens during the meditation), real magic—even miracles—can occur.

Understanding and Working with Energy

Underlying most of my work is the understanding of energy. For me, that understanding came as the result of being shot. What I learned at that time was that even those things around us that *look* solid actually are a form of energy. Our bodies are a field of energy; our houses are a field of energy, and so is the universe surrounding us. We are living in an ocean of energy with which we are constantly interacting.

I once visited Credo Mutwa, a head sangoma (or Zulu medicine man) in Bhophutaswana, Africa. He was one of the most profound human beings I've ever met; his wisdom ran so deep into the earth that he seemed to have tapped into universal knowledge. For example, one time we were sitting together talking, when all of a sudden his face and body contorted. He said, "Oh-hh-hh." I said, "What's wrong?" And he said, "The French have just exploded an underground bomb in the South Pacific." It was as if his sense of self was so expanded that it incorporated not only his body, but the entire universe—and he could feel that testing within his universal energy body. It was remarkable.

I work with this universal energy in different ways. In one group, I might be talking about the energy in homes, about how the objects in your home have energy. The way you place these objects affects you. In other groups, I might talk about reincarnation and past lives—about how who we are today is a result of who we once were. Or, I might talk about dreams, about how, within the night, we enter portals into ancient and sacred dimensions that dwell within us. But all of these seemingly different subjects emanate from the same source, which is energy.

Even though the topics may change dramatically, whenever I'm working with a group we collectively generate very powerful energy. And this isn't just my subjective point of view. After attending a seminar, many people notice that the magnetic strips on their credit cards have been erased. Others report that for three days after a workshop, they seem to have an effect on electromagnetic fields; for example, televisions turn on spontaneously when they walk by.

Spontaneous Healings in Groups

It is not unusual for spontaneous healings to occur in my seminars. For example, one woman had a cancerous tumor so severe that it was pushing on her optic nerve. She could hardly see when she arrived. In the course of the seminar, she regained her vision. Two years later, she was still alive and seeing well. Another person had used a hearing aid for fifty-two years; she had been nearly deaf almost from birth. In the course of a seminar, this person got her hearing back. Four years later, she still had her hearing. I always like to see long-term effects, because sometimes there can be an instant euphoria where a person feels better—but then the symptoms return.

A woman who came to one of my seminars in Australia discovered that the program was being held in a Japanese hotel. She had been interned in a Japanese prison camp during World War II, and had hated the Japanese ever since. Her continual stomach problems had started in the prison camps. During this seminar, she not only experienced a spontaneous healing of her stomach problems, she was also able, during the course of the day, to talk with several Japanese people. She found them to be friendly and kind, whereas before she had never been able to even look at a Japanese person.

These are not uncommon stories; events like these occur in every single seminar I lead. But I don't think that these so-called "spontaneous healings" are miracles; I think that they are the result of natural laws. And I don't think they occur because there is anything special about me.

I do think that, as a group, we are able to co-create energy. If you take one tuning fork and place it next to a second one, the second tuning fork will begin to vibrate. I think that, in a group, we become each other's tuning forks, co-creating and generating a life force energy. It's that energy that can activate the place of healing within each of us and allow us to return to the root or the source of our difficulties—whether or not we are consciously aware that this is happening.

There are times when I'm working with groups that I know I'm not talking to anyone but myself. I know that I teach what I need to learn. When I've really learned what I'm teaching, I probably won't teach anymore. So when I'm leading a seminar, I listen to what I'm saying because I know that this is what I need to learn. If I'm teaching people about loving themselves, it's because I want to love myself more deeply; if I'm teaching about forgiveness, it's because I need to learn how to forgive more.

Vibration, Drumming, and Healing

In my seminars, we are co-creating energy, and when you begin to enter into the realm of energy you gain the understanding that everything has a vibration. Science is validating that everything has different vibrational frequencies. Color, for example, has a frequency: Violet is a finer, faster frequency and red, at the other end of the spectrum, is a slower frequency.

After I was shot, I could look at a color and hear its sound; I could also hear a piece of music and see color flowing through it. When people set out on these inward journeys, they often find that the separation between their sensations of smell and hearing and sight begins to diminish, so that they can smell a color, see the colors of a smell, or hear the sound of a color.

A drum is not just a musical instrument; it is an object of power that can transport you into the realm of energy. Drumming—the rhythm of the heartbeat—is the most constant thing we're aware of for the first nine months of being in our physical body. It has been my experience that when there is drumming a body will absorb the rhythm that it needs. I believe this explains why drumming is so often used in healing rituals in earth-based cultures around the world.

In my seminars, I sometimes use drums. The people who are drumming decide what beat to use. As the energy generated begins to move them—and as they connect with the person they are drumming for—the drumbeat will often change. The drummers seem to almost disappear; at some point they are no longer deciding what beat to use—they are just allowing the beat to flow through them. And that's when healing can come.

When I drum, I ask people to look at where in their bodies they can feel the vibration. They may feel it in their throats, their chests, or their stomachs; they will usually feel it in the place where their body needs it most. I believe that the body naturally absorbs those rhythms.

In ancient times, and even in some modern cultures, the drum was thought to be a living entity. It was often buried with the medicine man or medicine woman who owned it. I talked to Credo Mutwa, the Zulu sangoma (or medicine man), about the importance of the drum in his culture. He said, "In ancient times, if someone touched the medicine man's drum they were killed. Now we charge them 200 rand—which is a lot of money for a poor Zulu."

My husband, David, and I hand craft ceremonial drums for people. When a drum is made, it really does feel as if it is being birthed—so we perform a naming and blessing ceremony for each drum we make. I named one drum "Moonshadow." My husband said, "That doesn't sound like a very good name." And I said, "I don't know, that was just the name that came to me; I know that it's the right name for this drum."

The woman who received it said, "Denise, this is so amazing. As a young woman, I wanted to have a healing center and call it Moonshadow. That was my dream. When I got married, my husband said that we could have a center—but he didn't like the name Moonshadow, so we named it Pilgrim's Rest. I never really liked that name."

This woman received the drum just after she had been divorced and planned to start traveling. She said, "You know, I now have my Moonshadow—my healing center—and I will be taking it with me."

You Don't Have to Suffer to Grow

I used to think that you needed to suffer to grow. How else could I make sense of the difficult experiences I had gone through in my life?

Years ago, when people in my seminars would regress back to an earlier age in their present lives, or into past lives, the experience was usually very emotional. In every seminar I led, someone would start really going through a catharsis, and pretty soon the whole room would be yelling and crying and sobbing, and I would think, "Yes! It's working, it's working."

Well, one day I led a seminar in Vancouver (Canada), and during the guided meditations everyone was quiet. I thought, "Oh, no. I've lost it." I called my husband at the end of the seminar and said "David, I'm going to have to find a new profession. It didn't work." At another seminar in Toronto, the same thing happened.

I became really concerned: Here were two seminars that I thought hadn't worked. Because I felt I'd lost the ability to effectively lead seminars, I started thinking about where to go next in my life. Then I began getting letters from the participants in those programs, telling me about all the wonderful things that had happened. And I thought, "How can all these wonderful things happen to people when they're not crying or yelling, when they aren't suffering, when they're having a good time?"

I never made a conscious decision to make a change in this area. But ever since that time, when people come to my seminars, they enjoy themselves—and their lives get better. I think that on some deep subconscious level, I must have realized that you really don't have to suffer to grow. You can have fun, you can enjoy yourself—and you can get the same results.

I have the feeling that, energetically, things are really speeding up on the planet. I think that there's a huge awakening occurring, and, within that awakening, I believe there will be the understanding that suffering is not necessary. In fact, when you have joy in your life, that joy spreads all around you. Like a pebble dropped in a still pool, its ripples are felt at the farthest shores. Joy actually generates an energy that can be much more profound—and much more healing—than suffering.

Fred Woody

Steamboat, Arizona

All is beautiful

before me

behind me

below me

above me.

All is beautiful

all around me.

—Excerpt from a traditional
Navajo healing chant

*T*he Navajo Nation covers more than twenty-five thousand square miles. Much of the land is located on the Colorado Plateau, in the Four Corners area where Arizona, New Mexico, Utah, and Colorado come together. The immensity of the space is hard to grasp and hard to describe: mountains, deserts, forests, sandstone, basalt, lava rock, craters, canyons, and cliffs are all housed here. Beautiful as well as diverse, the land is largely silent and largely empty. You can travel the two-lane highways that criss-cross the reservation for hours without passing another car or seeing another human being.

In this isolated and seemingly inhospitable land, a homeland they hold sacred, the Dineh (the name the Navajo call themselves) have not only survived but thrived. The traditional lifeways which helped them resist domination by Plains tribes and Spanish conquistadors in the early eighteenth century also helped The People survive a hostile U.S. government which did its best in the nineteenth and early twentieth centuries to first physically, and then culturally, eradicate the tribe. Reduced to fewer than ten thousand people in 1868, after a government-ordered three hundred-mile Long Walk and incarceration at Fort Sumner, New Mexico, Dineh rolls have swelled to more than two hundred thousand members. They are now the largest Native American tribe in North America.

We walked into this history and this landscape with some trepidation. We were to be introduced to Fred Woody by his granddaughter, Tamara, who had lived with Judith in Massachusetts during a cultural exchange program, and by her mother, Fred's daughter Laverna. Seventy-five years old at the time we met him, we knew that Fred was a traditional Navajo who had spent his life on the reservation, practicing his healing art for the benefit of his people for more than fifty years. We also knew that he spoke little English and that he had never before consented to speak to outsiders about his work. He would speak with us only because we had been brought to him by family.

We had learned just enough about Dineh culture to know that looking people in the eye and asking a lot of personal questions is considered rude. Compared to Anglos (whites), the Dineh are not big talkers. They choose words carefully and give details sparingly. Personal matters are to be kept private and sacred practices are not to be turned into stories to satisfy the curiosity of strangers. So we were nervous. How would we collect the information we needed while showing proper respect for the man and his traditions?

The interview took place near Fred's home in a remote area of the reservation. We sat outside, under a tree. Behind Fred's head were towering thunderheads. Miles away, a storm raged. Behind our heads rose another great storm, also miles away. As we watched the skies and listened to the soft musical sounds of the Dineh language, a language totally unrelated to the European tongues we were familiar with, we gradually let go of our attachments to the interview and the photographs. In that beautiful landscape, with that wise man and his gracious daughter, we sat for several hours, only vaguely aware of the mid-day heat.

At one point, red ants began swarming over Judith's sandaled foot. Not wanting to get up and interrupt the flow of the conversation, she wriggled a bit but stayed put. Minutes later, Fred noticed the ants. Using his walking stick, he banged on the ground, then drew a line in the sand between Judith's foot and the army of ants. For the remainder of the interview, not a single ant crossed that line.

At the beginning of our conversation, Fred refused to let Susan photograph him. By the end of the interview he agreed to just a few shots. She took some fine pictures of Fred standing alone and looking directly into her lens, and of Fred and Laverna standing side by side. When Fred turned to walk back to his house with Tamara, Susan snapped the final frame.

Our ongoing friendship with Tamara, Laverna, and her husband Javier, who feed and shelter us whenever we come within a few hundred miles of their Tuba City home, is a bright spot in our lives, an unexpected gift of this journey. In the end, we realized we need not have worried about the outcome of our meeting with Fred Woody. We got much more from that visit than we ever could have expected. Whether it could be translated into print, however, was another question.

This chapter differs from others in this book in two significant ways: First, Fred's words are not recorded in the first person. This is because our questions and Fred's answers were translated by his daughter, Laverna, at the time of the original interview. Later questions and answers were mediated by Laverna and her sister, Alice Mary.

Second, Fred doesn't go into great detail about his work. For this reason, a little background information about Dineh healing traditions may be helpful to provide some context for Fred's story.

Like many Native Americans, the Dineh see body and mind, the material and spiritual worlds, as inseparable parts of a unified whole. Health is considered a function *of inner and outer balance. Healing ceremonies, called chants or sings, are designed to address the cause rather than the symptoms of an illness and bring the elements in a person's life that are out of balance back into harmony.*

The Dineh medicine man, called a chanter or singer, is as much a tribal history-keeper as a healer. Because the knowledge he must master is oral rather than written, a singer's training is long and difficult. To be successful, a candidate must have a good memory, a strong voice, a spiritual nature, and great physical stamina. Because they must remember large numbers of prayers exactly as they have been taught (with no variation and no error), and reproduce many different sand paintings, freehand, in minute detail, most singers specialize in treating only one type of disorder.

The Encyclopedia of Native American Healing notes that the Dineh have more than sixty chantways for blessing, curing, and purification. According to this source, Fred Woody's specialty, the Evilway or Ghostway chants, are "purification ceremonies...employed to cure the patient...of illness caused by the spirits of the deceased. The idea behind these ceremonies is that it is necessary to avoid the dead, because contact with them can lead to illness or premature death."

One additional note: the Ghostway is specific to illnesses caused by Dineh spirits. Non-Navajo ghosts must be dispelled by another ritual known as the Enemyway or by the ceremonial Squaw Dances held in summer months.

What we need to understand first is that there are different types of medicine men. My dad is known for his Evil Chaser, what is called the Ghostway.

The spirit of the deceased that comes, it's not an evil spirit. It's a spirit that you kind of invite in your mind to take over your life. And, if you don't come face-to-face with it, it will continue to harm your health either physically or mentally. What my father does is put these spirits to rest. He asks and prays in a precise way for the spirit to stay away, to not invade the person's life.

Some previous writings indicate some association with evil things with the type of practice that my father performs. It does anger me, some of the things I've read. His practice is by no means evil.

Some people will come and say that this person is doing some witching, and ask if my dad can do this same thing back to them. But my father's sole purpose is to enhance one's spirit to continue on a positive journey, not to do harm to another person's spirit. The chanting he performs, the singing that he knows, is to help people get on with their lives again. It's not something that you can work against another person to do harm. His belief is in healing the soul. He is a healer—what he does is put the spirits to rest by his songs and by his prayers.

To Become a Medicine Man, You Really Have to Put Your Mind to It

He says the way you learn this practice is by following a medicine man, a close relative—it could be your father or your grandfather—and you travel to different places, wherever people need you. And he says like anything else, you practice and you become good at it, and you pick up what you need to learn in order to become a medicine man.

His father was also a medicine man. It's been carried on from generation to generation in the same family. During that time, there was no formal education or school on the reservation, so a lot of people were wanting to become medicine men. He told me a lot of older people used to come to his father and to his maternal grandfather to learn the ritual. While these men would be learning the prayers, he would lie there on the sheepskin. He would listen to these other people try to learn to sing and say the prayers. By listening all the time, he got it into his mind and he memorized all the chants and the prayers.

He says that he tried school, day school, when education first came to the reservation. He tried but it wasn't for him—it was too confining. His father told him that he could also make a living as a medicine man, be well known and respectable, and find a place for himself in the community. So, since he was already familiar with the Ghostway, he chose this path.

For a lot of the men, it was hard to learn and memorize the chants. I guess it's like learning the verses of the Bible. For my father, as a young boy, it was easy because he remembered the chants and the particular order that they came in. And then, when he was herding sheep, of course, he practiced a lot, using the sheep and the lizards as patients. He says it was easy for him.

The most important thing you need to learn is the prayers, the chants. The chants are handed down from generation to generation; they are all oral. He has mentioned before that he has maybe seventy-two different ways of praying and they are not written down on any paper or recorded on any tape. He has them all in his mind. There are maybe close to two hundred different songs you have to learn and also different kinds of sand paintings. He does a lot of different prayers in a lot of different ways.

So that's the most important thing you need to learn, the chants. And from there you learn how to apply different rituals to the person, the patient. The chants and rituals are interdependent; they go together. You also have to learn how to use a variety of certain types of herbs and plants.

It takes approximately ten years for someone to learn the type of ritual or practice my father performs. And once you think you have learned what you need to perform the ritual, you don't go off and start singing, just like that. You have to be initiated and you have to have a ritual ceremony done on yourself with the chants and prayers you have learned. The other medicine men perform this on you, and they will fix all the materials, the paraphernalia, you need for the ceremony.

Some people train just by following the medicine men around and they learn all the songs and prayers, but they will not fully become medicine men. In haste, they will begin to hold ceremonies without the proper initiation procedures and the ceremony will not have meaning or purpose. But if you've been initiated, and have all the chants and prayers and paraphernalia prepared for you, everything will work positively for you. When you do your chant and prayer, you will have been blessed with it.

What the Ghostway Heals

Let's say that a loved one has died and a person is grieving and depressed over the loss of a loved one. When some people lose a loved one, they can't get back to their old way of life. It seems like there is a block there and they can't move on. That's when they come for my dad, and that's how he helps them.

He chants and says prayers throughout the night, until the early dawn. He says that there are spirits around, especially toward the evening. They get into your mind and they tell you how peaceful and beautiful everything is, and they kind of entice you to join them. That's where he comes in. He has special herbs he puts on the person and he asks the spirit to stay away and to let this person continue on with his or her life.

If you allow the spirit to just come, let it take over your life, you can become both physically and emotionally ill. Physically, you may have aching bones late in the afternoon, be constantly urinating, have a bloated stomach or back pain, swelling in your legs and hands, double or blurry vision, a ringing sound in your ear, or some lightheadedness. Emotionally, you'll feel lonely, get upset easily, and cry all the time for no reason. You may see things like shadows.

He says that when the people come to him, their minds are usually completely preoccupied with a person that they have lost or with some other person who invades their dreams to the point where they feel that this spirit has actually come to do them harm in some way. If a woman has lost a husband, for example, the husband may return and the woman will have a dream that she is having a relationship with him. Sometimes patients will say that the person they have lost is constantly on their mind, and, if they are out somewhere, they see this person in the crowd.

This is how the evil spirit can cause you to become sick. These will usually be the spirits of loved ones, although you can also be affected by the spirit of any Dineh [Navajo] corpse. In a sense, they are not actually evil. They just kind of invade your thoughts so much that you stop living for yourself and you let yourself go. You become severely depressed and you don't eat. You're not functional, you're not social. You become closed and withdrawn.

Who Can Be Affected by a Ghost Sickness

He says the spirit doesn't choose someone randomly. You, yourself, invite it in. If you've had a relationship with a person and that person is in your thoughts all the time, you are doing harm to yourself; you are making yourself sick from that.

Other ways people can get this kind of sickness is if they look at a dead body, or if they go to a funeral and touch the corpse or put some of their personal belongings into the casket as a token of their love. This allows the ghost to come back to them and they can get sick from it. For a female, if you were pregnant and you lost the baby—if you touched that fetus, carried it, or buried it—you can be affected by the child's spirit. Women who are pregnant also can pass the sickness, or the spirit, on to their unborn child. And people who don't participate in the acceptable mourning period can pass the sickness or spirit on to their spouses when they couple.

In our culture, when a person passes away we're given four days to mourn and, after four days, we're not supposed to mourn any more. Usually, within those four days, people in the community that have known that person will come and try to console you and talk about what that person was like. When my grandfather passed on, we spoke a lot about his younger days with my uncle. It was nice to know about some of the experiences my grandfather had, so in a sense it was like a celebration, but it was a sad time, too.

They say that within those four days, the person who died is still fresh and the spirit is still around. So you have to stay inside the house with your relatives; you don't go out in the dark at night. You can go around during the day, but at night you have to be with each other in one place. My father says it was made for us to mourn for those four days because a long time ago when a person passed on there were only two persons allowed to carry out the burial and the necessary preparing of the body. They were given four days to protect themselves, to keep themselves from putting their lives in danger.

We always have everything in four—I guess it goes according to our four sacred mountains. The prayers are in four verses, the songs are in four verses, and we always have to say everything four times. After I've had a singing done for me, I have to be good with it for four days. For four days I can't take a shower; I can't cut my hair; I can't do a manicure because my dad has said a special prayer for me and I can't mess it up. That's how it usually works. After four days you can take your shower and clean yourself and drink some herbal medicine. You say your prayer with corn pollen in the morning and then you can carry on with your life again from there.

So, if you get this kind of sickness, it's usually because you have put yourself in a situation that allows a spirit to bother you. You bring it upon yourself, put yourself in a situation where it can affect you. If you don't have the singing done, it will hang on to you. But if you have the singing done for even one night it can help.

How the Chant Is Performed

My dad does two different kinds of singing: there is the one-night singing and the five-night singing. One-night sings are mostly for newborns or young children because they have never done anything wrong or hurt anything—it's just that the parents have gotten sick from keeping the child's spirit among them.

If, as an adult, you suspect that you may be affected by an evil spirit, you might like to have that one-night singing done for you. If you feel a lot better after it's done, you could start preparing for the five-day sing. If there is an emergency and the person needs the sing to be done right away, it will usually only last for one day. But if you want it done really carefully, and you want to be meticulous about everything, it takes five days.

When people come and ask him to do a prayer and chant on them, he goes out to a wooded area to gather all the plants and other things that he will need to use. Whatever herb he's going to pick, he has to say a small prayer to that herb to be able to make that person well. Sometimes the patient or the family go and get their own herbs, say their own prayers, and bring them to him so he can prepare them. The herbs can be used in many different ways, in the water in a sweat lodge, or as a drink.

A sing starts at about 3 o'clock in the afternoon and runs until about midnight. That's the small sing—one evening. When it's five nights, it usually starts up every evening about 8 o'clock and goes until midnight. It depends on what kinds of prayers the people want and what has been ailing them. I think that late in the afternoon is when people tend to be more lonely and depressed, and I guess that's when the ghosts really tend to invade their thoughts. That's why sings usually start toward evening.

For a five-day sing, he starts again at about seven in the morning and goes until about 10:00 or 11:00 A.M. It depends on how fast the helpers are. The helper is usually somebody who wants to learn, to practice the sing. Family members can help, too. On the final night, he'll rest from about three in the afternoon until about 11:30 P.M. so that he can stay up all night. He'll start at about midnight and go all the way up to six in the morning. Then he'll come home.

For a five-day sing, my dad goes and stays with the person, the patient, for five days. They'll have a special hogan [a traditional six- or eight-sided dwelling with the doorway facing east] for the ceremony. If there is no hogan, they'll make a place for him and he'll have the sing right there in the middle of their house. He'll have all his tools and his jish [medicine bundle] with him—and he likes to have a helper with him so the helper can get up and do things for him. Usually all the family will be in there, too, to help or just to observe. It doesn't matter how many come; whoever wants to sit in, listen in, can participate. They can go to the sing and get help there too.

In the morning, he usually builds a fire in the center of the hogan and they sweat all the bad things out, to cleanse themselves. He does that every morning right up until the fifth day. On the fifth day, he'll do some sand painting and set up these hoops, twelve of them, on the east side. The patient goes under a hoop and my dad says a prayer, then they go to the next hoop and he says another prayer—about twelve different prayers. Then he would come back into the hogan and do some more singing. By that time, it's about 2:00 or 3:00 P.M., and he stops. Then he starts again at midnight, and all the way from midnight through 6:00 in the morning he would do the chants and the prayers again.

To stay in good health, he has another medicine man do a prayer and chant on him every so often.

People usually pay you or give you something when they want to have the singing done for them. The fee for a ceremony depends on how you value yourself, and how much you want to heal so you can be with your family again.

My father is very busy. The medicine men are in demand now and a lot of our generation are not willing to become medicine men, so they seek him out a lot. He's gone from home quite a bit. Sometimes he's gone one night, sometimes he's gone for five. Sometimes he won't be busy for a month or two and then, all of a sudden, people will start coming around asking for him and he can be scheduled for months ahead. When we don't see much of him, we sometimes follow him to where he's singing and help him out.

It's Important to Tell the Truth

He says that he can see and he can sense when a spirit is around, especially when he is at a point in the ceremony where he is actually asking the spirit to leave. The prayer and the chanting is like asking the spirit in a kindly way to leave the person alone, to stay in its own world and let this person continue on with his or her daily life. It becomes hard when the spirit wants to stay around. He says that there are special songs, special chants, just for that particular time and special rituals that he does—I'm not familiar with all of them—that involve different herbs and different kinds of special objects that have meaning to them. So he uses one of those and he kind of draws a line. After that, the spirit cannot step over that particular line.

While he's singing, he usually has his eyes closed and he'll just stop singing and ask the patient, "Have you done this?" or "Did you do that?" Whatever he sees, you know, he will ask the patient. And sometimes the patient will be surprised—yes, he would agree he had done something—and then my dad can say the special prayer to get rid of that spirit.

He says that if a person comes to him and doesn't fully tell the truth about what is bothering him, if he leaves something out and doesn't tell the full story, then the spirit can keep invading the person's life. If the person tells everything, whatever needs to be told, then my father can use that information to ask the spirit to stay away. He uses the analogy that if you go to a doctor, and you don't completely tell the doctor what is wrong with you, the doctor may misdiagnose something and you're still going to have the problem.

If you don't fully tell the truth of how the spirit is affecting you, if you have just missed some details or are hiding information because you are ashamed to tell the truth, then the spirit can still invade your life. What he told me is that if the people who have come to seek his help have, in their minds, actually had sex with a dead spouse, or if they don't fully tell him that they are being bothered in this way or another, the spirit will continue to come and invade their dreams and their thoughts. So it's best to tell him what really happened. That's the only way he can say the certain name and prayer to make the spirit leave you.

A Personal Healing Experience

From what I gather, if you don't come face-to-face with whatever the tragedy is that happened, then it's like everything else: it takes over your life until you're not capable of anything anymore. That's basically what he's saying. I have experienced that myself, so I know that my dad can help.

I'm unable to have more children. I've had four tubal pregnancies and I used to get really bloated feelings in my stomach. It used to get really tender. I went to the doctors and they gave me medications, but they couldn't really figure out what was wrong.

So I asked my dad and he did a chant for me a few years ago, a one-night sing. He asked the spirit of the baby, the unborn child, to leave. He told it that there was a resting place for it elsewhere and to go to that place and not stay with me.

The thing my dad did, it just kind of woke me up. I needed to decide if I was going to hold onto this—the miscarriages, the tubal pregnancies, they were babies to me—or make up my mind to let go. Of course, I also had to let go because my wanting more children took over my life and it was harming me mentally. But once I made up my mind and I accepted that I couldn't have any more children, life's been better. All my symptoms went away. Every month I used to have female problems and I don't have that anymore.

The Prayers and Singing Do Work

When my dad says the prayer with the singing, the spirit does let go.

A lot of people will come back a few days or several months later and say that they felt a lot better after the singing was done for them, that they were now able to eat or continue on with life. That's how he helps other people and how he knows he has done a good job. Sometimes, when the singing has been done on people and they get better from it, they tell another person, "You know, I feel a lot better because so-and-so, this medicine man, helped me out when I was sick." Then that other person will come and ask my dad to do the singing for him, too.

Is there a healing that he feels most proud of? He says that there are no particular cases that stand out in his mind. The reason I'm having a hard time with this

question is that there really is no Navajo word for what I need to ask him, so we are going at it in a round-about way. I don't know how familiar you are with the Navajo culture, but we're not brought up to boast about ourselves and talk about how we can do something really well. We just kind of go with the flow.

He's been asked, but he's never really talked about his work before. But since we are relatives [who brought you here], he has allowed it. He doesn't like the exploitation of medicine and of our culture that is going on now. And he's very uncomfortable when he's asked to remember and talk about something that happened in the past. It is not good to talk of being perfect or wealthy, for example, because in the future you might fail or become poverty-stricken. That may cost you your life.

My father says that a lot of times he's kept private on these matters because he is, in a sense, being careful of his own well-being, his own spirit.

What the Future Holds

My dad says it's been a long lineage [of medicine men], but I think it ends with us. We have three brothers in our family and they all live in Utah. When they were younger, they wanted to learn about our father, the singing and everything. But now they are mostly away from home, away from the reservation. They have no desire to move back here and learn.

I [Laverna] have never shared my interest in following in his footsteps with him before. But that's why I'd like to move back to this part of the reservation. I could learn a lot and I know my father's getting old and my aunt is getting old…And he says we have a shortage of medicine men these days, so any people who are willing to really learn…I would love to learn, but a medicine woman? It's not accepted…I have an aunt who was an herbalist; women are allowed to do that.

I [Alice Mary] used to help my dad when I was younger. But as I grew older and got married, I didn't remember much. But now again I can help him. There are some females who are medicine women—there's one at Many Farms [a town on the reservation] that does a different kind of ritual ceremony, not the kind my dad does. Several times he has asked me if I would like to learn all his singing and I would like to learn a lot—but at the same time I feel it's not appropriate for a woman. I don't know why I feel that way…but I hope my little grandson will learn.

These Rituals Are to Be Respected

I think what my father would really like to put across is that the medicine man, the chant and the ritual that he performs, is not all "hocus pocus." It's the real thing. And he would like people to know that this work should be respected in the same way that a doctor's work, when he heals people, is respected.

I've noticed that a lot of the doctors practicing at the IHS [Indian Health Service] in Tuba City are not very sensitive to our culture. I've told him that a lot of doctors are not sensitive to our needs and he says it's true. And he says that a lot of medicine men are also out there now for material purposes. A lot of these medicine men are not doing the ritual right, the prayers and the chants. They're not doing it right and that could harm the patient. It's the same thing with the doctors—some of them are not very thorough either. They just try to treat someone quickly and go on to the next patient instead of taking the time to see what is really wrong.

He says that the way he sees it, doctors know a lot about how to mend a broken bone and stuff like that, but they don't know what's inside a person; they don't know the feelings, the state of mind that can make you ill. That's where the medicine men come in. They have a cure for that.

Grandmother Connie Mirabal

Nambé Pueblo, Santa Fe, New Mexico

Mother Earth is the greatest grandmother—
she nourishes us all. We need to thank her
and thank Creator for giving her to us.

In Native American culture, a grandmother is much more than someone's mother's mother. Although she may, indeed, have biological children and grandchildren of her own, a woman who carries that title is an honored elder, someone who has contributed much to her community. She is a woman whose wisdom and guidance are highly valued.

Grandmother Connie Mirabal, a Hopi elder, was born in Keans Canyon, Arizona, to the Snake clan more than seventy years ago. At fifteen, she left home to attend the Indian School in Santa Fe and never returned to her native land.

For many years, Grandmother Connie lived quietly, raising her five surviving children and working as a nurse's aide in Winslow, Arizona, and Los Angeles, California.

In 1985, Connie married Ernest Mirabal, a former classmate whom she re-met at a Santa Fe Indian School reunion, and moved to his home on northern New Mexico's Nambé Pueblo. Connie and Ernie serve the Nambé Pueblo as designated representatives for the Native American Graves Protection and Repatriation Act.

Grandmother Connie started attending multicultural spiritual gatherings in 1991. She now travels extensively, praying and speaking at gatherings from Maine to Australia. She will only participate in gatherings whose purpose is spiritual, and will not attend gatherings where drugs or alcohol are used.

Grandmother Connie looks for the positive in life, but she is no Pollyanna. She recognizes the negative and chooses to see the positive. This ability to shift perspective is what allows her to say that Indian reservations are not all bad, to see the beauty as well as the devastation in a strip mine, to share the tragedies that have struck her family and say, "My life is good." This ability to be with the difficulties in life—without slipping into despair or bitterness herself—is, we think, one of the gifts that allow her to help people heal.

We have visited Grandmother Connie a number of times and have always been impressed with her gentleness, her humor, and her deep commitment to "walking her talk."

Connie Mirabal is a grandmother in the true sense of the word—sharing herself and her wisdom with all who come to her. Her life is a testimony to the healing power of compassion, kindness, and love. We feel blessed to have had the opportunity to sit at her feet and call her "Grandma."

Many years ago, I went to a medicine man and he told me that I would find a bundle. But he didn't say what kind of bundle. Well, I was always looking for that bundle—a physical one, you know—until I started going to these gatherings. Now I know what my bundle is. It's to use the voice that Creator gave me. It's a wonderful gift and blessing.

That's what I do—I talk to people. I go to gatherings and if people need advice, if they want to come talk to me, or want to cry, I'll cry with them, or just listen, or hold them or whatever—just to ease their pain a little.

It doesn't matter who comes to me. At one gathering maybe it'll be just men and at another maybe nothing but young women. I've even had grandmothers come to me, so there's no age limit. If something is bothering them, they'll come and confide in me.

The first time I spoke at a gathering it was at an opening ceremony. I didn't think about it or anything—the words just came out of me. When I looked around and saw people crying, I thought, "What did I say? Where did those words come from?"

I was just speaking freely from my heart, so it was a wonder to me, too.

The Good Way of Life

I don't like to walk in front of people. I'd rather walk behind them. I don't like to be in the spotlight. When I was young, I was very shy. I still am shy, so I surprise myself now when I get up in front of people and just talk and talk…but that's what I'm committed to doing. The Creator's using me in this way and I accept it.

I don't like to talk about myself, because it's not about me. It's about making others aware of the good way of life.

What is the good way of life? Recognizing the Creator and who you are. Loving one another, sharing. Not asking for anything in return, just giving of yourself. In our Indian ways, when we have our ceremonies, it's not for ourselves or the family or the village—it's for the world. We include everyone, all living beings and things.

That goodness is what this world needs right now. We're so in chaos, you know. Nature's right there trying to wake us up, but nobody listens. When there's a natural disaster, a lot of people come together, even if they have never spoken to each other before. Their homes are in shambles, but they're alive so they relate to one another.

When we pass on, we can't take the material things with us. It's the goodness that our being becomes that goes with us. So live a simple life. Be humble and don't think you're better than anybody else. The Creator knows who's doing what, you know. He's the one who gives us the blessings, so just try to help others. I'm here for whoever needs me—that's my life, the way I'm living it now.

The Creator has done so much for me and now He's made me aware of how I can give back. He's given me that understanding of life, of how to share with one another. Once you get that understanding, you have to live it. And show it to others—let them know too. I'm in my later years, but I'm so happy inside because the Creator has given me that wisdom.

If you're at peace with yourself first, then you can share yourself with whomever needs you because that's what counts—that love. When you can relate to one another without any kind of interference, that is good.

Right now, I have this need to talk to more people, to reach more people. I have this great urge to do something to make people more aware of the good life. I really feel very strongly that I need to get to them.

The Gift of the Creator

Rolling Thunder [a well-known medicine man, now deceased] once told me that it's men's minds that are causing problems—bombs, technology, children in front of the TV all the time instead of out playing, moving their bodies. In our business world, too, there is no patience. Everybody wants everything *now*. In an instant. It's greed…They want more money, money, money.

I think we are a poor example of the good life. Look at our country. They say it's a free country, but I don't think so. The United States is a poor example of the good life of human beings. Everything goes. Anything goes. And it's the poor people who suffer, the poor people who do all the work. We need to get all our so-called world leaders together in a spiritual gathering and get them to start thinking of peace and what's good for the people.

What are they doing to our food, injecting things into animals, interfering with the Creator's creations? I always ask the question "Why?" Why are things the way they are? Because there's always a reason for everything. If there wasn't a reason for it, it just wouldn't be. But maybe it's not for me to know…

The pace is too fast right now. They want everything to go so fast. They can't stop to listen and just do things in a nice, slow way. It has to be now, now, now,

now. People are all stressed out. Why? Because of the fast pace. You can't keep up with it.

All this medicine that's man-made…They give so many people four, five drugs at one time, and that's not good because they may be counteracting one another—but that's for money again. And look at all the cars. There's so much pollution.

When they start cloning humans, that's it! That [cloned] person is not going to have a spirit. They are not doing right when they start making human life. That's wrong…That's not the Creator's plan. It might look good right now, but what will happen later on? You just don't know. That's a man's mind inventing these things, you know. It's not God, it's not our Creator. It's a man's mind and it's all for money again.

Now they're trying to get people up to the moon. Well, He put us on earth and that's why we're here. If He wanted us up on the moon, then we would have been up there…I just know I'm an earth person and I want to stay down here. That's life, you know. That's what life is about. He's testing us. How are we going to use the gifts that He gave us? For good or bad?

It doesn't matter what color or what religion you are. The Creator made you who you are. We should be glad and proud to wear the colors He has given us—red, yellow, white, black—you should be proud because He chose that color just for you.

Every organ, every cell in our bodies belongs to Him. He made this body just for you, gave you that life for that body. That's why I tell people, "Be happy with who you are. The Creator made you to be who you are…"

The Creator gives us the choice to be who we are—that's the gift of the Creator. Be proud because He chose that gift just for you, the gift of life. It's priceless. No one is above another. We are all the same. We each have to find the self within.

So how you treat the being inside that body is up to you. You make your own decisions about who you are and what you want to be. It's up to you to want the good life. You don't have to buy it. It's priceless. And it's very simple. Just be glad of who you are and remember to thank the Creator every day.

It's Time to Give Back

I'm a mother, a grandmother. I raised my own family and now, in the second phase of my life, I'm giving back. In our Indian ways, it's always there to give back—not just on Sunday but every day.

I never had a grandmother myself. I would have liked to have just gone to her, hugged her, eaten one of the tortillas she made. I yearned for a grandmother, but I never had one. That's one reason I think I've found myself in this position.

I go to spiritual gatherings and I meet a lot of wonderful people. Many people at these gatherings ask me, "Would you be my grandmother?" I tell them I'll be their grandmother. I will be there for them. So now I have many grandchildren all over the world. They all call me "Grandma," and if they have a problem and they want to talk it out with me, I try to advise them the best way I can.

I tell them that I will always be with them. If they have me in their hearts and I have them in my heart, then we're always together. There's no physical distance when we have that exalted position. You are in my heart, I am in your heart, we're always together.

It's the people who make me the grandmother I am, because it works both ways. It's me for you and you for me, and everything comes together in a good way. The more people you meet, the more blessings you get. They come into your life and you feel overwhelmed with love all the time.

The Focus Is on the Grandmothers

The spiritual gatherings I go to started in Canada maybe ten years ago. The young people were noticing that they were losing their culture, their Indian ways of talking, their Indian ways of doing things, their ceremonies. So they went to their elders and told them their concerns and the elders called a big meeting of different tribes in Canada to discuss these things. Out of that, they decided they needed to include all the tribes of the United States and Alaska, too, not just the people in Canada. So they called another gathering for the following year and they invited all the tribes.

At the second gathering, the tribes decided that the gatherings shouldn't be just for native people—they should be for all people. That's when the gatherings came down to the States. The first time a gathering included non-natives, it was held in the area where my husband and I live. At that gathering, we had more non-Indians than Indians. At first we called the gatherings the "Spiritual Unity of the Tribes."

Once we included non-Indians, we started calling them the "Spiritual Unity of the People."

Since then, we've held gatherings in Arizona, New Mexico, South Dakota, Washington, Alaska, New Jersey, Maine, New York, and on the Navajo land. These gatherings are bringing people together, regardless of what color skin they have or what denomination they are. They are just about being together and sharing spiritual ways.

The messenger who helped start the gatherings was from Alaska. His name was Jim Walton. Every time he saw me, he emphasized that these gatherings were about grandmothers.

He told me that we must always remember that they were to be that way, that we were never to forget the grandmothers. The reason they wanted to focus on the grandmothers is because the grandmother was a mother. She gives life. She bears children. And, as life goes on, she becomes a grandmother. She's still the main focus of a family. She holds families together.

"You're going to be a great grandmother, too. Everyone is going to know you," he told me. "And you're going to be traveling." I had just met him and I said, "What is this man talking about? I've never gone anywhere or done anything like that!" But it has really come to pass. This past year my husband Ernie and I took part in a gathering in Australia.

Different Things Come Out of Each Gathering

We never know what's going to happen at a gathering. Each one turns out the way it's supposed to be. It's a natural thing. It's all about simplicity, gentleness, kindness, learning how to live with each other, letting go of the past, letting go of negativity—focusing positively on the present and the future. When we come together, we come with a clean mind and a pure heart. We respect each other's ways.

We all camp out in the woods—that's where they usually like to hold gatherings—and we usually have an arbor made with logs and boughs. There's one opening in the arbor for the sacred fire. We always light a sacred fire that burns from the beginning of the gathering clear through to the end, usually four to five days.

The arbor is where we all congregate to start the day. Usually, someone will come with a pipe and do the sunrise service. We also have one meal close to the arbor where we feed everybody. Everybody eats together and there's a lot of talking, a lot of crying, a lot of laughter and prayer.

We have a lot of ceremonies at gatherings, too—sweat lodges, pipe ceremonies, talking circles—something for the children, and maybe something for women who are on their own. There's a lot of prayer, a lot of singing.

One time a gathering focused on the elders. Sometimes it's just for men, sometimes it's for women. Another time, in New York, it turned out to be for the men who had lost somebody. There was a man once who came to me. He was forty years old and said that he hadn't cried in thirty years. "But every time you speak," he said, "I cry." "There's no shame in that," I told him. "We have feelings and you can't bottle them all up. Crying means you're healing."

The good times are lessons, too. Laughing is a healing process, just like crying. We do a lot of hugging at these gatherings—that's how we bond. It's good to hug, touch, laugh, or cry because, whatever we do, it's a healing process.

Different good things come out of different gatherings. We never know what is going to happen, so we can never have an agenda. It will be whatever it's going to be.

Some people will come and stay two days and some will stay a day. We really don't have an accurate count, but I'd say maybe three hundred to five hundred people a day come to the gatherings. It varies. It doesn't matter how big or how small a gathering is.

Any Gathering Is Good If It's for the Right Purpose

We met a couple from Australia at one gathering. They had just come to Santa Fe for the summer and they heard about the gathering. Now they come to every gathering. They come back every year.

Those who want to be there will be there, you know...Some people come and say "I don't know what I'm doing here but I came..." And they find out why they came. They were supposed to be there.

At these gatherings, we can see the transformations people go through. I went to a gathering in New York one summer and I met a man there. He was all dressed up in a suit—he had to go to Seattle, or be at a meeting or something—but he came by to see what was going on. Four days later, he was still there, with no suit on. He was barefooted and he didn't wear a suit. He said, "I'm sleeping out under the stars, and I just feel great." Things like that happen to people. If they're there and they're ready for it, they feel it.

It's up to each one of us. What do we feel inside? Are we ready to change our way of life—or make that commitment to not wanting everything? Thinking of others before we think of ourselves? It's good to think of yourself, take care of yourself—but there's always that part of taking care of others first, then yourself.

"Things Happen If You Believe in a Good Way..."

I tell people that we're having these gatherings for a good reason, for a good purpose. We're trying to bring people together, to live among each other instead of fighting each other—just being kind, compassionate, tender, loving, and sharing our prayers with one another, you know.

For one of our gatherings, we got donations from the Ute tribe—they sent us some deer and elk. One of the men donated a cow and the Navajo donated sheep. Another man that we got to know furnished us with vegetables he grew. But in this society we also have to have money, because that's the only way we can get some things. We have to have insurance in case anyone gets hurt, and, of course, we have to rent latrines. So, to help fund these gatherings, we do raffles and make mugs or T-shirts and ask for donations.

A lot of things came up at our meeting. Should we take pictures or allow sketching or have people writing? When I thought the committee was going to okay something like that, my heart would just ache. So I would get up and argue with them, and they listened to me.

If you're there taking pictures, you're interrupting that good energy that's there—so we don't need that either. Someone else wanted to set up a stage and lights. They wanted a grandmother there, talking. And I said, "No. You're trying to do something like in the movies and that's not what it's about. You have to let it happen with no disturbance."

This writer wanted to be on the finance committee because he knew how to raise money. He'd done it before and he could go to all these people and companies to get the funding. But nothing happened out of it. Not one penny did we get through him. He wasn't in it for the right reasons, so it didn't happen.

It needed to come from us, the ones who were putting on the gathering. I got on the phone and, in twenty minutes, people who had already refused us once said they would send us three thousand dollars. So that was a lesson I learned—we have to do it ourselves.

There's always a way to do things, you know, so don't ever doubt. When you doubt, you're working against yourself.

I don't ever doubt. That's the great blessing that I have, and that's why I can be there for everyone. The Creator sees that things happen. He's always there. The question is, how good is your faith? Do you really believe in what you are doing? Things happen if you believe in a good way.

You Can Pray Any Time

When you pray, you are one-on-one with the Creator. He's the one who will hear your prayers. You don't need anyone else to pray for you. You just need to be in a space where you are saying your prayer and really meaning it, coming from your heart and nowhere else.

When I'm concentrating on a ceremony, I don't feel the cold because I know the ceremony is a prayer for the world, for all people. Because I want to give my energy to that, I don't feel the cold. Nothing can distract you if you're totally into a prayer. I can walk outside in my nightgown, with no shoes on, to say my prayers and I don't feel that coldness, either, because I'm out there for a better reason.

My church, or whatever you want to call it, is outside, where I can feel all that naturalness, where I can talk one-on-one with the Creator and all His creations. It's all right there. I don't have to wait until Sunday or some evening to go to a meeting. I can pray any time—whether I'm riding in my car or sitting up in the mountains or just waking up.

Your church is wherever you are when you have that urge to pray, you know. It's there all the time. You can see the beauty, smell the good smells, hear the good things. It's all there and you don't have to pay a thing for it. But if you're blind to it, you won't see it.

At one of the meetings, people were talking about "my land...our land..." and I told them what we need to think about is that the Creator gave us Mother Earth. She doesn't belong to any one person or any one group of people. Because she sustains life, she belongs to every one of us, to all living things.

Mother Earth is sacred and we are supposed to respect and honor her. It's not "This is my land...or this is your land," you know. We're all her caretakers. If you're living on her, then it's up to you to take care of her.

We were in Silver City [New Mexico] one weekend and we saw all that mining down there—all those fields just cut way down to the bottom. But I saw beauty in it, too, because I saw all the different colors. That's Mother Earth there, too, you know. If that mining is helping some people, then I have to thank her for that and pray that they will take care of her.

Why are people fighting over her when she's giving of herself so freely? She belongs to all of us. If people would see it in that way and learn to share, instead of saying "mine," "I," or "me" they would be saying "we," "us," "ours."

Mother Earth belongs to all of us. We can see her, the beauty of her, all the time. It's all there, if people just took the time to see her.

"Creator Is Always with Me...Mother Earth Is Always with Me."

I travel a lot by myself and my children worry about me. "Mom," they say, "you're always going somewhere by yourself. Be careful." But I always say, "Don't worry about me. I'm fine. The Creator is always with me. Mother Earth is always with me, too."

Mother Earth is with us every day of our lives. We take from her, we travel on her. She produces all the food we eat. She sustains all living things.

The Creator gives us life. That's the greatest gift—life. He also gives us a body to house that life. Mother Earth nurtures that body and it grows. In time, Creator will take back that life He gave us and our bodies will go back to Mother Earth.

She is the greatest mother, the greatest grandmother, of all. We can all learn from her. She doesn't discriminate against anyone or anything.

Ron Roth

Peru, Illinois

*I'm interested in taking people
from a sense of hopelessness to hope,
from faithlessness to a sense of trust,
from a sense of isolation and separation
to oneness, so that they don't ever
have to be afraid again. I just help people
develop a God-consciousness—
and that's what heals.*

*I*t's probably no accident that we had our first encounter with Ron Roth when we were ten thousand feet in the air. Idly passing time on a cross-country flight by listening to some old tapes of a Caroline Myss and Norman Shealy workshop, we were unprepared for the man they brought in to lead a brief but powerful healing service. As strains of the Hindu chant, "Om Namaha Shivaya," filled the earphones and Ron's voice began to invoke the Spirit of the Living God, tears began to run down our faces. On a worn and scratchy tape, Ron's prayer still had enough resonance to touch us deeply. Who is this man, we thought—and how can we find him?

We need not have worried. A few months later a flyer came to the door announcing the first East Coast appearance of Ron Roth, an Illinois-based spiritual healer. Ron was presenting a workshop in Providence, Rhode Island, on a weekend when all three of us were already scheduled to be there. When we called to see if an interview might be possible, Ron himself picked up the phone. Within minutes, he agreed to meet us at his hotel. Ron later acknowledged that he never took interviews, but a sign he had received the morning we called suggested he expand in this direction.

We were again unprepared for the high energy and good spirits of the man who opened the hotel door. We've spent many enjoyable days meeting and interviewing healers, but we have never laughed as long or as hard as we did in the hours we spent talking with Ron Roth and his long-time associate, Paul Funfsinn. We've also never had less control over the direction of an interview. Whoever was in charge that day— Ron or the Spirit that speaks through him—it was definitely not us!

Described by many as a modern-day mystic, Ron has led workshops and healing services all over the world and discussed religion and spirituality on radio and television, including the Oprah Winfrey and Joan Rivers shows. Telling uproarious stories on himself and his own misadventures on the spiritual path is one of the ways that he connects with his audience and raises the group's energy. Whether that group is three women with a microphone and camera or ten thousand people anxiously awaiting healing in the Anaheim Convention Center, Ron's great humor and stand-up delivery definitely help him get his message across.

We encountered Ron Roth again, a year later, when we attended one of his workshops in Scottsdale, Arizona. During the first part of the program Ron bounced about the room, entertaining the audience as he talked us through the five stages of spiritual healing. But an entirely different man took the floor during the second half of the program, when it was time for the laying on of hands.

There were no more jokes as Ron moved about the room, speaking softly with some people, touching others as the Spirit moved him. As he went by, some people smiled, others cried quietly; some remained standing, others slipped to the floor, seemingly unconscious. Having participated in healing Masses before, none of this struck us as unusual. What was unusual was that this time one of us—the most rational, in-charge intellectual one of us—was among the people lying on the floor after Ron passed by. And even that experience was not as we might have imagined it: there were no lightning bolts, no electrical shocks, no great revelations—just an all-enveloping sense of sweetness.

Ron Roth holds a B.A. in Philosophy, completed four years of graduate school in Theology in a Benedictine Abbey, and has earned both an M.A. and a Ph.D. in Religious Studies. Ordained in 1966, Ron served as a Catholic priest for more than twenty-five years before leaving the institutional Church in 1992. While some worried that his healing abilities might disappear along with his priestly robes, Ron held onto the piece of scripture that says, "God never calls back the gifts that he gives to people, whether they use them or not...the gifts of God, the grace of God, is irrevocable." He has never regretted his decision to expand his ministry to include people of all (or no) faiths, and has noticed no diminishment in either his healing grace or his own powerful connection to the energy he calls the Living God.

Founder of the Celebrating Life Institute in Peru, Illinois, Ron travels the world leading workshops, retreats, and intensive training programs which allow others to teach the same principles of spirituality and healing. He prays daily for people whose names have been called or faxed to him. Audiotapes of many of Ron's workshops are available through the Celebrating Life Institute, as are two books he has co-authored with Peter Occhiogrosso: The Healing Path of Prayer and Prayer and the Five Stages of Healing.

Although his files are filled with testimonies from people healed of "incurable" illnesses, Ron's colleagues say that his greatest gift is not hands-on healing but his ability to reconnect people to the Divine. Reconnecting the self to its true source, they stress, is what ultimately allows the healing to take place.

My mission is to help people realize that God, this Divine energy we call God, is for us, not against us. For most people, the biggest need for healing is on an internal level, to make a reconnection with this Divine energy, to make a reconnection with the oneness they felt with all Creation when they were children. That usually is enough to bring about some type of physical healing.

If you read the scriptures (or any of the sacred writings) with a mystical eye, you can see that oneness. If you read the scriptures from a literal point of view—and that's the way they are preached in most churches—you miss the whole point. So much has happened in the arena of religion to hurt people, to give them the impression that if you do this or you do that, you will be separated from God.

Now, we know from an energy perspective that no one can be separated from God. It doesn't matter what you do. The only thing that can separate you is what you believe in your mind and what you accept in your heart. If you believe that mistakes and "wrong actions" will separate you from God, then you will begin to suffer some very bad problems—not because God is doing it to you, but because you, yourself, are saying, "Well, I'm separated from this life force."

That's why it's so important to develop a conscious awareness of this presence, not only around you, above you and below you, but also within you. God is not a million miles away. God is right here, right now. At the core of your being is this Divinity.

Sharing the Joy of Healing

I don't move energy or project energy when I work with people. I just make the connection with God. And I do it very simply.

On one particular occasion, when I invoked the essence of God to come during a healing service, the word that came out of my mouth was "Adonai." After lunch, this gentleman came up to me and said, "May I talk with you for a moment?" I could tell he was welling up, so I said, "Yes. Let's go out in the hall."

He started to cry as he said, "I wasn't going to stay for that prayer stuff...I'm a Hebrew and I was not going to stay. But something told me to stay." Five or six years earlier, this man had been hit by a car going forty-five miles an hour. His legs were broken and he had been in constant pain ever since. He had tried everything to relieve the pain and nothing had worked, so he just assumed prayer wouldn't work either.

He told me that his medical doctor brought him to the program because the pain was so bad he couldn't drive. And he said, "My doctor was sitting next to me, and you said, before you offered the prayer, to take the hand of the person next to you, because we're all in this together. The spirit not only fills the world; we're part of this world and it fills us, too. Then, when you said 'Adonai,' an electric shock went through my body—and all I can tell you is that all the pain is gone. My doctor is crying because he can't believe it. I'm crying because I can't believe it."

"I only have one other problem," he said, "this leg, ever since the accident, is three inches shorter than the other one…"

"Well," I said, "Just sit against the wall…" I'm at my best with this sort of thing. All I do is just put the ankles like this. Then I just close my eyes and wait and do some secret things that stay secret. Then I watch my thumbs and I watch the leg just grow…

I asked him if he was feeling something pulling in his hip and he said, "Oh, my God, I feel it all through my leg…" Then he was crying again, and I said, "I'm going to leave you alone now. I want you to express your gratitude to God in any way that's comfortable for you, all right?"

And so I left. A little later, he came bouncing back into the room and I asked him if he would mind, at the close of the program, sharing what had happened to give the other people hope. He said, "I'd love to…" When he came down the aisle, though, I almost burst out laughing. Because he still had a three-inch lift on his shoe, he was limping! But he was so excited that he told the audience, "My doctor drove me here, but I'm driving him home!"

When people hear that, and they see that kind of healing, they feel such a sense of oneness. They applaud, they hoot, they holler, because they're feeling the joy that the particular person is feeling. I believe that if I share one story like that in a workshop when it begins, that's usually enough to center people.

I met a doctor at a program in Orlando a few years ago who said that he had called me about his daughter six or seven months ago. And I said, "Well, you never told me how she was." She had cancer of the mouth or something like that, so I figured that she had died. And he said, "Well, she got healed." And I said, "And you didn't call me?" He said, "No, but there are a lot people in the city where I live turned on now because they keep looking at my daughter and saying that this can't be possible, this can't be possible."

Another time a woman came up to me and asked if I remembered her. I thought she looked familiar, but you see so many faces....She said "I was in Denver when you and Caroline Myss co-presented at this workshop. You were at the two ends of the hall, signing books. I'm the one who kept standing last in line…" Then I remembered her, because every time I looked over, I'd see this gal saying, "You can go ahead of me…" I wondered what she wanted.

When she got up to me, she just looked at me and knelt down on the floor, because I was sitting. I said, "You don't have to do that." and she answered, "No, I want to be at eye level…I have an affliction that I can't deal with; it's very difficult for me. So I waited to be last in line so you would touch me."

Then I said to her, "Well, if that's what you want…but it's not important whether I touch you or not. What's important is that you just open to God's spirit." And she said, "No, I want you to…" So I touched her, and that was the last we heard about it until I was doing a service for the American Holistic Medical Association and this gal came up and asked me if I remembered her.

"You have no idea what you've done," she said. "I'm a medical doctor, and I'd been taking herbs and doing the alternative healing route as well. But the day you touched me I felt something different. And when I went back home to be examined, they couldn't find any trace of my multiple sclerosis."

The Difference Between Healing and Curing

For some reason, I've always done my best work in a group. In a sense, all I'm doing is acting as a conduit, a magnifying glass, if you will. I take the crowd's energy and give it to God, what I call God, and I take God's energy and give it to the people. And I usually do that in silence. After a couple of minutes, I usually just say, "Okay, this is what I'm going to do. Now let's see what happens…"

I can't make a guarantee. All I know is that on some level—spirit, mind, body— if you are in that room, you will be touched. You can sit there as skeptical as you want; the skeptics are usually the ones that get smacked first.

I usually think of healing as a process—but it's faster than the medical process. I mean, a person can break his arm and be told he has to wear a cast for seven weeks. With prayer, the cast could come off in a week and a half. A cure is the instant departure of a problem. Whatever the problem was, it's gone.

Cures usually occur on a physical level. Most emotional healings need additional help from us; we have to make some decisions and change our thinking patterns, our belief systems. Sometimes, when a healing service becomes emotionally hyped, there are what appear to be cures. But these effects often disappear in twenty-four to forty-eight hours, as soon as the person returns to his or her normal belief patterns.

To me, the greatest healings are those that happen in silence. I use as my reference the story of Elijah going up to the mountain to find God. The earthquake came and God wasn't in the earthquake. The thunderstorm came and God wasn't in the thunderstorm. The fire storm came and God wasn't there, either. Then Elijah heard this quiet, still voice—and that was God.

As a healer, you can lead people to a high or into a depth. Depth is more lasting.

Choosing to Heal

I believe very strongly that you don't have to stay in therapy for ten years. You make a choice. I mean, the Old Testament says, "I lay before you life, death, blessings, or curses. Choose life." But the choice is yours.

How many people laughed when Nancy Reagan said, "Just say 'No'?" But that's the beauty of healing. You have to *do* something. I choose this or I choose that. There is no such thing as "I had no choice." Not choosing is a choice. It's a choice! And I won't let people get away with that. They have a choice. If they want to stay stuck in bitterness then they have chosen to do that, no matter how hard it is for them to accept it.

You know, when I decided it was time to leave the Church, because over the years it began to be so political, the first thing I thought of was, "Okay, I'm going to leave, but I have to leave without resentment or bitterness," which meant, of course, that I had to stay another eight years. That's the truth.

For eight years, I wasn't dealing with the real issue. The real issue was, "What do you want to choose?"

"Okay," I said, "I choose mysticism because I love what the Church taught me about mysticism. I choose the energy concept of the sacraments rather than their ritualized form." When I do the sacraments at my intensive workshops, there are Jewish people, there are Christians, there are people of no religion—and they all feel the energy. It doesn't matter what religion they are. And I knew that I couldn't do that as a priest, that's forbidden. You can't do sacraments for people of other religions.

At that point, when I made the choice to take the mysticism, to take the prayer, to keep the things I loved and leave the politics behind, I was able to say, "That's it. I won't do this anymore."

The Path to Mysticism

If I were to define mysticism, and I've defined it differently on different occasions, I would say that it is a deep awareness of oneness.

Bede Griffiths was a Benedictine monk who established an ashram in India and brought the Hindu tradition together with the Christian. He explained the oneness that underlies all spirituality by saying that all the world's religions are like the fingertips of your hand. Out here, on the periphery, they are separate. By the time they all reach the palm, they are one. This is what true religion was supposed to be: the sign of a loving, all-encompassing, all-inclusive God.

A mystic, to me, is someone who is all-consumed by the presence of God. When I go in to do lectures, for example, all I'm given before I go onto that platform is, "Start with this sentence." That's it. And that to me is part of a mystic's training. "Okay. Here I am God. Use my mouth, use my eyes, use my hand, use whatever...but this is You now. You speak to this audience, because every audience is different."

Basically, that's not being taught anymore. I was fortunate to go through the seminary in a Benedictine Abbey. I had four years of theology in graduate school, four years of theology, and I'd say three of my professors were definitely mystics. They always had that smile, as if they knew something at a deeper level. So I said to one of them, "I want you to be my spiritual director, and whatever you have, I want." And that's how it began.

But I know that I had already been having mystical experiences when I was a child. It ran in my family; I never saw it as a big thing. My mother and my grandfather were extremely intuitive. I can remember the day we were sitting at the table and my grandfather was playing solitaire. All of a sudden he stopped and said, "My mother just died in Poland." Two weeks later we got the letter, and sure enough, it was on that day that she did die in Poland.

My mother would just know when certain events would occur. But my mother's big thing was to never mention these things outside the family. My biggest mistake was at age seven, when I went to school and told the nuns and the priest about dead relatives coming to me. I thought everybody had those experiences. I found out very quickly that I should keep my mouth shut!

I can remember my grandfather going to confession during Lent. He came home laughing because the Monsignor had bawled him out: "Reading the future, you know, that's of the Devil. You keep doing that and I won't absolve you anymore." I was sixteen at the time and I said, "So, what are you going to do?" and my grandfather said, "Well, if I go back to confession, I'll lie—because this is a gift and I must use it." He never hurt anybody with it. He never set up a shingle so that all the people in town would run to him. He used his gift mainly for the benefit of the family.

When I was eleven, I got extremely sick and heard a voice that said, "If you'll just put your hand up here, just for a minute, I'll heal you." So I did that, because I'd heard that voice before. I did it and I was healed.

I went with a gal when I was eighteen and I thought I was going to get married. We went together for two years and she had the same kinds of experiences. We'd sit in her house watching TV and the rocking chair would start to rock. That never bothered me. I'd say to her, "Do you see that?" And she'd say, "Yeah. That happens all the time." In those days, we were told that this was probably a sign of a deceased soul that's restless. Just pray for them and that will take care of it. And it always did.

As I got older and more sophisticated, however, I didn't want to accept those things anymore. By the time I went to the seminary, they had been completely blocked from my mind. Then I had this scripture professor, a man who was one of the translators of the Dead Sea Scrolls. This man reeked of divine, sacred energy. I mean, he was the first priest I ever saw celebrate Mass and smile all the way through it. And I thought, he knows something!

Then I took his course on the Book of Acts, the New Testament Book of Acts. And I remember the day he said, "Gentlemen, we've got to lose our wise sophistication...Look at what God can do, look at the love..." This was a man who had two Ph.D.s, and he said, "We've got to go back to healing, because that is the only thing that makes spirituality different from religion. People have lost the idea of

God's unlimited mercy and unconditional love and this is one of the ways to bring it back—through healing."

I can still remember the day he taught that. When the bell rang, nobody left. I skipped the next class because I had to take a walk outside and think about it, because something inside me was saying, "This is what you're supposed to do..."

"We Are All Wired for God..."

Whenever I discuss spiritual healing, I have to make the connection with religion, because my mission is to help people raise their consciousness. Most people are stuck; they don't feel fulfilled, but they don't know what to do about it. No matter what church you go to, you're going to hear the same thing—unless you happen to hit one where the guy or the lady behind the pulpit is really preaching spirituality, prayer, or even Divine energy.

Now that scares the living daylights out of most clergymen and clergywomen today. Energy? What do you mean? This is the Holy Spirit....Well, what is the Holy Spirit?

You can read about the various aspects of the Holy Spirit from the Book of Genesis to Revelation: The Holy Spirit is a Divine power. What's power? You know, it's dynamite—the word in Greek for dynamite is dunamis, which we translate as dynamic or dynamite. There's an explosion of energy whenever this Divine power is released. Well, what do you think this is?

If you want energy, that Divine energy that can come from sacred writings, take a look at a phrase like, "Be perfect as your heavenly Father is perfect..." Now, something in you will probably say, "Uhh," because the energy there is not sacred. That's because this phrase is not translated correctly from its original language. In the original language, the phrase reads, "Be all inclusive, as God, your Divine Parent, is..." Now, all of a sudden, you can feel an energy.

When people read, "God is love, God is light," there's something in them that says, "Well, what does this mean?" And that's where we have to get into re-learning—unlearning may be a better term—some of the things we've been taught.

One thing that I just want to touch on briefly is how we're all wired for God. We're not wired for competition. We're wired for oneness—not to compete against one another, but to bring everyone into this sense of inclusiveness.

Prayer As Communion with God

Most people have no idea that when they go to a workshop they're coming with other people's beliefs. They're not coming with their own beliefs, because they haven't sorted those out yet. All they know is what they learned from mommy, daddy, religious institutions, and schools. And, until they can say, "Now, wait a minute here. I've been praying twenty years without an answer. Could it be that I'm praying according to another person's belief whose life didn't work for him either?" they will remain stuck.

Prayer is not snapping our fingers, hoping that God will become our heavenly bellboy. Prayer is not even one's conversation with God. Prayer is one's communion with God. Prayer can take the form of conversation, of course, as long as there is a heart-to-heart connection.

I don't like to describe prayer as having different levels. But, when I do some general work with the chakras, I have to use that distinction because the lower three sacred energy systems are where all your "gimmee" prayers are coming from—and there is a lot of short-circuiting there. When your life isn't congruent with what you're asking—for example, "Bring peace to the family....But I'm still going to hate so and so!"—then the energy is going to be short-circuited. Prayer doesn't really take on its true definition until it reaches the fourth sacred energy system, the heart chakra. That's the point at which you are willing to pray for others and forgive.

When Teresa of Avila talks about the seven rooms in her mansion, to me she's talking about the evolution of one's communion with God—and she's running up the seven chakras, or seven sacred energy centers of the body. Whether she thought that or not, I don't know. That's not the point. The point is that authentic prayer releases a loving energy. The energetics of prayer, authentic prayer, helps you become aware of your connectedness, your oneness with God, and your oneness with all creation. That sense of oneness then alleviates the need to be resentful or bitter, to judge or condemn. I'm not going to say that this kind of prayer is easy...but it's extremely simple.

So, then, I define authentic prayer as your communion with God and your conscious awareness of your oneness. You can reach this communion in a morning devotional, at evening prayer, even when you're taking a short break. Thirty times a day for thirty seconds, try putting your hand on your chest saying, "Nothing, absolutely nothing, can separate me from God's healing love," and then go about your business. If you're at your workplace, you don't even need to put your hand on your chest. Just think, thirty times that day, "Nothing..."

Eventually, what's going to happen is the ego will begin to diminish and the spirit will begin to fly forth. And I mean *fly* forth! You will begin to see synchronistic, congruent acts occurring in your life, things that you may have prayed about for twenty years. Now they are happening because you are aware that if you have a desire for this, and it's good, it's not going to hurt anyone; it's going to help mankind, and it's going to heal the planet, then that desire is already there in the spiritual dimension.

Prayer is about tapping into the energy from the other side of the veil. There's a lot of help there if you can tap into it. You've just got to learn to bring it from there to here, which is really no big deal.

What I share in my book *Prayer and the Five Stages of Healing* is that if you have an attraction to a particular saint who has died, it is most likely that energy, that spirit, is calling to you from the other side to help complete that work. It may be just the simple work of the way that person prayed.

I find that the easiest way to tap into the energy of the other side is to take a certain saint's prayers, such as the prayer of St. Francis of Assisi, "Lord, make me an instrument of your peace..." and simply meditate upon that day after day—for months if necessary—until you digest it, assimilate it, and it becomes part of your being.

Just reading spiritual books, lives of the saints and things like that, isn't going to do the same thing for you. There has to come a time when you actually meditate on a certain section of that life or prayer that really resonates with you. The longer you ponder these things, the more they will become a part of you. Then you will start walking in the same energy that the saints walked in, which is the spirit of God.

Response-Ability

When people come to my programs, I tell them that I may, if I have the time, be able to respond to their needs three different times—but, after the third time, they're on their own. Because I figure if I give you the authentic principles of what I believe is a way to open up the channel for the human and Divine energy to meet, what else do you need? So don't bother me. Make your own relationship with God. I certainly don't want a bunch of groupies following me all over the world, giving *me* the responsibility of taking care of them.

You've got the ability—what is your response? Will you move on or stay stuck? To me, the story about Moses and the Red Sea is about reclaiming our spiritual power, about understanding that God is for us, not against us. Whether this incident really occurred or not is beside the point. The point to the mystic is always, "What is that story telling me?"

Moses is standing there. The water's there. The Jewish people are behind him, saying, "Do something!" And the Egyptians are coming with the chariots. So Moses starts crying out to God: "Help! Do something..." And God's response is powerful: "Why are you crying out to Me? Stretch forth your own hand and part the sea!"

Jesus knows the energy connection and commands it. To me, faith is the energy to command—"Be gone! Stand up! Stretch out your hand!"—because, if you really

know something to be true, you don't have to yell or shout or do all this theatrical stuff to get others to believe. It just passes through you. It's that simple.

I don't teach anybody to heal. Nobody taught me. I'm just here to help people develop a God-consciousness—and that's what heals. In my book *The Healing Path of Prayer* I tell people how to take the sacraments and be their own priest, how to use them for their own healing and for the healing of others. Because that was God's gift to all the people, not just a chosen few.

"Nobody Is the Opposite of God"

I don't believe in little horned, tailed individuals from hell. The Greek word that we have translated as "demon" is daemonae—and in Greek it means spiritual energies.

The Kabbalists refer to angels and devils as bundles of energy. Positive. Negative. The early Christians saw daemonae as spiritual energies, too; it was only later that they began to make a distinction between daemonae and angelic forces—but they were still spiritual energies.

I look at these energies from the viewpoint of deep, mystical Christianity which called these forms elementals, and believed that they literally came from the thoughts of individuals. A horned thing with a tail? No. But it's got that kind of power in a sense. It can keep you from moving through life. Resentment and bitterness are prime examples of negative spiritual energies.

At any rate, whether you call it a demonic entity, a bad habit, a spiritual energy or John Bradshaw's term that I love, "energy emergence," there has got to be a point where that energy emerges from your system.

Like a bad habit that you cannot break once it possesses you, you will probably need someone to help you break the hold of this spiritual energy. This to me is what Jesus meant when he said that the woman swept out the demon and the demon ran out into the desert. But the woman did nothing to fill up the gaps, so seven demons came back with the first one and her latter state was worse than when she began. That makes sense to me.

If you want a good book on this topic, get Elaine Pagel's *The Origin of Satan*. She points out that our enemies were always "the devils." If they didn't agree with us on this scripture passage or that, they must be of the Devil. (Of course, they were probably saying the same things about us!) And then we started killing each other.

The Crusades, the Inquisition: all of this because we're looking for devils, because we forgot that God is love.

If you read the Old Testament, you'll find that Satan is one of the angels that acts as an advocate, kind of like a prosecuting attorney: "Well, God, the only reason that guy is paying attention to you and praying and doing these spiritual things is so that nothing will go wrong in his life." And God will say, "Okay. If you want to, you can put some obstacles in his path—Job is a prime example—you can put some obstacles in his path, *but you will not harm him.*

When you look at it like this, you start getting a whole different picture. This energy isn't even a power, except here, in our minds. There is only one power and that is God. And what has religion taught? What's the opposite of God? Satan! That's not true. If Satan is the opposite of anyone, he would be the opposite of St. Michael the Archangel. Nobody is the opposite of God!

So…black magic, black energies…they do exist. And there are people who can gather together and project black energies to hurt other people if those other people aren't spiritually strong. But if the people that they are projecting this blackness onto have a very strong spiritual immune system, and their energies are being protected by the light energy, by the spirit of God, then that black energy is going to bounce right back on those who sent it.

Harry Edwards of London (he's dead now, but they claim he was one of the greatest healers since Jesus Christ) and I both have never done anything to consciously protect ourselves while we were working. And nothing has ever happened to us. I've always felt that if you pray, you're protected. Your protection comes from the awareness that you are one with spirit because you *are* spirit—and that's it.

We Are All Holograms of God

Sometimes, people misinterpret it when you say you are God. But in essence you are.

It's just like the sunlight: When you open a window in the morning and the sun's rays come through, that's not *the* sun coming into your room—but it is.

So we say, well, it's a particle of the sun—but that doesn't define it either. That sunbeam is not just a long distance light that doesn't carry any energy. That particle carries the whole essence of the sun. How else could you take that ray of sunlight, put a little magnifying glass over a pile of leaves or a piece of paper, and see it start burning?

We are God's essence. Whether that essence is this big or THIS BIG it still contains the fullness of God. Like a hologram, no matter where you cut it, it still contains the full picture.

You don't have part of God's spirit, you have the full essence—and I think that is what we're being called upon to develop while we're in these bodies: to become the full essence, the elegant spirits that we really are. Like that sunbeam, you are a burst, a spark of the Divine light that has never gone out. Your job is to develop that spark so that it burns more brightly.

Mitchell May

Castle Valley, Utah

Nature always has been a solace to me, the solitude,
the quietude. The forces of nature are very active.
I feel friendships with a lot of those forces.
I don't want to sound as if I'm putting
human characteristics to these things; I feel that
that's a mistaken way to relate to these forces.
But they are alive and they do relate and they respond
to honor, just as we do. They respond to respect;
they respond to generosity; they respond to awareness.
Anything that is alive responds to those qualities.

*D*riving *through the high desert country of southern Utah, en route to our meeting with Mitchell May, we were struck by the wild beauty and the power of the landscape that surrounds him. The natural world is still dominant here, we thought, still free, in large part, of man-made structures and influence. Winding along the Colorado River, through red rock canyons and over rugged cliffs to the secluded valley in which he has made his home for the last fifteen years, we thought we must have fallen into a state of grace and slipped into Shangri-La.*

We first became aware of Mitchell May when we read an article about him and his extraordinary healing in Yoga Journal. We tore out the article and tucked it away for future reference. A year or so later, when we were actively collecting interviews for this book, a friend called to say she was going to a one-day healing workshop in New York City. Would we want to come along to check out the person conducting the program? His name was Mitchell May.

We couldn't say exactly what it was, but as Mitchell stood there, telling stories, playing his flute and leading the group through breathing, movement, and visualiza- tion exercises, something happened in that room. It became palpably lighter and brighter. Although we had driven ten hours in heavy rain and sat for seven more hours in the seminar room, we experienced no tension, no fatigue, no anxiety or irri- tation—just a gentle sense of relaxed awareness that persisted for days after the pro- gram ended.

The day the three of us spent with Mitchell in Utah was more intense. Hours flew by as we listened to his words and followed the rhythmic sound of his voice. We were impressed with his passion, his humor, and his willingness to take risks, to go out on a limb to make a point. Mitchell not only answered all of the questions we asked, he answered some that we didn't ask. We realized, as we left that evening, that some force had been put in motion, some underground current stirred, some connection made that might not reach full consciousness until months after our visit. The expe- rience was different for each of us; what we shared was the clear awareness that we had been in the presence of a master.

Mitchell May made medical history twenty-five years ago when, at the age of twenty-one, the Volkswagen bus in which he was riding was struck head on by an- other car. Pronounced dead at the scene and then resuscitated, Mitchell awoke in the hospital in excruciating pain. His bones were broken in more than forty places and his lungs were punctured; he suffered severe muscle, nerve, and organ damage, and a two-and-a-half-inch piece of bone was missing from his right leg. Told at first that he was unlikely to survive the accident, Mitchell was later advised that even if he did survive, he would never walk again and be in severe pain for the rest of his life.

Several months later, after being examined by more than fifty medical specialists who advised amputation of at least one, if not both, his legs, May was transferred to the UCLA Medical Center in Los Angeles, barely alive but still steadfastly refusing to agree to the amputation.

At that time, UCLA was seriously engaged in the study of such phenomena as ESP, clairvoyance, and spiritual healing. It was there that Mitchell had the good fortune to meet healer and Parapsychology Laboratory staff member Jack Gray. After working with Jack Gray for just three days, Mitchell's unremitting pain disappeared, even though his wounds were still unhealed.

Continuing to work with Gray over time, Mitchell fully recovered from his injuries, regenerating muscle, nerve, bone, and organ tissue—a feat considered medically impossible, yet fully documented by x-rays and the reports of consulting physicians. Mitchell also became Jack's apprentice in the healing arts, working closely with his mentor until Gray's death seven years later.

Mitchell sees few personal healing clients these days, preferring to teach groups of people how to shift their consciousness and change their "stories" so that they can tap into their own healing potential. As CEO of The Synergy Company, May is also engaged in making the superfood formulas that supported his own recovery available to larger numbers of people. His work as a healer and nutritional pharmacologist has been studied and reported in a number of magazines and medical journals, including Yoga Journal, Explore, East West Magazine, Natural Health, *and the* Townsend Letter for Doctors and Patients.

My primary interest isn't healing—it's freedom. Healing just happens to be one doorway.

To me, we're here as a gigantic experiment. We're not here to learn a lesson. We're not here to get it right. We're not here to get enlightened. We're not even here to achieve world peace. As hopeful as I am that some of those things will happen, to me, we're here solely (as well as soully) to experience what it means to be alive, to discover what it means to create.

I'm interested in people being free to join the experiment. Free to live who they are. Free to make all the mistakes and all the successes necessary to continue on, to see who and what we are, who and what this life is. For each person, that freedom is going to be unique.

Snowflakes, when they've had the opportunity to form completely, are always six-sided—always. That's the nature of the physical parameters of water and ice and air pressure and gravity and whatever other forces come into play. However, you will never, ever see two snowflakes that are identical. Thousands of snowflakes have been photographed. They are all six-sided, but they are never identical.

So, within the limits, there is unlimited creativity, potential, and possibility. And, within what appear to be the limits of a human being, we have an unlimited capacity or potential to create and express. It has been reported that we use one-tenth of our brain. I think that is a very generous statement. We have the capacity to create so much and we're just barely beginning to learn.

Coming to Utah

I could have never imagined myself being where I am today. And, to me, that's one of the most wonderful parts of life: we have an opportunity to end up where we don't expect. Many people want to end up some specific place, and my hunch is that they are, in many ways, limiting what life has to offer them by dictating what they think is a good life or a spiritual life or whatever. I don't see anything wrong with that, but I'm much more into the surprise and the adventure of life.

When I came to Utah, I really came, in many ways, to reflect on my life. When I was in Los Angeles, many hundreds of people were coming to me for healing. And, though a lot of wonderful, good, and meaningful work was happening, it seemed to me that, in a certain way, I wasn't growing. There were a lot of assumptions about me, projections that somehow I was already complete, or I was enlightened or some other kind of nonsense. I didn't feel as if there was room for me to explore the fullness of my humanness. I wanted to integrate the day-to-day experience of being fully human into the spiritual awakening that was unfolding in my life.

A Lifelong Search

Very early on in my life, I felt a deep need, a calling to connect with some source that felt larger—larger than a connection to family, or a connection to the community, or a connection to any of the social structures that we normally hook in with. Somehow, those connections alone just didn't seem large enough for what life was really about. I still don't know what it's all about. I'm still discovering the vastness of life.

In that yearning, in that longing to connect and feel that aliveness, that Mystery, I began, in my early teens, exploring, searching out different ways that people had truly connected to something larger in life. But during that time, I was frustrated that most of the avenues that were available back in those days were woven into religion. So, even if certain individuals were plugging into a larger vision of life, what I noticed was that the collective consciousness of the people who gathered in those religions was not truly engaged with the Source, and certainly not in a "relationship" with the Source. Sure, I could get into some exotic or esoteric system, but I would, in some ways, just be trading one dogma for another. It still appeared to be a limitation of consciousness, not a pathway to freedom.

So I kept searching, but I wasn't finding anything other than moments. I had my ecstatic moments. I'd have my moments feeling rapture. I'd have my times of feeling a deep, intimate connection to the Mystery of life. But I never really knew what it was that cultivated that connection. It just sort of seemed to happen. And I didn't know how to make that a way of life.

In my search, I put out a request to life—the essence of which was, "I'll do anything to know You." And I meant it, even though I didn't know the full ramifications of what I was saying because, at that time, I was just too young to know. So I put that communication out there—and whether my automobile accident had anything to do with that or not, I don't know. But three days later I was in the accident that forever changed the meaning and focus of my life.

"Life Is Totally Creative"

It's my experience that life will use whatever circumstances are present to assist us in the experiment. Life doesn't say you're going to get into a car accident or you're going to fall off a roof or you're going to marry the most spectacular person in the world. Life is not so robotic. Life and the Mystery are not automated. Life is totally creative and will use whatever resources are there in the moment to achieve the fullest potential that is possible for who we are. We may have certain tendencies, because of our past conditioning, to realize certain possibilities in our lives, but the specifics of what happens are unpredictable.

All the great teachers that I've learned from have taken advantage of circumstances that many people would have thought of as terrible or traumatic to propel themselves to the next step of their evolution. The knee-jerk interpretation of, "Oh, something's bad, something's wrong," that we lapse into only reflects our own internal dynamics. And then we blame our disappointments, our misfortune, on life.

I don't think life has that kind of a value system. To me, life just *is*. Life itself doesn't judge us. Life itself doesn't have a preference for hot or cold or fast or slow. To place our values, our judgments, on life is, in a sense, creating God in *our* image and likeness; it reflects just how limited and habitual our thinking is.

So the accident happens and the bottom line is that it's such a major wipe-out that the medical synopsis is: "You are never going to walk again, and you're going to be in pain for the rest of your life. You have to lose one, if not two, legs. You will lose most of your hearing and most of your vision. Your organ systems aren't going to operate properly. Your immune system isn't going to operate. You'll be in a wheelchair the rest of your life..." and on and on and on.

Making the Decision to Use the Situation

Somewhere, somehow, I made a decision to use the situation. Making that choice is where the power is. I didn't have a choice necessarily in deciding what was going to happen, what the outcome was going to be, whether I was going to suffer, whether I was going to walk. Where I did have a choice—and we all have this choice—was whether or not to fully be with what happened, and to take total responsibility, not for what *had* happened, but for what *is* happening.

I was fortunate. So many people have come to me burdened with a false sense of responsibility—that they alone are responsible for their circumstances, for their health, for their illnesses. People have come to me and told me that their anger caused a tumor, or a terrible accident happened to them because they had rejected their soul.

I find that there is no truth to this way of thinking. Certainly our consciousness, our psyche, habits, and patterns all have an influence on what happens to us—but we, alone, are just one of many influences. We are in a *relationship* with life. We are not autocratic dictators who decide how it's all going to be. In my opinion, that form of thinking is based upon fear and a false sense of control.

Use what your life is—that's where all the energy is that you need to do whatever your life is about. I didn't know if I'd live or die. I just knew that what had happened to me was huge. I was terrified. I was in pain. I had high fevers. All of these things are signs that you are very close to something, very close.

When your life shatters, when you can't hold the whole picture together of who and what you think yourself to be, then and there is where you need to be. That's what is so valuable about the experience of being so sick or so depressed, so discouraged or despondent. Yes, there is suffering and that's a very difficult part of life. But it also means that there's a crack in whom we know ourselves to be. And that's when a genuine, gifted healer or a teacher or a wizard or a shaman or a lover or a friend can help crack it open further—not plaster it up. That crack, that opening, is an opportunity that, if taken, allows us to expand and evolve from whom we know ourselves to be to all that is beyond our imagination, to all that is possible.

Getting "Lucky"

I believe in luck. The reason I like luck is that you don't have to be anybody special to have it. You don't have to have your karma cleaned up. You don't have to be a holy person. You don't have to be a saint. Luck can come to anyone and everyone—it's not about being worthy enough before it comes to you.

Don't allow anyone to tell you, "Well, the reason God didn't heal you is because you're not pure enough," or because "You don't pray enough," or some other inanity. Anybody who professes such, in my opinion, is a liar and is miscommunicating about the Great Mystery. And I don't like that because it scares people. It erodes people's trust in life and in themselves. Few of us think or feel that we are "good enough" to fit the standards of what most people say you need to be a good person or a holy person or a sanctified person, And many whose prayers have been answered were neither "pure" nor "good enough."

With luck, you just have to be alive. That's the only qualification. To me, luck is there all the time; the trick is to be aware of it. When you let yourself be open and aware of more possibilities, you have more options—and often you will choose a new, previously unknown option. People who don't realize the options that exist may think you are so blessed, or you're under grace—when really, it's only because in their own lives they're not looking for or opening up to all the options and all the possibilities.

Luck has to do with using the full spectrum of who you are: your senses, so you sense what's possible; your intuition, so you have the inner guidance of where to go and what might be valuable for you; your logic, to explore the many possibilities. Your friends and family have ideas and can help you. A class, a tape, a book—really whatever comes before you can be luck and can be of assistance. So I believe in luck. I just know the possibility is there, that there are things that I wouldn't have thought of, things that I couldn't even have imagined that are going to come into my life.

Really, my job as a healer is to help other people become aware of the truly unlimited possibilities in their lives. People may think I heal other people. I don't. I have never healed anybody. When people become aware of new possibilities, new insights, new opportunities—Boom! Life unfolds and new opportunities and new resources surface. Now there's more to it than that, but that's the gist of it for me.

When the circumstances of my injuries required that I return to Los Angeles, I was dismayed. I didn't want to go back to LA, because that's where I grew up and I certainly didn't want to be dependent upon my parents.

But it soon became clear that I was going and that it was in many ways exactly where I needed to go. I didn't have any money. I didn't have health insurance. This was going to be a long haul and I was in a cast from my neck down to the bottom of my feet. At the time, it seemed so unfortunate that I had to go to LA and back to the care of my parents. But, at this point, I had to make a decision. I chose to trust the unknown. I chose to go to LA.

Well, had I not gone to LA, I wouldn't have had the good luck to meet Jack. That's the thing with life. When we want something, we usually want it to be a specific way. In wanting something a very specific way, we interfere with all else that is possible. We don't allow for the Mystery of life to show itself when we're fixated on how it "should" be, on how we want it to be.

Meeting My Healer

So, in Los Angeles, at the UCLA Medical Center, I met Jack Gray. He was being studied by the Parapsychology Department because of his extraordinary capacity to help other people heal, people who were in impossible medical circumstances, people whom the medical community had given up on.

I knew nothing about healing when Jack came on the scene. I grew up in a well-educated, very scientifically oriented family. Things of this vein, spiritual things, so-called psychic things, were not a part of my upbringing or my life—until my mother contacted Dr. Thelma Moss of the UCLA Parapsychology Department.

So, when Jack came on the scene, I had no idea what to expect. I'd seen healers on TV and in movies and I really thought a healer would be someone in a purple cape.

Quite the contrary!

Jack was just an average-looking 65-year-old. I hardly expected a "healer" to be someone wearing a tie and a polyester leisure suit, driving a Pinto. There was nothing exotic about Jack. I never imagined what I was seeking would come to me like this—and then he put his hands on me.

Touched by Life

I had never been touched like that before. And it was not because he had so much energy or anything like that—it was more the quality rather than the quantity of energy. His touch was as if *life* itself was touching me. There was no inhibition, no restriction, no—I don't want to define it only by what it wasn't. It was Life completely coming as him. I had never felt that in a touch before, or by simply being in someone's presence. And I had no idea what he was going to do with that touch. But he went right to work.

At a distance of two or three inches above me, his hands traveled lightly, sensing areas of weakness, strength, and pain. And, as I slept, Jack talked to me, knowing that my subconscious would be aware of his voice as he continued to make magnetic passes over my body with his hands. Within three nights, the pain that had tortured me was gone. Within two weeks, I was off all the painkilling medicine.

In the days and weeks that followed, along with the talking and laying on of hands, Jack used various forms of hypnosis, meditation, and sounds to shift my consciousness. He used colored lights and encouraged me to join him in strange chants and guttural sounds which took me into different trance states.

I knew that this man had the knowledge and the understanding and the passion of life I was looking for, but I didn't know how to cross the bridge between where I was—desperate, sick, and full of toxic medicines—and where I yearned to be.

Jack met me exactly where I was. He met me with all my fear. He met me with all my longing. He met me with all my sickness. He met me with all the pain. And when I say he "met me," I mean that he didn't need or want me anywhere else, he didn't want me to have any other experience than the one I was having.

He wasn't afraid of it. He could touch it. And that's so often what each of us needs: to touch that which has been untouchable in our lives; to touch wherever we have shame; to touch some part of our physical being that hasn't yet been able to heal; to touch our relationships. And he touched me with no restrictions, no limit.

In working with Jack, I realized that here was my golden opportunity to fulfill all the yearnings and longings and dreams and desires I had. I wanted a fuller, deeper relationship with Life, with no filters, without anything in between.

On one level, what happened to me was witnessed with horror. My life had been taken away. My leg, my health, my future was irrevocably changed. And yet, on another level, it was an opportunity to experience the unexpected, to experience a gift, a blessing, a miracle. My accident was the one opportunity for me to hold still long enough to be in Jack's presence.

If I had met Jack walking down the street, I would have just passed him by. Had I attended a lecture by him, I would have said, "Who is this goofball? Look at him. What does he know? Some seventy-year-old coot!" Or, I might have thought that what he had to say was interesting, but I wouldn't have given it my full attention. And, until you give something your full attention, it has no power in your life.

The Power of Attention

One of the greatest abilities we have as human beings is our attention, and the choice as to where we place our attention.

Where do most of us place our attention? It's usually scattered, often hooked into a lot of things from the past, or focused on our desires and needs. For most of us, 90 percent of our attention goes there. What we have left to live our lives with is 10 percent.

Jack was intense. But he also knew how to contain and modulate that intensity so that what would come forth from him to whomever he was communicating or interacting with was at the appropriate level. Wherever my attention was, Jack was

right there with me, whether our attention was focused on a piece of information about Tibetan cultures, ancient foods, or facing habitual thought patterns that he could sense that I was in. Whatever and wherever it was, he met me there.

How often do we feel met, really, in our day-to-day experience with people?

I don't think most people feel met as an everyday experience. I don't think people usually feel met with their partners. I don't think people feel met in their religions. I don't think people feel met in their work. I don't think people feel met with their children. That, to me, is so very sad. Because that is what is really going to revitalize people: being met—being face-to-face with whatever is. That's what is going to heal.

Jack understood all of this. I could see that he wasn't afraid of what my circumstances were: he knew how to enter my experience and touch it and he knew that, together, we could transform it.

We began to do that together. And it was in the "knowing" and in the "doing" that bone regenerated, nerves regenerated, muscle regenerated, organs regenerated, my eyes regenerated, my kidneys regenerated, my hearing regenerated.

Entering into My Apprenticeship

After about three months of doing this very deep, powerful, and intensive work together, Jack told me he'd been waiting for an apprentice for many years and he felt that I was the one. He gave me three days to think it over. And I knew that this is what I wanted to do. It was what I wanted to dedicate my life to. I didn't know where it was going to take me. I had no idea of what was involved or what the ramifications would be, but I knew I wanted it.

So I said, "Yes," and the whole nature of our relationship changed on the spot. Boom! No longer was he going to heal me. I had to learn to heal myself. He would be there to coach me. He would be there to show me where I was going astray, but the responsibility, in a sense, was mine. I had to learn for myself because the only way I could help others was if I really learned and lived the experience from the inside out.

That was a very big shift for me, to really take that responsibility on. I had been doing the work, but I was really counting on Jack, which is very appropriate in many stages of healing.

A Healer's Responsibility

There's the popular premise going around that you "gotta do it for yourself," that you've got to heal yourself. I don't buy the premise that we are solely responsible for our circumstances, our illnesses, and our traumas. Nor are we solely capable of healing anything and everything. There *are* other forces involved. If you are not ready or don't know how to take these on for yourself, then a healer can assist you in learning to do that. If the healer you've chosen does not recognize that there are forces beyond you, then I would suggest that you find another to assist you.

The field of psychology knows the value of transference and projection. You cannot transform what until now has been a nontransformable situation unless it is imbued with power, unless you give it some magic and a sense that "there is more than I know here."

There are different stages in healing, just as there are in any other part of life—like learning to ride a bike. The first stage is learning to get on the damn thing. The second stage is falling off. The third stage is going for five or six feet with somebody holding on. A good healer, a mature healer, knows how to use that projection and knows how to guide you through the steps of the healing process. A good healer can recognize and help you to best utilize the magic, the abilities, and the power that you already have within you.

Trust is a tremendous responsibility and an absolute requirement to the healing process. For the healer, it necessitates being absolutely respectful and cognizant of what it means to have somebody who has a need come to see you. The incredible responsibility a healer has is that here is another soul, another human being, asking for your help. And to give that person anything other than truth isn't fair; to give him or her your trip rather than truth isn't fair. So, if someone is giving the healer a projection, it needs to be very skillfully managed. It needs to be honored and used, but not abused and not disregarded.

In the healing process, there's a point where the healer can move with the energy or essence of a projection, and a time when the healer hands it back to people. There is an appropriate moment when the recipients' containers, their beings, their development, their maturity, are ready to reincorporate these parts of themselves into their lives. And that's part of the healer's work: taking on a projection and skillfully handing it back. You don't want to dissipate that transference, because it has a lot of prospective healing energy. It is one of the components needed for magic to happen.

That's how a shaman operates. People come to a shaman because they believe the shaman has contact with the unseen world, has contact with the forces that have a lot to do with how this world operates and can influence those forces or intercede on their behalf. Without that belief, that projection, that leap of faith, the magic wouldn't occur. The shaman would lose his or her power and the person coming for healing wouldn't receive healing.

Accessing the Unseen World

Usually, we only invest in what it is we know, not in what we don't know. My job is helping people open up to what they don't know and cannot see, so that ultimately they learn how to invest more of themselves in that place of the Mystery and in their relationship with it.

Jack was always pulling the rug out from under me. He taught me that whatever you think you know, you can be pretty sure you don't, especially with matters that go into the vastness of life and being. We don't really understand those laws and we don't really understand the workings of the human soul and the spirit and all these unseen realms—we just don't. What's disproportional is that the unseen world makes up 99 percent of reality, but we place 99 percent of our attention upon the seen world.

A great deal of healing is helping somebody access that unseen world. You help somebody access it by being familiar with it yourself, valuing it, honoring it, knowing your way around it, and being comfortable in it. When people feel that you know your way around that unseen world, they feel safer with you and they are able to trust you as their guide.

The imagination is the doorway to the unseen world. There are other portals, but the unseen world and the imagination go together. That's where mythology lives. That's where our stories live. With the story we create the world, because from the unseen world comes the seen.

What's an atom? It is unseen, and yet it creates us. It is this floor. It is this house. But you can't see it. I'm also talking about the unseen beyond the atom. But even at that literal level, this whole world is created by a lattice work and a blueprint of the unseen world. When you influence that unseen world, you influence the seen world.

An amazing example of this occurred during my healing. After eight months in the hospital, x-rays of my leg showed that the bone was healing—actually regenerating. Jack cautioned me not to place my weight on it, because what the x-rays were, in fact, showing was but a blueprint of the growth to come. Eleven months later, the bones had aligned and solidified enough to bear my weight—despite the fact that they had never been set and despite the fact that this was medically impossible.

There is so much going on in the unseen world between us, everywhere, all the time. One way to know the unseen is to recognize that every act of physical creation has its roots in the unseen world. So, if you're not sure how to know the unseen, get to know the seen. Look at the creation, the form; learn to track it and you will trace its root back to its creative source, back to the unseen.

A creation does not exist separate and apart from its creator. Everything that we see and everything that is—whatever facet of life created it, whether you call that God or gravity, whatever the creator is—it continues its involvement 100 percent with its creation. And the creation forever carries the creator's imprint.

So we are 100 percent, fully invested with all the forces that created us. *Everything is.* And that's what we need to tap into: the knowledge that what created us is still 100 percent here, with and within us. Creation didn't "happen." Creation *is* happening and we don't know where it's going next.

Sir Laurens Van Der Post, the South African writer, once asked Carl Jung, "Do you believe in God?" It was at a psychiatric conference and all these psychologists were giggling because, of course, psychologists don't believe in God. Many professionals in this realm have lost touch with the meaning of the word *psyche*, even though their work, day-in and day-out, revolves around it. Psyche is the root word for soul.

Jung reflected for about twenty seconds, then he said, "No, I don't believe in God...I know."

My heart, even now, vibrates there. You just know. If you need to believe, you don't know yet. And there's nothing wrong with believing, nothing wrong with not knowing. You need to believe in the possibility to begin with, before you know.

I want people to *know.* I want people to know the Great Mystery directly. I want people to have the Mystery as their best buddy, as their lover, as their blood, as their breath, as their brain, as everything. I get a little concerned when I speak this way because it sounds real high-falutin', but this is the truth of the matter for me because I know what it has given me. This Mystery is my life source.

Strengthening Our "Spiritual Muscles"

There are practices or things you can do to help yourself understand and relate to the unseen world more. That's what every system of esoteric knowledge or mysticism or spiritual teaching is really all about. They all have a different way of going about that. You should only follow a path that suits you. One is not better than another. It either works or it doesn't. That's where it's at.

For me, the foundation of any daily practice must begin with the physical body. Taking care to nourish and train the body so that it can tolerate more and more energy—be it physical, psychic, or spiritual. I value lifeforce and vitality in my food, water, and breath. I want to feel the communication with that which has not been altered by unconscious behavior. Over-processing, chemical contamination, and pollution destroy the inherent lifeforce and vitality of our food, our water, and our breath.

When chemicals are dumped into our water, that's a whole system of unconsciousness that I don't want. I want consciousness—water that comes out of the earth that hasn't been contaminated has something to offer me. Food that is pure and that hasn't been altered from its original state, genetically engineered, infused with chemicals and hormones, or over-processed has so much more to offer me.

We have a need for spiritual nourishment, too, just like physical nourishment. There is a cosmic energy that we literally need to thrive. Most people are only surviving; very few people are actually thriving. When you thrive, you glow—and you can only thrive if you're getting nourishment from the unseen world.

Sure, you can be healthy and vigorous and you can run a speedy mile and all that, but that's just your physical energy and vitality. To really glow, to really be ecstatic, you need to have all of your other bodies nourished as well.

Beyond our physical bodies—which to me are the expression of our soul—are our other bodies: the emotional or psychological body that deals with our personal and tribal history; the mythological or imagination body, which is the realm of the unconscious and archetypal energies where much healing takes place; the spiritual body, where our deepest essence is and where we have our relationship with the soul; and, finally, the energy/luminous body that nourishes and informs us with spiritual energies.

You need "spiritual muscles," so to speak, because there is so much to deal with which requires strength and stamina. There's so much exploring and experimenting to do in our lives. If you don't have your spiritual feet underneath you, every time a wave comes by, you're going to feel knocked over. So you need practice in that unseen realm, just as in the physical realm.

Developing a Practice

The way to begin that practice is by first acknowledging the existence of the unseen; then begins the work of cultivating a relationship with it. Have a dialogue with the unseen just as I am having one with you. Ask it questions. I don't expect it to speak as I do, to speak "English." Remain open and alert because it may not always speak in words. It speaks Life. That's the universal language here, Life.

Energy is another part of the language. Energy itself is not what heals; the energy carries the information. Energies bring forth information and, in a sense, we remember and that's what heals us: remembering who we really are, what we are really about, and what we were doing before we were a part of this human experience.

When we take on this physical body, we seem to develop a kind of amnesia. We forget that we designed this show. We forget that we were part of the experiment long before there were physical bodies, long before the earth existed. We forget—meaning Mitchell forgets and Susan forgets and Judith forgets and Pat forgets. But there's a part of us that doesn't forget. It has never forgotten. We just don't pay much attention to it.

In our culture, we are not taught to cultivate or foster this awareness in our lives. Few of us have daily practices where we can connect to this Mystery. Yet, as we begin to pay attention to it, the more we remember—the more all of us begin to remember. As we join our daily practice with our daily life, we begin to feel less separate—we don't feel so torn, so split between realities. I don't like to separate spirit from matter, or my daily life from my spiritual life.

Certainly, there are as many different ways of accessing the unseen world as there are traditions, and each has its own unique offering: martial arts, meditation, prayer, movement, dance, being in nature, and so on. Everybody needs to find what it is that helps you personally to connect to that greater sense of life, to what I call the Mystery. I'm more comfortable with that word than with "God." The word, "God," has been so misinterpreted that it actually limits our experience of God, rather than expands it. So "the Mystery" works a little better for me. It's hard to put your finger on a mystery.

I practice every day by acknowledging and valuing that the unseen world is alive and real, as alive and real as what we're doing here. And what you place value on in your life will grow in your life. It's that simple.

For me, breathing is a very important component of the practice because breathing really is that bridge between the conscious and the unconscious. Breath can happen automatically or you can have a mindful relationship with it. All day, today, we weren't even aware we were breathing, but you can now be aware of it. When we come into conscious relationship with our breath, we can make contact with that place where the seen and the unseen touch.

In all cultures that I am aware of, the breath is some way considered equivalent to the spirit: the Breath of Life, the Spirit of Life, Prana, Mana, and chi. God breathed Life into mankind. Many practices use the breath as a vehicle to enter altered states of consciousness. It is something we all have access to. It can be either conscious or unconscious.

By consciously using our breath, we can control our brain waves, our autonomic nervous system, and we can control the amount of oxygen to the brain. The breath is designed to fuel the brain and the body.

The brain feeds on oxygen, and most people are not getting enough. The brain will reduce oxygen and blood flow to the rest of the body to be sure there is enough oxygen in the brain. Not only does our breath take in essential nutrients, it also eliminates toxins from our bodies. In fact, 70 percent of all the body's toxins are eliminated through the exhalation of our breath—and, if not, then other organs in the body will have to work harder to detoxify and eliminate the waste.

Yes, you can make an occult, esoteric, metaphysical science out of how you do connect to your Source, and there are practices that will help you do that. But to not recognize, to not cultivate an individual and intimate relationship with the Mystery makes it mechanical.

When ceremony and ritual become habitual and mechanical, they don't have the power to take you to a different state of awareness, a different state of consciousness—which is what they are intended to do. Unless they're fully passionate, unless they're alive, unless they're fresh, they won't take you any place. Or, if they do, it's a place you've been to a million times before so you're only going someplace you already know. I don't really think that's what it's about. To me, it's about going to a place or an experience that you don't know, as well as to where you do know, having free access to go wherever you need to go, rather than where you only allow yourself to go.

A Healing Story

Before I built this addition to my house, I had a very tiny room upstairs with a ladder going up there. And a dear friend of mine fell down the stairs, really wiped herself out. She thought, and I did too, that she'd broken her wrist and her arm. She was bleeding and had lots of cuts. It was a bad fall.

I didn't know if she needed to go to the doctor or not. So I said, "It's your call; let me know if you want to try to work with this right here, right now, and see how we can use the energy that's here—all the pain, all the fear, all the confusion." And she said she was willing to try that.

The first thing she needed to do was to acknowledge all that was there for her, in that moment. She had to release the fear, which meant she needed to cry, which meant she had to look at the anger she had at herself. She said she was stupid. She was a massage therapist. How was she going to make a living? She had to really be honest, bring up all the concerns and fears and express them. The self-judgment, too, because she didn't really like her body. "I'm too big...If I was more graceful...If I wasn't so overweight..." or whatever it was. It took about ten or fifteen minutes to move through that. And that's not easy energy to move for a person who is in the midst of it.

From there she needed to go to the place of forgiving herself, the place of really connecting to simply loving herself for what had happened right there in the moment, a place where there was no judgment that it should have happened or it should not have happened. "I love myself even for being a klutz. I love myself even for all my terror and all my fear..."—whatever was there.

And in the process of going deeper into that place, life flowed back through those areas that had been injured. Life flowed back through her body and you could see, before your very eyes, the black and blue marks literally disappear. We watched the swellings just go down. We watched her cuts begin to close. It was awesome. And it was because we were using everything that was present in that moment.

I don't know if she actually had fractured her arm or not, but within twelve hours there was literally no residual sign of anything having happened. And this was a fall that, with "normal" healing, would have taken two to three months to reach that point, maybe longer.

Seeing the Divine Everywhere: Business As a Spiritual Path
The most challenging spiritual road I've ever been on is being in business. I had no

intention and no desire to participate in the business world. But I came to realize that what I needed to do was to face it and to embrace it in order to heal myself, in order to see the Divine everywhere.

When I was living and practicing my healing work in Los Angeles, I could go into hours of ecstasy—until I realized that, in some ways, I was really hiding from the world. I didn't have to deal with relationships. I didn't have to deal with what it really means to make a living. I didn't have to deal with the rest of the world beyond my own work. I could use the spiritual path I was on to insulate myself from those things that I didn't want to deal with in my life.

This realization was excruciating for me because I was afraid of the world; it hurt to put my physical body and my consciousness into the many places that people place their lives and minds into—day in and day out. It was at that point—when I realized that I was using my spiritual path to avoid life—that I left Los Angeles.

When I first came to Utah, this valley was exquisite. I was meditating and doing my daily practices; it was really splendid. But eventually I realized that what I really needed to do was to go where I was afraid. My spiritual work would be found where I was consistently afraid and resistant. Not the momentary fear of crossing the street with a car coming, but the fear that, in a sense, doesn't give you freedom, the fear that interferes with where you can go in life.

So, I'd think, "Where am I afraid? I'm afraid of business. I'm afraid of what I perceive as the lying and the deceit and the manipulation and the ego and all the games that go along with that. And I'm afraid of what it means to really try to pour myself into business, into money. What does that really mean?"

I looked at the world and said, "Sure, people can come to me and I can put my hands on them and I can do my hocus-pocus and maybe it will help; it seems to have helped many, many people. I love that work and some really magnificent things have occurred. But that's within a small subculture." My real goal was to reach out far and wide, to touch the whole world.

What touches the whole world today? Business and the people who are in business—IBM, AT&T, Nestle! When they make a decision, millions of people are affected.

Being in business—talk about the demonic realm! I love it! I have to confront it every day. Every day there's a temptation. Every day I deal with somebody who probably isn't telling me the full truth. Every day somebody offers me a deal that if I just slide a little bit here or there I can make a lot more money.

All that has to be dealt with. It's very demanding. It would be so much easier to be in business without my ethics. It would make life so much easier. That to me is where karma surfaces.

When you don't know what you're doing, that is really a very different kind of karmic situation. But when you know what your actions mean, that's when you generate karma. It's just cause and effect: when you cheat somebody, life responds. That's how it is. It's no different from when you touch a hot stove, you get burned. When you "burn" somebody in another way, you make a statement to life and life meets you exactly where you are. It's not as if life is getting even with you. Life is simply responding to you. That's all there is to it. There is nothing esoteric here.

I learned a lot of that from Jack. To him, one of the deepest teachings was to really live by your needs, not your wants. If you really go by your needs, your true needs, you will have everything that you need. If you go by your wants, you may get them, but you may not get what you need. I see that with people. They may be getting their wants, but their needs are not being met. And, in many ways, inadvertently, they're interfering with other people getting their needs met. This is because their consumption and their wants are so great and so disproportionate to their true needs and to others' needs.

One of the reasons why I got into business was because I want to generate enough resources so that I can help people whose full attention has to go into survival, into just feeding and sheltering themselves. I want to help people to meet their basic health needs, including their basic nutritional needs. If you don't have the basics, you simply cannot truly pursue freedom, your own individual freedom.

I don't have an answer to all this. I just know that my way of healing now, strange as it may seem, is to do business. That doesn't mean I don't also teach another side of healing, because I do both. But I need to bring the principles that I've learned from my mentor and from my own life experience into the world.

Part of my goal, on a truly literal level, is to support our human evolution. I want to support the full use of our nervous system and our senses and everything that we are physically, emotionally, and spiritually. I want to put together life-enhancing products and services that address these issues and assist us toward our highest capacity of function, our highest evolution.

Creating "Pure Synergy"

In my own healing process, I knew that I needed support on many different levels. Essential among these were the healing I received from Jack, the allopathic medical treatment I underwent, and optimum nourishment for my healing body. I wondered if there were certain substances that carried archetypal information that you could consume, that would pass that native information (meaning primal or cellular knowledge, cellular integrity) on to our bodies, on to our cells, at an energetic core level. I sensed the importance of what I put into my physical body would profoundly affect my healing process on many different levels.

Because Jack and I were at UCLA under the auspices of the Parapsychology Laboratory at that time, we had access to very sophisticated equipment. So we began looking at different substances, plants, mushrooms, and algae using electron microscopes, photomicrography, polarized light fields, Cymatics, Chromatography, and Kirlian photography. Jack taught me that foods have a vibration, a frequency, a life force—and so we played with this concept. With these instruments, we discovered that each substance had a very specific energy pattern and structure that carries the energy or life intelligence of the substance. And guess what—when we ingest the substance, we also ingest that life intelligence.

Then I began seeing what would happen when I combined a variety of things together. It's that relationship—the formula, or the alchemy, or the synergy of putting two or more things together—which creates a new dynamic. The first part is the science. The second part is the art of combining things, like arranging flowers or the Feng Shui, so to speak, of a good cook. These concepts went into the creation of Pure Synergy™. Creating and refining the life-enhancing superfood formula that I called Pure Synergy was a fifteen-year project.

While still formulating Pure Synergy, I experimented on myself. I began eating it to see what would happen to me. I really felt terrific. So I took the experiment further. I stopped eating food altogether and began living on Pure Synergy. I wanted to see what effect it would have on my consciousness. I thrived. (Of course, it's nothing I would recommend to others. Jack had taught me many techniques to consume energy from sources beyond food—from the air, from lying on rocks, from many different kinds of things. I meditated a lot. I did a lot of healing work.)

For almost two and a half years, I consumed only a small amount of sprouts, some carrot juice, water, and significant quantities of Pure Synergy. Long before Pure Synergy was available to the public, I specially prepared this green formula for friends, family, colleagues, and many health care professionals. Without exception, the results were phenomenal and everyone wanted more.

What I really want to see happen with the Synergy Company, if we can continue to be as successful as we've been fortunate to be, is to create projects that are much more directly involved with meeting and alleviating human hunger.

Most Medical Problems Are Preventable

To me, 80 percent of our medical problems are preventable, or treatable without heroic means. Cardiovascular disease can be remedied by simple lifestyle alteration. Arthritis, certain forms of it, can be alleviated and remedied by lifestyle changes, as can many forms of cancer. What a waste of human creativity to wait until things get to the point of crisis before we intervene!

Almost everything that we need is already within us. We don't need to look for answers beyond ourselves, beyond what we as human beings already are. The intelligence, the technology, the capacity to access the unseen world—all of that information already exists. We're just not using it. I hope that I can help in that process.

I want to see all of our different resources being used wisely and collectively, synergistically. We must consciously choose to use the power of nutrition, the power of medicine, of surgery, of drugs, the power of medical intuitives, the power of healers, the power of shamans, all together, in unison. We could then, in cooperation, resolve many issues that have proven intractable when any one of these systems has tried to deal with them alone.

Our consciousness is the fundamental building block of our experience. It is a wide-open arena complete with surprises, adventure and, ultimately, an exploration of our freedom. That's my goal—for people to experience freedom. Our bodies are designed to experience ecstasy, but we need to raise our consciousness so that we can sustain it.

Jonathan Goldman

Boulder, Colorado

Sound is awesome! It is magical. It is sublime!
To resonate with the energies of sacred sound
is to attune with the vibrations of the Creative Source!
We are all born with this ecstatic ability to create
our own sounds and experience Divinity.
It is a gift to be able to reawaken and empower others
with this consciousness of sound. I give thanks.

*T*o sit with Jonathan Goldman is to be washed over, engulfed with sound. Almost every sentence he speaks is punctuated with sounds—a mantra, a chant, a tone, a harmonic. When he's not sounding with his own voice, he's emphasizing his point with tuning forks, bells, bowls, recordings of traditional and esoteric music—a delightful experience and altogether appropriate behavior for a man dedicated to using sound, particularly the human voice, as an instrument of healing and transformation.

We had taken a "Healing Sounds" workshop with Jonathan in Boston a number of years ago and were impressed with his warmth, his humor, and his mastery of both the Western scientific and Eastern esoteric traditions regarding the nature and uses of sound. He taught us to resonate our chakras with vowel sounds and led us in group chants that gave us the experience of being all one voice.

When we met again in Boulder to interview him for this book, Jonathan demonstrated another healing technique called overtoning. Using his voice to sound Judith's aura and locate an area of the body that needed to be balanced or unblocked, Jonathan directed a long, strong tone into her body.

Judith describes the experience as extraordinary. She remembers closing her eyes and disappearing into the vibrations, losing all sense of the boundaries of her physical body. She later reported sensing heat and seeing geometric shapes as the vibrations moved through her. As we were leaving Jonathan's studio, Judith insisted that she was quite fine and that she wanted to drive. The only problem was—she couldn't remember how to get in the car! She had, quite literally, been "blown away" by the sound.

Jonathan Goldman is no stranger to the healing professions: his father, grandfather, and brother all are physicians. But Jonathan went his own way, majoring in film at Boston University and playing in rock 'n' roll bands—until "the Light of God" struck him one night while he was onstage and an awareness of the power of sound to heal and transform entered his consciousness.

Today, Jonathan is an internationally recognized authority on sound healing. He is the director of the Sound Healers Association and president of Spirit Music, Inc. As a performer, Jonathan has been featured on film soundtracks and appeared with such artists as Kitaro, Steven Halpern, and Robert Gass. A pioneer in the field of harmonics and overtoning as a healing technique, Jonathan has been empowered by the Chant Master of the Dalai Lama's Drepung Loseling Monastery to teach sacred Tibetan Overtone Chanting.

An author as well as a musician, Jonathan has produced three books—Healing Sounds: The Power of Harmonics, Shifting Frequencies, and The Lost Chord—and numerous CDs and tapes, including Dolphin Dreams, Gateways: Drumming and Chanting, Trance Tara, and Chakra Chants, which won the 1999 Visionary Awards for "Best Healing-Meditation Album" and "Album of the Year." Based in Boulder, Colorado—a part of the country he describes as a "sound center"—Jonathan lectures and teaches two-day Healing Sounds workshops and nine-day Healing Sounds Intensives throughout the United States and Europe.

We invoke the spirit of Shamael, Angel of Sacred Sound.
May the sound of light surround us.
May the light of sound guide us.
May sacred sound come through us for the harmony of all.

I first encountered Shamael, the Angel of Sound, on my 42nd birthday while I was in a deep state of meditation. This luminescent being said to me: "I am Shamael, Angel of Sacred Sound. You are to be a conduit for my energy."

It was an extraordinary experience. I was bewildered and, at the same time, skeptical. I had heard of various archangels—Michael, Raphael, Oriel—but Shamael? Never heard of him. After the experience, I remained in this state of wonderment mixed with skepticism for about two weeks. Then a friend gave me a book called *A Dictionary of Angels*.

I looked for Angel of Sound and there was nothing. I breathed a sigh of relief—just some sort of discarnate entity trying to play tricks on me. Then I looked up Shamael and it said: "Master of Heavenly Song and Divine Herald." The book referred to Shamael as being an aspect of the Metatron energy. There it was—third dimensional verification of the energy I had encountered. It was real!

I believe the energy of Shamael is the same energy as that of the creative source that assisted the manifestation of the universe through sound—the Divine Herald of the Angelic Choir, similar to the Hindu Goddess Saraswati, from whose mouth came the Bija Mantras, the sonic building blocks of creation. I believe that Shamael has made its presence known because we're working so much now with sacred and healing sounds that those of us in the West need an angelic form to work with and tap into.

Life Is a Wave

Modern scientists are now validating what the ancient mystics have known for many a millennia: everything is in a state of vibration. From electrons moving around the nucleus of an atom to planets moving around suns in distant galaxies, everything is in vibration and is creating a sound.

Sound is measured as a wave form. Sound travels as a wave form. This wave is measured in frequencies or cycles per second, also known as hertz. Technically, sound as we know it is audible from around sixteen of these cycles per second to around twenty thousand of these cycles. That's the range of human hearing.

Dolphins can receive and transmit three-dimensional holographic information on sounds that travel at about one hundred eighty thousand cycles per second—this is about ten times beyond our range of hearing and many more times beyond our ability to transmit sounds vocally. Yet, to a dolphin, it's sound.

The Hindus have said that the world is sound. All is sound—all is vibration. Everything is in a state of vibration and that includes the chairs we may be sitting in and the pages of the book that we might be reading. I would like you to perceive that perhaps all is sound—whether it fits within our limited ability to hear or not—and that includes our bodies. Every organ, every bone, every system, every part of the body is in a state of vibration.

We call the normal, healthy vibrations of an object its "resonant" frequency. Resonance is the natural vibratory rate of an object. When we are in a state of health, all the different parts of the body are putting out different sounds—different pulsations, different frequencies that combine together to create this overall harmonic of health. In other words, we are in a condition of "sound health." We are vibrating in a state of ease and harmony. However, when we are vibrating out of balance, we call this out-of-tune condition "dis-ease."

If you like, you can think of the human body as an extraordinary orchestra playing the symphony of the self, the suite of the self, whatever you want to call it. What happens if the third violin player loses his or her sheet music? He or she begins to play out of tune, out of harmony. Pretty soon, the entire string section sounds bad. Soon enough, the entire orchestra sounds off. This is a metaphor for disease.

I come from a family of medical doctors and have great respect for the medical tradition. But continuing with our metaphor, currently traditional medicine deals with disease by either feeding the string player so many drugs that he or she just passes out and is no longer part of the orchestra, or else taking a broadsword and cutting off the head of this string player. This also removes the player from the orchestra and, in one sense, alleviates the problem of the string player without his or her music.

But what if you could somehow give the sheet music back to the violin player? What if you could somehow project the correct resonant frequency back into that organ, bone, or tissue that is vibrating out of harmony and cause it to vibrate back into wellness? This is one of the basic principles of sound healing.

Today, as the whole field of sound healing continues to expand, there are many, many different ways of projecting sound into the body to effect this type of healing. There are all sorts of machines and tapes and recordings designed to help do this. But it is my belief that the most powerful instrument for healing is the human voice, and much of my work is dedicated to re-empowering individuals with this power of the voice.

The Road from Rock 'n' Roll to Sound Healing

In 1980, I was playing in a club in Marshfield, Massachusetts. I had been playing professionally in rock 'n' roll clubs since I was around sixteen years old. For some reason, on this night, I looked out at the audience and became aware that the ambiance in the club was one of negativity, anger, and violence. No doubt, the alcohol and other intoxicants that the people were imbibing were contributing to this atmosphere. But there was also no doubt in my mind that the music I was playing was helping to create this effect.

Now, I had been performing professionally for nearly fourteen years and this situation must have manifested numerous times in the various clubs in which I had played. Why, on that particular night, did I notice it? Why, on that particular night, did I think, "I wonder if music could make people feel better?"

The idea of sound healing never entered my consciousness. That followed soon after. But on that particular night, something happened that changed my awareness of sound. I like to say that the Light of God struck me on stage that night. I don't really know what did occur, but I do know that it was powerful and life-changing.

Within a week of having that experience, I took a workshop with Sarah Benson, an extraordinary sound healer in Massachusetts. After that, doors just began to open. A few weeks later, I had met a number of other people involved in using sound and music for healing. Soon after that, I founded the Sound Healers Association.

The Sound Healers Association (SHA) was incredible. Many extraordinary teachers, healers, musicians, and scientists would come and freely share their time, teaching us about using sound and music for healing. There were people like Dr. Peter Guy Manners from England, who invented the Cymatics Instrument, which uses direct application of sound on the body for healing, Kay Gardner, John Beaulieu, Randall McClellan, Steven Halpern, Don Campbell—the list goes on and on. We held meetings once a month for over seven years and it was quite an amazing education for me.

In fact, much of the information I received at those SHA meetings was applied when I went to Lesley College in Cambridge, Massachusetts, and received a masters degree in independent study researching the "Uses of Sound and Music for Healing." Most of that information is still extremely relevant today—there is very little which is not the basis for the new developments in the uses of sound and music as educational, therapeutic, and transformational tools. The master's thesis I wrote for the program at Lesley became the basis for a number of my articles and books.

In 1992, I was living in the mountains outside of Boulder. A friend, who was a Hindu swami as well as a writer, called to tell me he and his wife had recently become editors of Element Books. He asked me if I had anything that might be of interest.

A week before that, I'd been deep in meditation when I heard a voice tell me that I was to write a book. The book was to be composed of a certain number of chapters and cover specific information. I even received an outline of the book during that meditation.

So, when my friend called me a week later, I gave him the outline I already had. I added a synopsis and a sample chapter and the book was accepted. Basically, the book was exactly what I was told to write in meditation, except for the title. I was told the book was to be called *Hermetic Harmonics*, but the publishers said, "No. We own this now and you'd better come up with another title because we're not using that."

So I came up with the title *Healing Sounds: The Power of Harmonics*. I actually am quite grateful for the title change. While the beings on the other side may be quite aware of content, I guess the publishers on this plane are more aware of marketing and promotion. At least it seems that way sometimes.

I've been amazed at the popularity of *Healing Sounds*. It has gone into its second edition and been translated into many different languages. I consistently get letters, phone calls, and e-mails from throughout the planet about it. It now seems to be considered a classic in the sound healing field, which is very, very gratifying.

Teaching Is My Great Love

The more the book began to sell and the more people began to contact me, the more I began to teach—and that is really my great love. I seem to be able to empower people with a certain understanding—a certain experiential knowingness about the sacredness of sound—and give them an experience of the Divine through sound.

My expertise is not working as a healer on a one-to-one basis, although I do know how to do that and many consider me quite a conduit for healing energy. My expertise is more in teaching people how to use sound to work on themselves or on their clients.

It's the old story that if you give people fish, you feed them for the day; if you teach them to fish, you feed them for a lifetime. So I'm teaching people about their ability to use their own self-created sounds to shift their frequencies and heal and transform. They in turn can work with others and, in this manner, the work really grows.

I particularly love the experience of making sound in a group. I tell students that I can sit and do a mantra for a very long time and experience certain effects. But if I do it in a group, it's much more powerful and awe-inspiring. It becomes very synergistic—a one plus one equals three phenomenon.

Many people have never experienced being in self-created repetitive sound, such as chanting or toning for an extended period—a half-hour or an hour—especially in a group setting. While it is a very simple concept, it is an extremely potent experience which can result in life-changing experiences.

When I teach, I facilitate this experience. Often, one can see colors, lights, spiritual figures, and geometric forms either during the experience or in the silence following the sounding. Many times the sound continues despite the fact that the chanting may have stopped. Angelic voices may be heard. Spirit guides can come through. It really can be quite transformational.

Acquiring the "Tibetan Deep Voice"

In 1986, Tibetan monks from the Dalai Lama's Gyume Monastery came to the United States for their first historic visit. During this tour, it was my honor to assist in making their first recording in a modern studio. This was in Boston, where I was living at the time.

I took the tape of their chanting home with me and put it in my crystal grid—a deep meditation energy field which utilized twelve very large crystals in a specific geometric pattern designed to enhance higher dimensional consciousness. I listened to the tape all night and fell asleep with it running.

When I awoke the next morning, this deep, growl-like tone emerged from me. It was the same "Deep Voice" that the monks chanted with. The sound is extremely deep and bass-like and feels like an aspect of one of the original creational sounds—a very, very, long wave that seems almost inhumanly low. Included in this Voice is another sound, a harmonic that is quite high, almost like a soprano voice. It is an extraordinary sound and somehow I had received it.

I was so excited, I raced to the recording studio. There I found my friend David Ison, who had helped record the monks. I said, "David..." Before I could say anything more, he turned to me and sounded forth with the same "Deep Voice" that I had received.

The Gyume Monks had left Boston after their recording session the night before and did not return for a month. When they came back, David and I were again in the studio. The Rinpoche (the head lama) and his interpreter walked through the door. We sounded forth with the "Deep Voice." The Rinpoche laughed and said something to the interpreter, who said to us, "Rinpoche say 'Best in West.'"

That is how the "Deep Voice" of the Tibetan monks came to me. I believe it is an example of harmonic transmission—of an almost magical ability being instantly transmitted through sound. It seems quite divinely inspired. It is supposed to take a monk anywhere from two to ten years to get the Voice and you're supposed to have made an offering to the Buddha in a past life. But here was an almost instantaneous transmission.

In dreamtime, I later remembered my initiation for this. It occurred in this immense hall filled with Tibetan monks and other beings of sacred sound. Among the things I was told was never to use the Voice as a party game, a macho tool, or an ego device because the Voice is a very, very powerful and sacred gift—not to be abused or used for one's own amusement.

While the "Deep Voice" of the Tibetan monks is an extraordinary sound, it is not one which I ordinarily teach. I have done this on occasion, but there are difficulties with teaching it and potential hazards that I feel are not therapeutic for most people.

I find that many similar effects of the Voice can be achieved with another form of overtone chanting which I call "Nouveau European" Vocal Harmonics. This form of vocal harmonics or overtone chanting is fairly simple to learn. It is based upon the sacred vowel sounds, which I also teach in conjunction with learning to resonate the chakras with these vowel sounds.

Most people can learn the fundamentals of how to create two or more notes simultaneously in a one-day workshop with me. Learning to create these harmonics actually changes the way we create sound, the way that we hear and—since hearing is one of the most powerful senses that we have—the way that we perceive reality. People use these vocal harmonics to resonate their chakras, activate portions of their brain, and send healing energies to others. It is quite profound.

Healing with Sound

A quote from *The New York Times*: "Sound shaped into dazzling new tool—can make, break, or rearrange molecular structure and levitate objects."

Most people normally think of sound as an energy that just goes into your ears and into your brain, and this, of course, is true. Sound does affect our brain and is able to entrain, or change, our brain wave activity, our heart rate, and our respiration.

This by itself is extraordinary, since it means that you can induce different states of consciousness through sound. But sound affects much more than that. Sound is capable of rearranging molecular structure. Think of what this means. There's virtually nothing that cannot be changed or fixed or shifted with sound. This is very powerful work.

I've had my own personal experiences of working on people and having students who have learned the overtoning technique from me come back with extraordinary reports of healing. As an example, a nurse who took one of my workshops made sound into a patient who was due to have surgery for the removal of kidney stones. The next day they went in to do the surgery and there were no stones.

People ask, "Jonathan, do you think this is possible?" Of course!

I have made sounds into people who have been very, very ill—sometimes terminal—and sometimes seen the imbalance disappear. I've witnessed remarkable healings through sound. Pick an ailment from A to Z, from asthma to eczema, and I could tell you stories about people healing themselves using sound, or being healed by others who have used sound.

The technique I've developed which I call "overtoning" uses sound to scan the body and the auric field and project a healing tone into an area that needs it. It's quite powerful—perhaps the most powerful technique I've encountered. After all, if you can rearrange molecular structure with sound, virtually anything is possible.

Yet, I always wonder, "What is going to happen five years from now? Is the imbalance totally gone or will it return? Have we gotten to the source? Does it matter?"

I had a relative with a debilitating imbalance—a niece with headaches so severe she'd been in bed for the last ten years. I had gone into deep meditation and was told to work with my niece, so I asked her to come visit me in Colorado.

Over the phone, I perceived that the problem was a blockage to her crown chakra. I thought that when I picked her up at the airport, I could touch her head and she'd be healed. That didn't happen.

I did a tremendous amount of work with her—very deep and profound work. The energy medicine field was totally new to her and I'm sure it was a little unnerving, to say the least. But she stayed with me for a month and experienced my work, as well of that of a number of other really excellent healers. What was interesting was that each healer would see the problem from his or her own perspective. If the person was a nutritionist, it was a nutritional problem. If the person was an acupuncturist, it was a matter of low chi. If the person dealt with Pleiadian implants, it was a Pleiadian implant problem. And so on.

After a month, my niece had about all she could take. She thanked me for all the work that she'd had. "Uncle Jonathan, you've given me more than a lifetime's worth of experience. But I just want to go back to the life I had before."

I asked her to try to remember to practice some of the techniques and exercises that I and others had shown her. But I doubted that she would, and knew then that she had made a decision which would ultimately affect her continuation on the planet. She died fairly recently. It was quite tragic. I honor her now by telling her story.

This experience left me truly aware of how little I knew about the healing process. I'd been able to assist others, and yet I couldn't help my own family.

What did I learn from this experience? That the whole concept of healing is so very complicated. It is so unique and individualistic. There are so many deep questions: Why has this person chosen this condition from a karmic level? Why has this person gotten into such a situation? How is the imbalance serving the person? Is there a lesson he or she has chosen to learn? Is this person willing to go to the source of the problem in order to initiate healing? Is it necessary to go to the source or is this person, on some deep core level, willing to release whatever is creating the imbalance without ever knowing what it was or why it was? Does the modality of healing even matter?

I have seen people with extreme imbalances go to healers and that is it—the imbalance is gone for good. And I have seen others go to healers, have an intense remission, and then the imbalance comes back five years later, perhaps because the forces that created the imbalance hadn't been dealt with. Permanent healings usually require a change of lifestyle and a change of consciousness. But I've also seen miracles that don't require anything—not even a belief in the person who receives the miracles.

One thing I've learned is not to create too many boxes to put things in because, sooner or later, you'll find things that won't fit in the box. I've seen too many things that I cannot categorize or systematize. Yet, at the same time, I know that sound is an extraordinary tool for healing. Given the right time and the right place, with the right person, anything can happen. Sound can create miracles.

Working with Sound
When I utilize the overtoning technique, I will make a sound and a harmonic will come out. I'm not generating it—the harmonic comes out as an interface between the voice and the energy field of the person I'm projecting the sound to. It's almost as though the harmonic is a living energy form, and I'm simply a conduit for the sacred sound that is coming through me. When you're working with sound you

want to get out of the way of ego, which can get you into problems. I believe the same is true of any healing modality.

Before I use sound for healing, I will say an invocation to Shamael, Angel of Sound. "I invoke the spirit of Shamael, Angel of Sacred Sound. May the sound of light surround me. May the light of sound guide me. May sacred sound come through me for the harmony of all."

I have many techniques for creating and projecting healing sounds, but I believe that the process is much more than that. I have found this invocation to be quite effective in assisting in the process of opening and becoming a conduit for sacred sound. That's so important and something I will stress again and again—that we need to be channels for transmitting Divine energies: "Lord, make me an instrument..."

There are so many ways that sound can heal and transform. One of the most inspiring stories about the healing nature of sound does not involve the overtoning technique or mantric chanting or anything like that. It involves *Dolphin Dreams*, a recording I created many year ago for the birth of my son. *Dolphin Dreams* has since been used not only to assist in the birthing process but also to calm babies in hospitals, heal infants with croup, and reduce stress in adults. Both parents and children love it. It's really designed to open up the higher brain functions in children.

About eight years ago, I received a phone call from a woman. She said "My name is Betty. I had electroshock therapy fifteen years ago and since then I have been unable to sleep at night. My doctor told me I should get *Dolphin Dreams* because he thought it might help me. I put it on one of those auto-reverse cassette players..." she was in tears as she said, "and all of a sudden, for the first time in fifteen years, I am able to sleep through the night. Thank you so much."

It's so gratifying to be able to assist people. I'm so thankful that some of my recordings seem to do this. My latest recording, *Chakra Chants*, combines several different systems for chakra balancing and resonance and is designed for healing. It recently won the 1999 Visionary Awards for "Best Healing-Meditation Album" and "Best Album of the Year." It's quite an honor!

I've gotten many phone calls, letters, and e-mails from people telling me of outrageous experiences that have resulted from their listening to *Chakra Chants*, but that experience with the woman and *Dolphin Dreams* really moved me very deeply. I was in tears myself by the end of the phone call and I doubt I will ever forget it.

I would say that working with sound, you can heal anything. And that's true…depending upon the time and the place and the need of the individual. Sometimes you can use sound and nothing happens. As I said before, I believe the whole process of healing may be more involved than anyone can imagine.

People are always wanting to hear miracle stories, and I have great difficulty with this because then other people will expect miracles—and sometimes miracles simply happen because a person was at the right place at the right time. Sometimes, the person is there, he's ready and you can make a sound, you can give him a light, you can give him a crystal, you can give him an herb—you can give him X, Y, or Z—he's ready for the shift and he'll do it. It almost doesn't matter what you do.

It has been suggested to me that most of the healing in the twenty-first century is going to be interactive. This feels quite accurate. That's why I like to teach people how they can create sounds that can shift and change frequencies rather than having someone else make the sounds for them. Sure, there are times when you need to be "jump started" by someone else. There's no question about that. But, when you have a daily practice such as sounding your chakras and resonating different parts of your body, you are taking responsibility for yourself as opposed to giving it to someone else.

The Human Voice As an Instrument of Healing

We are all graced with the most extraordinary healing instrument. It's an instrument that is user-friendly, cost effective, and doesn't require batteries or electricity. I'm describing, of course, the human voice. We can all use our own voice as an instrument of healing, as an instrument of frequency shifting. It doesn't have to be a beautiful voice. It doesn't have to be a loud voice. And it doesn't have to be an "on key" voice.

I'm not talking about entertainment—I'm talking about entrainment, which is actually an aspect of resonance. Entrainment was discovered in the sixteenth century by a Dutch scientist who set a room full of pendulum clocks in motion and came back the next day to find that all the pendulums were locked in step with the rhythms of the most powerful pendulum.

Entrainment is a phenomenon of physics in which different systems seems to like to resonate together—it may have something to do with the conservation of energy. It's observable within the human body in terms of heart rate, respiration, and brain waves: all these different pulsations can be shifted and changed using sound. Being able to entrain using the voice means learning to shift your frequencies. That is, learning to change your vibratory rate with your own self-created sounds.

One can see how this works by experimenting with the vowel sounds: a, e, i, o, u. This is a simple self-healing technique that I teach in my book *Healing Sounds*. Try sounding for three to five minutes on any one of the vowels sounds. Do it in a place where you won't get disturbed. The sound can be gentle—it does not have to be loud. If possible, sit while making the sound with your eyes closed.

You may see colors. You may see geometric forms. You will certainly notice changes in your nervous system such as your heart beating slower. Note whether your hearing is more acute. See if you notice any changes in your senses. I can guarantee that all of a sudden you'll be more aware of the light, more aware of the sound. You may also experience a change in temperature in the room—probably making it hotter—simply because you will be generating more energy with the sound.

Sensing changes like this helps people to realize that sound isn't just a thing that goes into your ears. Sound goes into our ears, into our brain, and into our physical body. It goes into our etheric field as well.

The Effects of Noise Pollution

External frequencies go into the auditory pathways and entrain the brain. These sounds also affect the nervous system, our heart rate and respiration, and all our organs. I am convinced that many of the imbalances that occur today are a result not only of electromagnetic pollution, but also of noise pollution.

Years ago, two similar demographic populations were studied—one living in a pastoral setting and the other living near an airport—and it was found that there was a 65 percent higher incidence of stress-related illness in the group by the airport: cancer, stroke, heart disease, you name it.

This may be because loud sounds trigger what is called the fight or flight response—increased adrenaline, increased heartbeat, respiration, brain waves. There also seems to be a suppression of immunological functions as well.

Just think of how a car horn can jar you—everything in your body just tenses up. What happens if we are continually exposed to loud and unwanted sounds?

After a while, our conscious mind begins to ignore it, and our body habituates to it. This does not mean we're not being affected by the sounds, but simply that we're not aware of it anymore.

The people who lived near the airport in that test had a much higher incidence of stress-related disease whether or not they were consciously aware of the noise. Incidentally, loud sounds, even if they are consciously created, such as the high decibels coming from personal stereo units, car or home stereos, or "ghetto blasters" can produce the same results.

There are a number of different ways of working with loud sounds and noise pollution, such as playing soothing sounds while you're exposed to loud noises. You see a lot of the New York City population, for example, walking around with headphones. That's noise masking. Unfortunately, while the noise may not be going into your ears in that situation, it's still going into your body and having some effect.

Shifting Frequencies

An ideal solution is to learn how to shift frequencies and become fluid with the external sounds so that these sounds no longer adversely affect us. It really involves learning how to use our consciousness to change the way that we interface with the sound. Here's an example: I was on a New York subway on my way to teach a workshop when I noticed a woman sitting opposite me. She was grimacing, with her hands jammed over her ears. Clearly she was being influenced and upset by the sounds of the subway.

I broke a cardinal rule of subway riding that says you never speak to anyone on a subway you don't know. I just couldn't help it. This woman was in pain. I wanted to help. So when the subway made a stop, I went over to her, smiled, and said, "Excuse me, but I couldn't help but notice that you're being adversely affected by the sounds of this subway." And she was. She was so tense you could see that the sound was just breaking her up.

I said, "Maybe you could pretend that you're listening to this incredible dance band, which is really the sound of the subway. You could move with the rhythms of the subway and make it your friend, your ally, and not your adversary." My colleague, Dr. John Beaulieu, first suggested this to me years before when we were discussing the effects of New York subways.

I continued speaking with this woman. "Transform the sound with your consciousness. Focus on it. Travel on it. What is the source of the sound? What is it trying to teach you? Hum along with it. Dance with it. Make the sound your friend."

The woman looked at me, smiled, and nodded her head. Then the subway took off and I watched as the woman jammed her fingers back into her ears, gritted her teeth, and fought the sound. I shrugged my shoulders and reminded myself not to speak to strangers on subways again.

Another example of transforming sound: When I lived up in the mountains outside of Boulder, a sound that I had great difficulty tolerating was the buzzing of a chain saw. Due to the normal quiet of this forested region, the sounds of chain saws traveled for great distances. Not only did I find the actual frequencies of chain saws to be a disturbance, but—whenever I heard them—I would also picture someone cutting down trees and causing pain to Mother Earth.

No doubt about it. I definitely had issues with chain saws—until the day when I was building a tree house for my son. I had to cut some large tree limbs to use for the tree house. A friend, who had a chain saw, helped me by cutting these limbs with his machine. During the five minutes or so that the chain saw was on, I was humming along with the buzzing tool, marveling at the assistance this extraordinary device was giving in terms of the creation of the tree house.

This time, the sound of the chain saw did not adversely affect me despite my proximity to it. It was a major learning experience for me in terms of transforming an unwanted sound and turning it into an ally. By using our own sounds—I was humming during the time—and our imagination, we can become fluid and truly shift our frequencies.

Now, I'm not guaranteeing that the next time a chain saw starts buzzing next to my ear, I'm not going to freeze up, but this one time was enough to show me the possibilities and ways that we can work with external sounds.

Another method of dealing with unwanted external sounds is to immediately release the sound with your own voice. Say you're walking down the street and a car horn honks at you. Your body absorbs it and if you don't do anything about it, you'll stay with the stress created by the sound. But suppose, instead, when the horn honks, you turn around and honk back at the car? That allows you to release the sound and the stress from your body. It may sound silly, but it truly works.

It's quite possible that by being exceptionally fluid with external, unwanted sounds, the sounds will not be as hazardous as they could be. If you can learn to be fluid—tone with the sound and change your consciousness about the sound—then potentially negative sonic fields may not be detrimental to you. We may also find that by vocalizing and visualizing in this manner, other types of fields, such as electromagnetic, may be less detrimental to our bodies, our brains, and our auric fields.

This is one of the concepts of shifting frequencies—that we can alter our own vibratory patterns in order to move more easily with the changes that seem to be occurring on planet Earth at this extraordinary time.

Frequency + Intent = Healing

When I first started doing the work for my master's thesis, I was impressed with the relationship between sounds and the chakras, which are the seven energy centers that are transduction points between the etheric fields and the physical body. The word "chakra" is Sanskrit for wheel. The chakras are seen by psychics, clairvoyants, and others sensitive to subtle energy as spinning wheels of light. And the chakras are sensitive to sound.

The first time I looked into this relationship between sound and the chakras, there seemed to be a very simple system that resonated the chakras. This was the major scale—C D E F G A B. There were seven chakras and seven notes. It was very simple, or so I thought at the time.

As I began to research more, however, I found dozens of different systems that people used to resonate the chakras. It was very confusing because none of these systems agreed. The mantra, "Om," for example, could be used by one spiritual master to resonate the heart chakra. Another master might have it resonate the third eye center. Still another might have it resonate the solar plexus center or the crown chakra.

"What is going on?" I wondered. "This doesn't make any sense. How can the same sound affect different chakras and how can different sounds affect the same chakra? How can this be?"

As I meditated on this conundrum, the information came to me that "It is the intentionality of the person as well as the frequency that creates the effect of the sound." This made perfect sense to me. Intentionality is the energy behind the sound—the consciousness which rides upon the sound when it is created. I came up with the

formula: "Frequency + Intent = Healing." I share this with as many people as possible so that they may understand this phenomenon.

You can hear some amazing swamies and other spiritual beings chanting and their voices are so off-key—but the energy that they send upon the sounds can be so healing. And you can have somebody who's got a perfectly trained voice and they make sounds and nothing happens. It's just ego on the sound, nothing more, and that's all you'll receive.

Sometimes people say, "Well then, it doesn't really matter what frequency I use or what sound I make, because it's all in the intentionality."

I laugh and say, "Well, yes...That is true if you can bi-locate, levitate, or do all the different siddhas and miracles that the masters can."

There are spiritual masters, saints, sat gurus in various parts of this globe who can sigh, groan, moan, belch, or whatever and heal you of any disease because their energy is so extraordinary. But for most of us, this is not the case. The rest of us have to be aware of the frequency that we create as well.

If it is my intention to calm someone down and I shout in his or her ear, the results of my shouting will have the same effects we discussed with any loud sounds—it will increase heart rate, respiration, and brain waves. Despite my intent, my shouting will do anything but create calming vibrations. This sound, 99.9 percent of the time in this situation, would create stress.

One has to take into account what the "psycho-acoustic" effects of sound are—how sound on the physical plane operates in terms of the brain, the auditory pathways, the nervous system. We need to be aware of the physiological effects of sound as well as our intention. Until we have achieved a level of consciousness that allows us to operate from a higher dimensionality, it is important that we pay attention to both frequency and intent when making a sound.

And I may get up tomorrow and say, "You know, it is all intentionality..."

We Are All Unique Vibratory Beings

It is my belief that we are all unique vibratory beings—in other words, that the sounds of one person's chakras may be very different from the sounds of another person's chakras. We can change and shift our frequencies as we become more evolved.

Since I believe that we are all unique vibratory beings, I don't think that we can create just one sound that would correct an imbalance for all people or restore health to an organ for everyone. We can certainly create a generic frequency that might work for a majority of the people, but it is not going to be as refined and effective as a specific frequency which was created for an individual. Therefore, we need to try to get as uniquely individualistic as we can in terms of understanding the particular effects of resonance and the interface between sounds and each person.

When I have a workshops of forty people and I say, "Anybody here allergic to penicillin?" two or three people usually say, "Yes!"

So, if we all took penicillin, some of us would get healed and some would get very sick or die. What I'm saying is that even in terms of the allopathic medical model, we don't get 100 percent response to any remedy. The same thing is true in Ayurvedic medicine, which has different body types who require different types of food, etc.

I believe that in terms of creating a generic frequency for everyone, about a 70 percent response would be about as good as it's going to get. This comes very close to some of the new percentages that are demonstrated by what mainstream Western medicine calls the placebo effect. The placebo effect is frequently found to be 35 percent effective, but recent studies have shown it to be much more effective. I think the placebo effect, incidentally, really demonstrates the mind-body connection and the power of our minds to influence us.

Any Music Can Be Therapeutic

It is my belief that not only are we all unique vibratory beings—I also believe that any music, depending upon the time, the place, and the need of the individual, can be therapeutic.

For example, when I lived nine thousand feet up in the mountains and I was trying to get home on a snowy night when the roads were quite dangerous, I would not put on soft, gentle music that would relax me and help put me into a stupor. Instead, I would put on loud, fast rock 'n' roll to stimulate me. I wanted to be alert. I wanted to be on the edge of stress and have my adrenaline flowing—that was therapeutic and healing for me under those circumstances.

About fifteen years ago, a woman called me to say that she was putting together a catalog of all the beautiful healing music in the world. "Great!" I said. "What types of music are you using?" Well, her catalog of beautiful healing music was all classical!

I said, "I really honor that you are doing this, but do you think an eight-year-old black boy in a hospital in Selma, Alabama with severe burns is likely to respond to that? Michael Jackson might be a lot more therapeutic for taking his mind off his pain than Mozart. And in India or Bali, I have a feeling that people would respond very differently to classical music than we do in the West. I love the idea of your catalog, but I think you may be a bit culturally biased."

I think we do that a lot——especially in the field of sound and music healing—

get very biased about music. You get people who will tell you that "Only this music is healing!" or "These are the best healing sounds on the planet." I think that's nonsense. I believe it's very individualistic. It's important not to get locked into any one type of music as being the be all and end all of healing music.

There's a lot of emphasis on Mozart right now. And Mozart is wonderful. But I would like to suggest that when the real research is in, you'll find that many different classical composers have very similar effects to Mozart. And if we look at other types of music, we'll find powerful and beneficial effects as well—depending upon the time, the place, and the need of the individual.

Now, of course, not all music is going to create the same results. What is your purpose for listening to music? Some music slows you down. Some music speeds you up. Some music enhances creativity. Some music stimulates concentration. Some music makes you want to dance and some music makes you want to relax.

We live in an extraordinary spectrum of different sounds on this planet—an incredible variety of sonics, all with different abilities to influence and effect our lives. I don't think the Creator would have given us this extraordinary candy store of different sounds if we weren't supposed to experience them all. So I remain skeptical about any research that says that any one type of music is *the* major sound healing form.

I very much hope that, regardless of how much information we collect on the psychoacoustic effects of sound, no matter what additions are made to the science of sound, that music will always be, at least in part, a intuitive, god/goddess, divinely inspired and created form.

Because, if we get locked into "this is the way it must be," not only are there no surprises, but we've created a dead-end, a loop that does not allow for creative and conscious evolution. For continued creation, we need to be able to shift our frequencies with new vibrations.

A Visit from the Dolphins

I was in Los Angeles a few years ago to present a workshop called "The Dolphin Shamanic Extraterrestrial Angelic Sound Connection." The title was a bit tongue in cheek, but I had literally pages and pages of notes on the relationship between dolphins, angels, extraterrestrials, and shamanic sounds.

As I was walking on Venice Beach, California, trying to get some last minute thoughts together about my workshop, I was drawn to the water. At the time, the beaches in the area were shielded by a wooden wall due to damage that had occurred from storms, and I had to climb over the barrier in order to get to the ocean.

While I was doing this, my mind was racing about the presentation I was to give that evening. I was wondering if the dolphins came from Sirius, or if angels and extraterrestrial were sometimes the same—that sort of thing.

Then, I was at the water's edge holding a crystal. A moment later my shoes were off and I was standing in the surf sounding forth with the "Deep Voice" of the Tibetan monks. Whew! Talk about frequency shifts.

All of a sudden I saw a dorsal fin cut the surface. Now, being a city kid, I got scared. I thought it was a shark. Then, there were two dorsal fins. Then three. Then four. In a few moments, I realized what was going on: a dozen dolphins basically materialized out of this totally clear ocean and were leaping and playing about thirty yards in front of me. It was outrageous!

I immediately established some sort of telepathic contact or rapport with them—or I perceived that I did—and I asked them what planet they came from and how they evolved from there.

And the dolphins communicated: "The questions you are asking are not important. What is important is that you humans must stop polluting the earth. You must unite together to clean up the planet and make it safe for your children and their children. This is what you are to talk about tonight. Tell them this is a message from the dolphins. Do not be concerned about what planet, what solar system, what angel—or anything else that fascinates your mental body. That is not important. What is important is for you and others to do the work to assist in cleaning up the planet."

I share this story because it was a powerful one. I went on to give my presentation that evening and I said, "I have to tell you people what happened to me today. As a result, what I want to talk about now is how we can unify together and reach out to others for the good of all on our planet."

I proceeded to talk about how sound can do this. Sound can break through our isolation. Sound creates connections. Once we sound together with others, we realize our oneness as we resonate together. When we sound together in a group with combined intentionality, we can create ecstatic shifts and changes. We can change the world. We can change the universe.

Another one of my formulas is: "Vocalization + Visualization = Manifestation." This simply means that through combined self-created sounds, coupled with specific imaging, it is possible to achieve amazing creations. When our consciousness and our sounds work together, anything is possible. Miracles can and do happen.

Healing the Earth

At every workshop I've ever done, at the end we do an "Om" for the planet Earth. It's very simple, but very effective. We send the sound that we have created into a quartz crystal in the center of the circle and then visualize the sound being transduced into beautiful gold and pink energy which travels around the outside of the planet and filters down to all the beings on the surface of the planet.

At the same time, this wonderful gold and pink energy riding on the "Om" sound goes back down into the crystal, into the heart of the Gaia matrix, to let the Earth Mother know that there are beings on the surface who are working to assist her. It's a wonderful and powerful experience for all.

At more advanced workshops, and particularly at the Healing Sounds Intensive, we use specific sounds, pitches, ratios, harmonics, colors, and geometries in order to create a multidimensional form that acts as a gateway between the planes. I call it a Group Merkaba. It is very powerful. And we use this, of course, for assisting personal, planetary, and even galactic healings.

At the Intensive, we generate a field of love and light through sound for nine days, beginning early in the morning and ending late at night. It is extraordinary what can be achieved through sounding together like this. We experience initiations into various realms of consciousness, resonating with different divine energy forms. We learn how to use our own self-created sounds to shift our own frequencies and assist in shifting the frequencies of the planet.

It is truly the most amazing and life-changing experience one can imagine. The only difficulty arises when we conclude the Intensive and must go back to our normal lives. We carry the experience with us, but no one wants it to end. Perhaps, someday, we can all be in this field of love and light through sound together and we will create a new world.

If you take a pebble and throw it into the water, you get these amazing ripples that will reach the shore of the body of water. These ripples are much greater than the waves you started with. In the same way, a group of people making sound together will create ripples that reach much further than the actual acoustic field that the people are creating. That is the power of sound coupled with consciousness—vocalization + visualization.

I think, ultimately, my work is truly geared toward assisting both personal and planetary vibratory and evolutionary shifts. What does this mean? You heal yourself and you heal the planet! You heal the planet and you heal yourself!

By beginning to shift your frequencies, you begin to open up to higher and higher levels of light and love, higher and higher levels of consciousness. We begin to realize the illusion of separation that we have been taught—the separation between ourselves and other humans, separation between ourselves and all of life, separation between ourselves and the Divine.

I like to believe that, through helping initiate people with the experience of sacredness through sound, these barriers of separation will drop by themselves, and we will resonate together as this extraordinary harmonic of love and light.

Marty McGee Bennett

Santa Fe, New Mexico

We learn from all our animals, but llamas are so foreign to most people's experience that they really can cause a more profound and more dramatic level of learning than other animals. Working with llamas can really make us look in the mirror in a different way.

*S*usan is so devoted to the small herd of llamas lounging outside her Maine studio that we nicknamed her "Our Lady of the Llamas," and joked about how she would surely try to slip a photograph of llamas into this book.

Sitting over breakfast in a coffee shop in Tuba City, Arizona, she got her chance. Passing through the Navajo Nation on our way to Utah, we were musing about the varieties of healers we had met to date and the kinds of people we would like to meet in the future. Someone mentioned people who work with animals and Susan fairly shouted, "Marty McGee!"

Susan believes that the workshops she took with Marty not only helped her establish the kind of relationship she wanted with her llamas, but also empowered her to become first a photographer, then an artist, and finally a woman who is able to stand on her own two feet. No one, Susan insists, leaves one of Marty's training clinics without undergoing some sort of transformation—and the changes usually have little to do with long-legged woolly mammals.

Watching Marty working in a pen—with or without a llama—it's easy to believe Susan's assertions. Balance, truthfulness, clarity, and confidence seem to permeate every step she takes, every word she speaks. Whether she is telling funny stories about herself, analyzing a behavioral pattern, or responding to participants who disagree with her training techniques, she stands tall.

To stand in balance with your animals, Marty points out, you must first be able to stand in balance with yourself. Healing your relationship with animals points the way to healing your relationships with other humans. Working with Marty, you simultaneously are reconnected to both your animal nature and your higher self. It's no wonder that the stories of Marty's ability to effect "miracle cures" are legendary among llama owners and handlers!

Born in Virginia, Marty McGee Bennett received a degree in animal behavior from the University of Georgia. She served five years in the United States Army before moving to a farm in upstate New York, where she spent ten years breeding llamas and writing for Llamas Magazine and a variety of llama- and alpaca-oriented publications.

In 1992 Marty began a study of what was, at that time, considered a controversial new approach to animal training with Linda Tellington-Jones—an approach based on partnership and understanding rather than dominance and repetition.

Today, Marty lives in Santa Fe with her husband Brad, their dog Rocky and cat,

Ulu. Doctors and nurses are the primary focus groups for Marty's newest workshop, "Learning from Llamas," a program which uses llamas to teach health professionals about working and being with other people. She offers her "Doggy Different" training services to clients in the northern New Mexico area and conducts her "Cutting Edge" llama and alpaca training clinics across the United States and in Canada, England, Australia, New Zealand, France, Switzerland, and Germany.

My work begins with the assumption that all animals can learn quite well, that they don't have to be "conditioned" into learning new behaviors and that they would prefer to do things the easy way, if they can understand what the easy way is. Treating animals kindly and respectfully is a big part of the training.

Animals learn better when they're not afraid, so we humans have to learn to conduct ourselves in a way that doesn't frighten them. That's how a lot of people would like to handle their animals, that's what attracts them to this approach in the first place.

The bottom line is that training works better this way because, when animals and humans are frightened, they don't think. And it's much harder to teach an animal who's not thinking than it is to teach one who is thinking. So kindness— teaching animals in a way that's respectful and understands their point of view—is not only good karma, it's practical.

When you learn to lead and nurture and husband animals—as opposed to dominating them—you can't lose!

Getting Started with Llamas

I was one of those kids who was pretty much born saying, "I want a horse." I wore my parents down and got a horse when I was about fourteen. I was also pretty determined that I was going to be a veterinarian. That was the only career I would entertain. My mom would say, "Wouldn't you rather be a doctor? You're smart enough to be a doctor." And I'd say, "No, no, no."

I went to college with that goal in mind and started down the pre-veterinary track. But, at that point in time, the "powers that be" did not want me to become a veterinarian. I got really good grades, thinking that surely would get me more encouragement. It didn't get me into veterinary school, but it did get me an ROTC scholarship. So I ended up in the army with a degree in animal behavior which, as it turned out, was a pretty good degree for ending up in the army!

I met my former husband in the army and we thought that when we left the army we would raise animals you didn't have to eat—so we decided to raise sheep. At that point, I was very naive. I thought that you could raise sheep and not eat them, but that's not the case. If you raise sheep, a certain percentage of them have to go in the pot. That's just the way it goes.

But I learned to spin and weave, and I got interested in specialty fiber animals. That's what got me started with llamas. I had seen an article in *Smithsonian Magazine* back in the early '80s with pictures of llamas and I was completely enthralled. We found out where the closest herd of llamas was and went out to see them. When I saw them, it was all over. I just knew that llamas were part of what I was looking for.

The llama community was very tiny back in 1982—there were only about two hundred to three hundred people in the whole United States doing something with llamas. So, knowing something about fiber, I became an instant llama fiber expert.

I started writing about llama fiber for the only trade publication at the time, *The Two LL Llama Newsletter*, which later became *Llamas Magazine*. As the magazine and the llama business became more sophisticated, the magazine became full color and I became a contributing editor.

Concurrently, I got another horse. He was a big, black thoroughbred stallion and I thought that I had the skills to train him—and I didn't. So, as I was looking around for a way to train him, this guy, Francis Livingston, came into my craft co-op wearing riding boots.

I was very anxious to talk about my horse and I kind of harassed him into telling me what he was doing wearing riding boots. He was quite resistant, but finally shared with me that he was a rider and knew about this wonderful training method. He said he would send me some information about it.

A couple of weeks later, after I'd forgotten about the conversation, a package of information arrived in the mail. I looked through it and there was a picture of this woman, Linda Tellington-Jones, working with a camel. And I thought to myself, "Well, golly! If this stuff works on camels, maybe it would work on llamas...maybe I could write an article for *Llamas Magazine* about this training method and get a free horse clinic out of it...." I didn't really think I needed any help training my llamas at that point. I knew everything there was to know, or so I thought.

So I called her and she was home. This was another serendipitous thing, because Linda Tellington-Jones is never home. She answered the phone and I said that I had llamas and wanted to come to a clinic. And I asked if she would come by after her horse training and train my llamas so I could write an article about it. Right out of the blue, Linda agreed to do that. That's what basically started the whole thing.

Meeting My Teacher

When I first met Linda and went to Australia with her, I was married to a man who was twenty years older than me, and he really influenced me heavily. His ideal woman was the Earth Mother, so I obliged him. I gained about sixty pounds, stopped shaving my legs, and quit wearing make-up. I really looked nothing like I do now. And that was how I looked when I met Linda and went to Australia with her on this trip called "Transformation on the Trail."

When I called to sign up for the trip, I said, "Listen, I want to go to Australia, but I'm worried. Am I going to have to like roll around in crystals naked or something? I'm not going to do that." And the woman on the phone just laughed.

I had been brought up on the East Coast and in Europe in a very conservative environment. I had just spent five years in the army. And then I run into these crystal-toting vegetarians, talking about energy fields and Reiki and I was thinking, "I just want to know how to use my hands like that woman does. I'm not interested in the personal growth, transformation thing. That's for someone else. Not for me."

And lo and behold, I went on this trip with Linda and, of the nineteen people I traveled with, I made the most complete about-face. That trip changed my life in every way possible.

The TTEAM Approach to Training

Linda Tellington-Jones began as a horse kid. She approached horses from a very traditional place, which can be quite forceful and violent because that's the way people thought that training had to be done. Violence and force tend to be reactions when you're afraid. And horses are frightening; you can get hurt quite easily by a horse.

And Linda, after being in the horse world for quite a while, got really tired of being around all of that and decided to do something different. Moshe Feldenkrais was an Israeli physicist who was doing some human potential work Linda had heard about, so she took some time out of the horse world and became a Feldenkrais practitioner.

In the process of learning that system of body work, Linda was, of course, still riding horses. So she was out working with a horse one day and, almost by accident, started doing some of the things that she had been learning in her Feldenkrais course. She wiggled this horse's ears and did something with its tail. This happened to be a difficult horse and the person who owned the horse later said to her, "What in the world did you do with this horse? She isn't hard to bridle anymore and she doesn't mind if I touch her ears. She seems like a different horse...."

Linda put A and B together and realized that what she was doing with humans was also applicable to animals—and that became the jumping-off point for the Tellington Touch.

Now Linda, quite brilliantly, recognized that not everybody who wants to work with their animals is going to take four years to become a Feldenkrais practitioner. So she simplified everything and came up with some basic touches that people could learn quickly, touches that were much more directed and focused than petting and scratching, which is what we typically do with our animals.

When I first met Linda, "TEAM" stood for the "Tellington-Jones Equine Awareness Method." But, almost at the moment that I met her, Linda was poised to move beyond the horse world, so someone suggested the name of the training be changed to the "Tellington-Jones Every Animal Method." And then it became TTEAM, the "Tellington Touch Every Animal Method." Linda is now working with wild animals, dogs, cats, and horses. She pretty much leaves the llama-alpaca world to me.

The touch isn't deep tissue massage or anything that is likely to be frightening to an animal. We work with animals in a way that can be profound without being painful, or even suggestive of being painful. The touches basically describe different ways to use your hands on the animal. The last time I went to a training with

Linda, there were probably sixty different kinds of touches and we started naming them after animals—the "Clouded Leopard Touch," "the "Butterfly Touch," the "Octopus," and the "Python Lift," for example.

When I'm working with llamas—especially if I'm doing the body work on them—the touch becomes a very meditative thing. The work that I'm doing on the animal settles and focuses me and allows me to get into a place where I can communicate more effectively with the animal and be more empathetic to the animal's point of view.

The bottom line is we are not endeavoring to do anything with the muscles. We are working with the nervous system, so the touch can be very light. As a matter of fact, sometimes the lighter your touch, the more interested the nervous system becomes. The touch works extremely well to focus an animal, to build a relationship of trust, and to solve behavioral problems. It's also a really nice way of relating to your animals. From a mirroring point of view, you get as much as you give.

Polly "The Problem" Llama

I have probably taught at half the vet schools in the United States. That's my pro bono work, my gift to the animals and the veterinary students. And I'm very grateful now to be on this end of the animal business. Rather than sewing up animals or cutting up their reproductive parts, I'm teaching veterinarians about handling animals.

When I am at the vet schools, I work with the llama teaching herds. The animals in a teaching herd are usually donated to the school because they have a behavioral problem or a physical problem. Then, when they get to the school, they become the practice herd for the new students to work on so they get stuck and prodded even more. If the animals' attitude wasn't good to start with, nothing that happens at the vet school will cause it to improve.

So I've had some really interesting experiences with these teaching herds. The most recent was with a llama named Polly. She was considered the worst of the worst—a kicker. She wore a bright red halter all the time to indicate danger to the students. Polly would kick for no reason. Everyone thought she was just nasty and awful and mean.

So they brought her in and I had them put her in a pen. Part of the work that I have developed with llamas is that before you can actually touch them—and have the touches mean anything—you have to figure out how to get to them. That's a piece that I've added to what I learned from Linda.

I found that the most important thing to a llama is an escape route. Actually the most important thing to anybody is an escape route. So I came up with this one-two-three-four body placement routine that describes positions inside a confined area, places where you can stand and still allow the animal to feel safe.

What I found is that if you stand behind the animal's eye, at a 45° angle or so behind the hip, you give the animal the largest possible escape route. So when I go in with an animal like Polly, that's where I stand—even though standing at a 45° angle off the hip put me in line with her back feet, her stated problem.

I believed that the reason she was kicking was because people were trapping her in a corner. Animals run forward, not backward. By standing behind her eye and giving her an escape route, I was able to eliminate her reason for having to kick in the first place. Then I caught her by maneuvering her into a rope instead of grabbing her around the neck—which is what most llama handlers do—and I started to do body work on her.

One of the places that animals hold tension is in their mouths. They breathe out of their mouths. They eat out of their mouths. Mother Nature tells them, essentially, "If you mess up your mouth, you're dead."

The animals have been worried their whole lives about having their mouths handled by a human. They've had this scary thing—a halter—put over their heads and they come up with escape and evasion routines to keep the halter from touching their mouths. A lot of times, the animals end up knocking the person on the head or hitting their own head on the side of a wall or a pen. It doesn't have to be, but haltering can become really awful for them.

What I tell people is that working with an animal's mouth, in a way that feels safe, is something scary that the animal and I can do together. It's kind of like bungee-jumping. We bungee-jump and, when everything turns out okay, we've done this really scary thing together. It forges an immediate bond between me and the animal.

I work with the mouth and usually what happens is the animal relaxes down into my hand, begins to loosen up the jaw muscles that have been really tight. It will chew a little bit and it will give me a couple of slow blinks. That means, "Wow!

Instead of feeling tenser when a human being is touching me, I'm feeling better. I can't believe it."

Polly did this for me and I realized, in the process, that she had on this really horribly fitting halter—and she'd had it on for at least a year. She had sores underneath her jaw and calluses on the bridge of her nose. She couldn't chew very well in this thing, either, because it was too far forward on her nose, impeding her ability to ruminate. And she had a whole bunch of old food stuck in her molars, behind the halter.

I suppose Polly hadn't been worked with often and this halter was just left on for safety purposes. So I unbuckled the halter and took it off. Polly stretched out her jaw and got all this junk out of her teeth—then she looked at me like I was an angel. I can't really explain that moment other than to say that this llama looked at me with a knowing and a gratefulness that makes being away from home worthwhile.

It wasn't that the people who were taking care of her didn't want to do right by her. They just didn't know how to handle her. Llamas have very tiny heads compared to horses, and they're difficult to fit appropriately in a halter. So I ended up working her mouth some more and comforting her and then I put on a halter that fit. So that was a nice, happy ending to all that. And Polly never kicked at all—not once. She didn't exhibit that behavior because she had no need to.

It's amazing to me that—so far as I know—there is not a vet school in the country that includes animal handling as part of the official curriculum. So the vets graduate with a seat-of-the pants, by-guess-or-by-golly approach to restraint or catching or haltering or whatever. And the ironic part of it is that when most of us lay people are shopping for a veterinarian, we make a judgment about whether or not we want a vet by how well he or she can handle our animal.

We can't judge how well a potential vet can diagnose an illness. What we want to know is if this person can get a rectal thermometer into our dog without putting a muzzle on him.

You Teach What You Need to Learn

The animals that bring humans to clinics are usually the most difficult ones in the herd. And they fall into one of two categories—they are either the smartest or the dumbest in the herd.

Animals are very honest. Some of them want to be in control and our standard approach in training—and in public schools and the rest of society—is that you have to be willing to give over a certain amount of control in order to get along. And these "problem" animals just can't do it.

If you work with them in a way that allows them to participate and understand what you want from them, they feel in control and they can go along with it. But if you approach them with an attitude that says, "You're going to do what I say, so just shut up and don't ask any questions...," they just can't do it. So they start acting out and bring a whole lot of grief on themselves. They can't help themselves. They just have to do that.

I identify very strongly with those animals that have a hard time with the "just do it because I say so" approach. I was continually acting out in the army, slinking around buildings so I didn't have to salute people and figuring out ways not to follow the uniform code.

Doing this work, I've learned as much about my own animal nature as I have about the animals. I have learned, for example, that I have a tendency to behave instinctively much more of the time than I thought. Before, I would have said that I was thinking almost 100 percent of the time, unless I was swerving to miss a car or something like that. I never realized the large degree to which all human beings are behaving instinctively.

The four responses to stress that animals use are the flight response, the fight response, the freeze response, and the faint response. Most animals will gravitate to one of those behaviors first and then flip back and forth between the others. In general, the flight response is the one that they pick first.

I skipped by the flight response and went into the fight response a lot. I was very angry and confrontational a lot of the time. Learning about animals and having the animals mirror my behavior back to me, I have learned how to override my instinctive responses and begin to think my way through situations. And that's what I am teaching the animals to do.

So, in the process of teaching them, they've been teaching me. Every single day, I see myself mirrored in my work. As they say, "You teach what you have to learn."

Allowing an Animal to Be Different

In the past year or so, I have been finding myself saying to a lot of people, "You have to let your animal be different." They will pigeonhole their animals into slots—this animal is a spitter, this animal is a kicker, this animal is aggressive—and then that's the way the animal behaves for them.

When I start giving owners or handlers different alternatives for their own behavior, things begin to change. If they maintain the attitude that the animal is a spitter or a kicker, though, it will get in the way of creating a different relationship, which is what they say they want.

I can give you an example from my own life. I went to a llama conference last year and met a woman there who knew me more than fifteen years ago, before I started doing any of this training. When I first started out in the llama business, I was very scared. I wouldn't have termed it that way back then; but now, looking back on it, I can see that I was really afraid that I was going to get overtaken, eaten up by all of the big guys who were coming into the llama business.

We had worked really hard to build up this little herd and we were just about ready to sell animals when big time investors got interested in the llama business. One minute we were the second largest herd of llamas in New York and the next minute we were a bit player.

In those days, when I got scared I got feisty—and I started behaving from that place. I started trying to take control over as many things as I could. I would be really obnoxious at llama meetings and put forth my point of view and not back off. I just wouldn't let go of things.

It's been a long road and I have really learned a lot since then. I am a lot different than I used to be. But, when I ran into this woman at the llama conference, she would not allow me to be different.

To her, I was just the same as I was fifteen years ago, the last time I saw her. I had quite a long conversation with her and she made all of these sneery little comments about the way I would react to things that were happening in my life now, or things that were happening in the llama business now. She couldn't have been more off-base about the way that I felt, but it didn't matter. That was the way she held me—forevermore, probably.

The interesting thing was that when I was talking with this woman, I really started going right back there, back to those old feelings. And I found myself slipping back into all that old behavior. Being around somebody like that put me in the same place I know the animals are often in, where they are labeled and not really allowed to change.

I think the same kind of thing happens inside marriages or between parents and children or with our pets or whatever. We often deny them the ability to change or the recognition that they are changing. It's a shame.

The Impetus for Change

Animals only respond to our lead. If we let them alone and just left them in the pasture, we wouldn't have a problem with them. The only time there is a problem is when we have to deal with our animals—so the onus is on us to change the way that we deal with them.

The example I give to people in trainings is this: If you always do things the same way, your llamas will always respond the same way. You can just about count on the fact that your llama is not going to go to bed at night and say, "Tsk! I've been having trouble with Pat. I think I'll try a different strategy." They don't do that. So if you don't like what the animal is doing, the easiest thing to change is your own behavior.

Here's a really simple example: I was doing a clinic ages ago in Maryland and this man was telling me, "You know, my llama spits all the time. She's horrible. She just spits at me." This spitting thing cuts right into humans. Spitting really does insult us and push deep buttons of fear, humiliation, and embarrassment. It's the kind of stuff that only llamas can do, and it's one of the things that makes them such great teachers for us.

What I encourage people to do is see that this animal is one that spits occasionally as opposed to making that behavior the entire identity of the animal. Then, when I come and work with those animals, people can see, quite dramatically, that the problem behavior is not necessarily consistent. It may be consistent with them, but it's not consistent with what I do.

If you don't behave in the way that provokes the behavior, you don't get the behavior. Teachers could learn a lot from that, too. If *you* don't behave in a way that provokes certain kinds of behavior from the children, you don't get the behavior. So is it fair to label the child? Or the llama?

Anyway, I said to this man, "Okay, let me just get a picture of what we're dealing with here. When does the spitting happen?" And he said, "Well, I can just about count on it when I'm picking little bits of stuff out of her fiber."

And I thought for a minute—and I know the guy was probably put out by my answer—but I said, "Why don't you not do that?"

Because that's how simple it was. He just needed to stop pestering that poor llama by picking stuff out of her wool. A lot of people don't realize it, but it really does drive llamas crazy to have even one little piece of stuff pulled out of their fiber.

When I had long hair, sometimes I would put a rubber band in my hair and there would be one hair that wasn't right. It was just the most aggravating thing. And pulling little bits of stuff out of a llama's coat is the same kind thing. She was just saying, "Please stop that." Running away wasn't an option because she was tied up. So the only other way that llama could talk to this man, could stop him, was to spit. When he stopped picking, she stopped spitting. It was that simple!

Remember Polly the kicker? She was only kicking because everybody cornered her to catch her. By making that one shift, by standing behind her eye instead of cutting off her escape route, we were able to stop the kicking. Sometimes the changes are so simple, so very simple—but they really can net a really profound change in behavior.

Often, at the lunch break, people who have been watching me work at a clinic will come up to me and say, "So, I have this llama at home..." And they'll give me all kinds of information—she's this old and she used to live here or there or the other place. Then they'll ask, "Is she too old to change?"

And I'll say, "Well, how old are you?" And the person kind of looks at me funny. "Well," I say, "If you're not too old to change, she's not too old to change!"

If you ask me, "How long is it going to take me to train my llama not to spit?" my answer is, "How long is it going to take you to stop behaving in a way that provokes that spitting? How attached are you to this habit that you have?"

Sometimes people get it and sometimes they don't. Sometimes they get part of it. I have a pretty good idea, when people leave a clinic, how it's going to go at home. But sometimes I'm really wrong too. Sometimes I'll watch someone as he leaves a clinic and I'll think, "Boy, I don't think he got it." And then he'll show up at another clinic a year later and he's really gotten it.

Llamas and Alpacas As a Metaphor for Life

A while ago, I wrote a book called *Llamas and Alpacas As a Metaphor for Life*. It was based on a talk I give. I think part of what the talk and the book do for people is put into words the feelings that people have about their animals. It helps them explain to others why their animals are so important to them.

Animals really are our teachers—and people will go to great lengths to be with or stay with someone they perceive as their teacher. I moved to Santa Fe, in large part, because Linda Tellington-Jones was here. When you find a wonderful mentor in your life, you really want to stick with her until you feel like you've gotten what you are supposed to get from that person.

I think in-laws, husbands, wives, and kids are a little flummoxed when a person close to them will change their life so radically to allow llamas or alpacas to join them. The book and my talk kind of settles them down and helps them realize that, in fact, the relationship that they have with their animals is really, really important—that it isn't just being self-indulgent or it isn't just being a weirdo that causes them to seek out and maintain this connection; this is something very, very important to their personal growth. The fact that I put it down in book form helps them legitimize it to a certain extent, and helps them explain it to other people.

What People Can Learn from Llamas

One of the things about llamas that people find very perplexing is that llamas and alpacas do not behave like dogs, or even like horses. A horse allows most people to pet it. A dog allows most people to pet it. Even cats, to a certain extent, allow people to pet them. Actually, cat people probably hear some of the same things that llama people hear—"It doesn't do anything. It's not affectionate. It doesn't do tricks. It doesn't want to be with you all the time. You can't take it in the car. You feed it and it doesn't even care about you. What's the deal?"

Llamas are like cats times five, but they're much bigger and they've got this wonderful, touchable look to them. They've got these big eyes with long eyelashes and they look sort of like cartoon characters. But they don't want just anybody to touch them. As a matter of fact, they don't even want their owners to touch them unless the owners really understand how to approach a llama.

So one of the metaphors that I have found that works quite well with people is this: "When you overwhelm someone and chase him around and you're too available, you end up getting ignored. When you live your own life and have your own interests and you don't pander, you become more attractive to everyone."

I think a lot of women could learn about that from llamas because our tendency, as women, is to make our men the center of our lives. We put everything else on hold and we make them our absolute priority and what we get for our efforts is ignored. Because we're always there.

And llamas really make that obvious. When you start to ignore your llamas, they don't like that. Maybe "don't like" isn't a good choice of words. Let's say that llamas respond real differently to people who ignore them than to people who chase them around. You can see pretty much an immediate shift when you start behaving more respectfully. Then the llamas say, "Well, it looks like this is safe to me. It looks like I'm not going to get trapped if I play with this person." And they begin to be much more forthcoming.

Alpacas do this too, but in a different kind of a way. Llamas are more attached to themselves as individuals. Alpacas are less interested in people and more inter-

ested in being attached to a bunch of other alpacas. But both animals respond really positively to not pandering, not chasing, not trapping. That was a big one for me to realize.

Force Is Destructive...And It Doesn't Work

Another big lesson we can learn from animals is how destructive force is and how force doesn't work. Llamas will stand quite nicely and allow you to do some fairly unpleasant things to them. As soon as you tie them up, however, they have to fight. Animals are not fighting getting a shot or having their toenails trimmed or being shorn. What they are fighting, in fact, is the restraint.

I think human beings often fight the same thing—not whatever it is that we're trying to do to them, but just the fact that we're forcing it on them. Human beings might be totally amenable, say, to doing a particular thing, as long as it feels like it's a choice or they have some input in the decision. When we are put into a position where we are made to do something, however, we sometimes don't even know what it is we're fighting. We just know we have to fight because we're being forced. That's quite often what llamas will do—and people are very, very surprised to see things change.

The Value of Confusion

I used to think confusion was a bad thing, but confusion is really a gift. When I'm confused, I know that I'm thinking as opposed to reacting. Confusion is when new possibilities can happen.

When an animal is in a pen and people have been cornering it for a number of years, as soon as the person comes in and begins that process, the animal right away thinks, "I know what's happening here and I know how to respond to it. I also know how I feel about this human. I don't like him." What I have found is that if you go into a pen with an animal and you do something that confuses it but doesn't frighten it, you can create a situation where the maximum amount of learning can happen. When I'm working with a human that I'm having difficulty with, that is also the approach that I take.

For example, one of my students was talking about how she was working with this veterinarian, someone who was well known in the business, and she was getting so frustrated because he wouldn't try the handling techniques that she wanted to use. Now her habit with this veterinarian was to talk, talk, talk, and whine, whine, whine, and get very frustrated and angry. And she was always telling him how to do things her way. So I suggested that the next time this guy came out to work on her animals, she agree with him and say, "You know what, let's pop this llama in the restraint chute right away. I don't think that he'll be able to handle anything else."

This would confuse this guy because that was behavior completely unlike this woman—to be decisive and to be willing to put the animal in a restraint chute without an argument. What happened was that the vet then suggested one of the alternatives that was more amenable to this woman, and it all worked out quite nicely.

Sometimes doing something totally out of character is what it takes to shake people off of their path and get them confused enough to consider an alternative.

The Difference Between Leadership and Domination

One of the things that we're told with traditional training is that we have to win—particularly with dogs and children. We have to show them who is boss. That was always the advice and it inevitably leads to resistance.

I do believe that animals and children need to have clear leadership, but there's a big difference between leadership and dominance, in my mind.

I think that animals and children come to their dealings with adult humans with the expectation that the person will lead. If that person assumes leadership and begins the dance—and it has a rhythm and a flow that feels comfortable—then they go along. If, on the other hand, the person begins to hurt them or drag them or make them feel uncomfortable, they will fight that dominant approach. If the person doesn't assume any leadership at all and sort of stands there quaking, most people and animals can't stand it for very long—so they fill the vacuum themselves and take over the lead.

So the line to walk is leadership that feels comfortable—and that means thoughtful leadership that takes into account the needs of the "being" you're leading. It's leadership that's firm enough and logical enough that people and animals feel comfortable going with you.

How quickly you have to assert your leadership depends on the animal you are working with. Llamas abhor a vacuum, so usually the faster you step in, the better.

That's why a lot of people are having difficulty with their animals—they either don't have a plan or they have a plan and they're not willing to change it. Either one of those things is going to get you into trouble when you go into a pen with an animal.

Animals expect leadership, but they're frightened by domination, so reducing fear is the first step of effective leadership. In other words, we first have to behave in a way that the animal finds non-threatening.

After that, all bets are off. It depends on what the animal does next. It's like playing chess. I make my first move and I have an idea of what my second, third, fourth, and eighth moves might be, but I certainly couldn't tell you until the animal responds exactly what I will do next.

There are lots of animal trainers out there who say, "I train them all the same way, treat them all the same way." That would be tough, because they don't all act the same way. And I think that's what we do, to a large degree, in our oversized public school classrooms. We don't have enough resources to treat all the children differently—or even to treat them in three different ways—which probably would solve 90 percent of our school problems.

We are a species that is attached to short-term rather than long-term results. That's something else that the animals have taught me—that the quickest way to do something today is not necessarily the quickest way a few days later. I have become more and more willing to invest time up front to save myself time in the long term. The thing that's interesting is that the more proficient I get, the quicker that investment comes back to me.

Often people will bring animals to me that they've been having problems with for years—sometimes for as long as ten years. And they tell me that the animal always, always, always, does a certain thing and it's always terrible. Usually it's a haltering problem. I've had animals that had to be sedated to have their halters put on. I've had people who have had to use a winch to put the halter on. Or they just leave the halter on forever. It's usually something small that has become such a bone of contention that it is now a really big issue.

So I'll have an animal arrive at a clinic with a particular behavior. I'll go in and do my thing and, within five minutes, the animal has got its old halter off and a new one on—and everything's cool because I've done things completely differently.

And the person will say, "How long is it going to take to change my llama?" And

I say, "Well, how long did it just take? Five minutes?" That's the good news. The bad news is it's taken me fifteen years to get good enough to do it in five minutes.

The good news is that when you learn what I know, every single llama and alpaca in the universe is easier to handle, because it isn't about training them. It's about training you. All you have to do is train one entity, so it's really quite cost effective.

Essentially the whole waterfront is covered in the animal training business, just like it is in the people training business. We have the behaviorists, we have the dominators, and we have what I do. Probably the way that I would differentiate what I do is to say that I focus on empathy and understanding, leadership and personal responsibility.

And I will often tell people, "Now if you're going to mix and match what I'm doing with a dominance approach, I think you're making more of a mistake than if you just go ahead and do the dominance routine, because it's just too confusing." I don't think you can use both approaches at the same time. As a matter of fact, I think you end up creating psychosis when you do that.

Expanding My Practice

I feel like I have the tools and the skills to make a difference for dogs as well as for llamas and alpacas, although I would rather be on the preventative end, working with puppies. People get so goal-oriented. If they are having trouble trimming toenails, they invite five friends over to sit on the dog. So it's just a matter of backing it up and chunking it down and reestablishing the trust the dog has lost in your behavior, by making a shift in your own behavior.

With llama people, the animal lives in the barn, so there's not quite so much "mommy, daddy, honey, angel, snookie" stuff. That will often get in the way of a respectful relationship. You have to be able see the animal in a way that allows behavior to change. It is an art, settling dogs. It's about putting them into balance and containing their energy.

I've also had a number of people over the years in the health care professions come to me and say that they were profoundly affected by a llama clinic.

People in a hospital, people who are sick, are really inclined to behave instinctively. By understanding, first of all, that patients and family members are behaving instinctively, and understanding how to shift things and think ahead of them, doctors and nurses can structure things so that they aren't trying to teach when people are not available to learn. If doctors and nurses can learn to approach people in a way that doesn't provoke the patients' fight or flight response, they can help them more quickly and easily—while at the same time saving time and money. Sometimes the body work will help bring people back to balance so that they are more willing to cooperate.

I've also had cards and letters from teachers saying that they never realized it before, but little Johnny in the third row was in his fight response all the time. And they saw how the things they kept doing would provoke that fight response. After the clinic, they realized they could change their approach.

Figuring out approach angles and flight zones and non-habitual behavior and creating confusion on purpose—these are things that these people probably had heard about or read about in other places. But, somehow, seeing it happening right there with the animal made the connection stronger and made their own behavior more apparent, enough so that they realized they wanted to make a shift.

Humans rely on words to communicate and become oblivious to body language. Even though llamas and humans are different, it is amazing how body language cuts across species lines. Doctors, nurses, and teachers working with llamas have to let go of their competence in one area and learn to listen and observe very closely to pick up the information they need to communicate with a llama. I just know working with llamas will help them communicate better with the humans they must deal with in difficult circumstances. So my next project is to invite health professionals to learn how to handle llamas, even though they may never have touched a llama before. That should put them in a non-habitual place for learning right away!

My intuition is telling me not to do things too differently; not to beat participants on the head by finding the metaphorical connections between working with animals and working with people. Just let it happen and then leave people enough free time to discuss what happened with each other.

Looking for a True Connection

The llama many people meet is what llama folks call a "public relations" llama. This is a llama that has been extensively handled or bottle-raised and has either lost or never had a normal llama's reluctance around strangers.

People meet these PR llamas and think, "Ohh...I have to have one of these. They're so wonderful." When their llama arrives, they are surprised to find that a normal llama won't let anyone near him. They are determined, though, to have a relationship with this magical, aloof animal and their llama quite literally leads them to me.

What I've realized is that dogs will let you have the illusion of a connection because they don't run away from you. They sit around and they want you to pet them—in fact, they haunt you in some ways. But a lot of people, even though they can physically relate to their dogs, are not really connected to their dogs. And they miss a lot of what a dog has to offer. But when people are looking for a true connection with a dog or a llama or another human being and find out they lack the skills to make that connection, that's often what starts them on the path to enlightenment.

Working with llamas has given me a totally different connection with my dog. This is my fourth Golden Retriever, and I would say this dog bears no resemblance to any dog I've ever had before—and that is because of the differences in me. The same goes for my relationships with people. Nothing else in my human experience has caused me to stretch in the way that llamas caused me to stretch.

Cat people probably have more of an understanding about what's required. A woman I know was explaining the differences between dogs and cats. She said that dogs think, "Wow, these human beings—they feed me, they take care of me, they take me for walks, they buy me a bed—they're so wonderful, they must be gods." Cats, on the other hand think, "Wow, these people—they feed me, they take care of me, they buy me a bed—I must be a god!"

That's a llama's attitude too: "They feed me, they pick up my poop, they build me a barn, they keep me warm in the winter, cool in the summer—I must be a god." And they act like it.

The Importance of Balance

Settling and focusing an animal is probably 60 percent of the magic that I do. I can go in a pen or take the lead or the leash or whatever and—because I know about bringing an animal into balance and I pay attention to my own breathing—I can get the animal to come into the present moment, come into its body, and begin to focus. When an animal can focus, it can learn.

One of the many things that I learned from my teacher, Linda, is role-playing games. To help people learn to empathize with the animal, I actually have them put halters on each other's heads and lead each other. I have people pick up each other's feet and find out how frightening it is to have someone else completely in charge of your balance.

So what we do in a clinic is learn to balance each other. We put ropes around our waists and teach people how frightening it is to lose your balance. I have someone stand inside a rope and have another person hold the two ends. Then I have the person lean away. And what happens is that you find out you are totally vulnerable to the person who's holding the line because if he or she drops the line you fall down.

That's essentially what llamas and alpacas do to themselves all the time. Because they're afraid of the human, they lean away. So, when the person holds onto the rope or holds them around the neck, they find themselves between a rock and a hard place. They don't want to get any closer to the human, but they also intensely dislike being at the mercy of the person who's holding them up—so usually they start jumping and bucking and moving and twisting and fidgeting.

If we simply bring them into balance over all four feet, at arm's length, the animal takes a breath, comes into balance and begins to think about its situation—and finds out that being with a human is not so frightening after all. Balance is the key to the whole business.

Can you bring an animal into balance without being aware of your own balance? No. Absolutely not. I use words, metaphorical words, actually, when I'm talking to people. When humans are holding the rope and the animal is leaning on it, they are, in fact, co-dependent. They're in balance, but only because each chooses to do this dance with the other—this leaning away thing or leaning toward thing.

What I'm after is bringing the person and the animal into an interdependence—as opposed to a codependence or complete independence, where there is no connection. In order to have interdependence, you both have to find your own balance.

In effect, the animal teaches the person how to find his own balance. And then, a lot of times, that sense of balance extends into realizing the importance of work, love, play, food, drink. The whole issue of finding a balance then permeates the rest of your life.

The Dance Never Ends...

I know I'm not in balance all of the time. But what the animals have shown me is I can actually be out of balance for a while, realize that that's where I am, and bring myself back into balance. In a sense, the only way that you know that you are in balance—or that you were in balance—is when you fall out of it.

When you're just cruising along and everything's wonderful, you don't have an appreciation of, "Wow, I'm in balance." You only have a hindsight appreciation for how nice it was when you realize that you have lost your balance.

The beauty of this is that the animals provide you with an immediate behavioral biofeedback loop. If you're standing in a pen with a rope around a baby llama who's never been handled before—and your arms are locked and your knees are locked and you're not in balance—that baby is probably going to be jumping up and down. As soon as you come into balance and begin to breathe, the baby settles down.

So I tell people to think about their breathing, not to lock their knees, to move back and forth between their feet. You know that you're standing in balance when the rope between the two people, or between the animal and the person, has slack in it. But the real learning comes from the animal telling you, "We are, in fact, in balance together now."

You can never be in perfect balance all the time. The dance never does end. It's just about reaching more and more successive approximations of perfection without ever actually getting there. It's not the destination, anyway, it's the journey.

Dayashakti
(Sandra Scherer)

The Wave Work™, Housatonic, Massachusetts

> *We know deep inside us what to do*
> *and how to be. That knowing is imprinted*
> *in every cell of our being. It's right there*
> *in our body and in our whole process.*
> *We need only to trust it—*
> *and for that we need support.*
> *We need a safe and loving container,*
> *someone who sees us and says, "Yes!"*
> *Then it's just a matter of time*
> *until our true nature is revealed.*

We heard about Dayashakti from a friend of Susan's who had taken The Wave Work seminar and reported that, in one week, Daya's process had taken her to a much deeper place than her long-term meditation and yoga practices, and had brought her more insight than years of psychotherapy. When she shared that she felt directly connected to her soul by this work, we were intrigued, and impulsively called Daya to arrange a visit.

Dayashakti describes The Wave Work as a psychospiritual process for integration which reawakens us to our innate capacity to heal ourselves. Grounded in the deeper teachings of yoga and meditation, The Wave Work is a unique, body-based process which uses attention, breathwork, and dialogue to allow a shift in consciousness.

Enrolled in graduate studies in human ecology at Cornell when she met her guru, Dayashakti dropped out of academia and moved into the Kripalu ashram, now the Kripalu Center for Yoga and Health, in western Massachusetts in 1973. In 1974, she took formal vows as a renunciate, or nun, in the lineage of yoga master Swami Kripalvanandji. For more than twenty years, Dayashakti lived in the ashram, practicing an intense, kundalini-type yoga and teaching and mentoring others.

In that time, Daya learned a great deal about the way energy works from her teachers, from her observations of others, and from her own experience. When her blissed-out state threatened her physical survival, Vinit Muni—a swami and disciple of Swami Kripalvanandji who came from India with him—taught Daya the value of balance, taught her how to ground and contain her energetic experiences, so that she could live as successfully in the material world as she lived in the world of spirit. This sense of balance, of alternately expanding and contracting energy, is an important foundation of The Wave Work.

Susan took a weekend workshop with Daya and found the work to be both simple and profound. Following the waves of sensation as they moved through her body, Susan believed that she did, indeed, encounter her soul. Contrary to her expectations, though, no angelic choirs accompanied the event. Instead, she found the experience to be deep, rich, and devoid of emotional extremes—almost impersonal. And Judith, after a one-on-one session with Daya, reported feeling both relaxed and energized. She could feel energy moving throughout her body and felt totally aware of every part of her body, from her fingers to her toes.

The literal translation of her Sanskrit name, which Dayashakti received when she renewed her vows in the mid-'80s, is "awakened spiritual energy of compassion."

When she left Kripalu and the renunciate order in 1993, Daya kept her Sanskrit name because she had used it for a long time and because she felt it suited her. We would agree. When we met her, we were struck by the stillness, the grace, and the strength of her presence.

Dayashakti remains closely associated with Kripalu and leads most of The Wave Work programs at the center. She also teaches and lectures internationally, maintaining a private psychospiritual practice with offices in New York City, Boston, and the Berkshire Mountain area of western Massachusetts.

"As in the macrocosm, so in the microcosm." What does that really mean? To me it means that all of the wisdom of the universe is within each one of us. If that is actually true—and not just some story we've been told—then once we become adept in The Wave Work—or any work, for that matter, which puts us in direct contact with the universal life force—we will be in contact with universal wisdom. The Wave Work is about contacting that wisdom, that universal life force. I get to witness this miraculous and yet completely natural process daily. It's such a privilege.

As a coach in this work, my role is to help people learn to trust what is present within them and to let whatever is present move in its own completely intelligent way. I am not moving energy through them. I'm actually not even trying to heal them in any way. Their energy will heal them. I'm just holding a safe and sacred space for them so they can trust their process.

I don't belittle the role I play. It's important and even crucial at times because, in order to go into these deep internal spaces, we need containers. We need somebody who can say, from a knowing place, "You're safe, you're absolutely safe—I'm right here with you—I will be a witness to this."

To have somebody actually see you and understand you is very important. To get the truth within you, then to be able to speak it out loud—to the universe, to another Being—and to have it be received and understood is very healing.

What I really want to say to people about this work is that it offers a doorway, a possibility. Try it and see if it rings true for you. If it feels good to you, if it gives you more space, if there is an expansion, a warmth, then chances are your soul is saying, "Yes!" It's important to pay attention to what feels good, to what creates space in us. Because that's how our soul guides us. It actually uses very simple and tangible signals. If it feels good, chances are that it's in alignment with our highest Self. If it doesn't, it's not. It's not as mysterious as we think.

The Same Energy That Orders the Stars Orders Our Experience

The Wave Work is a methodology or a technology, if you will, about how to be present moment to moment to moment to moment. It is based on the belief that the soul—or the higher Self, or the inner wisdom, or the higher power, or whatever name you want to give it—orders our experiences.

The same energy that orders the stars, the universe, and the galaxies is also ordering our internal experience. This is what the yogis teach. Each thing that floats up into our awareness in any given moment floats up under the direction of this deeper Self, the intelligent wisdom Self. And each experience is brought to us for a very specific reason, to evolve our consciousness in a very specific way.

So moment by moment things float up. It may be a thought, a memory, a physical sensation or an emotional feeling—or just energy or perhaps a sound we hear. Whatever it is, it is there for a purpose. A very important purpose. And, if we can be there with that one little thing that floats up, it will move through us in the most perfect way. It will move through the body in a completely intelligent path. What comes up won't be too much, it won't be too little; it won't be the wrong thing; it will be exactly the right thing—the thing that we are meant to experience in that moment, and it takes us to the next step in our evolution.

This work is deep because you're in direct contact with your self. People feel safe in it because of the safety the coach provides and because there is sort of a map of the energetic experience—which is generally outside of the control of the mind—through the model of a wave. It gives people a picture of how the energy moves and where they are in that experience, so it helps.

Trusting What Is There

Let me give you a picture of what the work looks like, so you can get more of a feel for it. The people doing the work usually lie on a massage table, fully dressed. They close their eyes and just focus inside and notice what is there, what is present in their field of awareness. Then I ask them to describe what they are seeing, what they are noticing.

The first thing that might come up could be something in their body—they might feel warm or cold, or their jaw might feel tight or some part of their body may feel uncomfortable. Or they may have a thought or a feeling present—say a thought of their mother or their brother or of work or their loved ones...anything. Whatever it is, I coach them to just trust it, that the very fact that it is present means they can trust it; that it's the right thing to be present at this time; that the soul brought it up, so just allow it.

In other words, it's fine to feel whatever they feel, whether it's an emotion or a physical sensation. Thoughts are fine too. It's okay to think and to have the thoughts they have. It doesn't mean they'll act on what they think, that they'll do what they are thinking about. We make that distinction—the difference between thoughts and action, feelings and action—very clear. The two are very different.

I coach them to allow whatever is there to be there, to just give it some space. "Just let that sadness be there. It's all governed by the higher Self. It's absolutely safe—it won't be too much or too little."

So, with my holding space for them, with my containing for them—which is my role—they learn to allow whatever is there to be there. They begin to feel safe in their feelings, which are more fluid or energetic because they are held in a very still and safe place. I'm holding a yang place, a steady, grounded place. A place of concentration.

In yogic terms, we say we are holding the chitta for them. We are holding our minds steady, focused and concentrated. This creates safety for them, safety for the movement that is happening within them. And we tell them, too, that it's safe. "This is absolutely fine, you are absolutely safe. I'm right here with you. See if you can allow this to be present—just be present with it and see how this sadness feels to you. It's absolutely fine—it won't be too much."

I'm containing for them, reminding them that I'm right here and that they are not alone, at the same time teaching that any experience that is not from learned concepts is not from the will, but comes from the soul—and that the soul is monitoring, pacing, and perfectly designing the entire experience—that they can trust it and allow it, that it is ultimately safe and intelligent.

I'm Not Trying to Heal Anything...

If we say, "Oh, I really want to get in touch with my anger..." and we start to do something to bring up that anger—for example, by doing cathartic breathing or certain movements with the body—then we're acting from a willful place.

Will is not bad. It's helpful, even crucial, in the right place. Many powerful healing modalities that have served so many so well have that as a central piece in their technology. But this work is not that. At least not the part of it I'm describing right now. It's about non-willful work. It's about radical trust in the power and intelligence of the Self.

This modality is not trying to heal anything, not trying to fix or alter or change anything. It's about being present and trusting what is present.

Let's take an example of how I would work with the emotion of sadness. First I would suggest they notice that sadness is present, then to trust it or honor it by giving it room, by giving it space to exist and not to try to get rid of it in some way. Then to move toward it with their awareness, coming as close to it as they can, and then to just feel it. How does this moment of sadness actually feel? Sometimes I'll say, "Just pull up a chair. Just sit right next to it. Give it some room. Let it be there and just be there with it."

I ask clients to breathe through their mouths through the whole session—not willful breathing, not necessarily deep breathing, unless your body actually needs to breathe deeply at that time. Not any particular kind of breath. Just regular breathing, only through the mouth—the way you would if you had a cold and couldn't breathe through your nose.

Breathing through the mouth in a non-willful, uncontrolled way is very key to this process. This kind of breath is less controlling than the nose breath, especially when it is a controlled nose breath. It's an "allowing" breath. It allows what is to be there. It won't make things come up, but it also won't make things go down.

If you're sad or angry or whatever and want that feeling to go away, all you have to do is close your mouth. But if you just let your mouth be open and let the breath come naturally—however your body needs to breath in that moment—then whatever is trying to come through will come through, because it's allowed to.

Simply closing the mouth begins to close down the whole experience. It's amazing! First the mouth closes, then the throat closes, the chest tightens, then the diaphragm begins to clamp down. It's a whole series of shut-downs which starts with the mouth, which holds everything in stasis. It's not "bad" or "wrong." It's usually just that people get scared and are creating safety for themselves.

There is a time when it's appropriate to close down. But when you are in a safe space—when you are actually doing your soul work—it's helpful to allow that process to continue as much as you can because it's happening organically. It's not something we've drummed up or stirred up or are trying to make happen. We are not saying, "Oh, now I have to let go of this. I have to get this stuff out of my body..." We're going with what is natural, with what is "of the Tao," if you will.

The Less You Do, the More That Gets Done

Although this work is not about changing anything, paradoxically, change occurs. Change is a universal law—nothing is static in the universe. So we are simply allowing that change to occur. We're going with it. We're cooperating with it. If we are authentically, energetically present, change definitely will happen. It's scientific.

So transformation happens, but not because we're after it, not because we're saying, "Okay now I'm going to do it and I'm going to choose what to do because I know what I need to do." It's not about working from that level, although willful practices—like eating a good diet and exercising—are important too. They are the umbrella under which the non-willful practice sits.

But—when you're really wanting transformation at a cellular level—the less you do, the more that gets done. If you can just let your organism do it, if you can just let the energy do it, then it will bring the right thing up and it will move it smoothly through you. Just like a wave, it comes up, it gets bigger, bigger, bigger, larger, larger, higher, higher, more energetic, faster, hotter, more movement in it...and then it will crest, coming to the very top of that experience—where a lot is happening on a cellular level—and soon it will begin to ease off and integrate and you find yourself in a whole other place.

You start in homeostasis and you end in homeostasis—but you are in a completely different homeostasis. You are a different person. And you're different at a fundamental level, at a cellular level, in the DNA. There's no way to prove that, but it's what I believe. It's the theory, or the hypothesis, if you will, that I'm presenting. I don't know that we have any way to research such internal energetic experiences yet. What we do have is subjective observation, which the yogis have used for centuries. We may or may not someday be able to prove this scientifically, with instruments. But perhaps the important thing here is that observable and fundamental change does occur, cellular or not.

And that core level transformation happens through non-volition, through just being present with what is there and allowing it to move through you at its own pace. I call it "riding the wave." For instance, to use the example of the sadness: allowing the sadness to go through, just "riding" that sensation, the sensation of feeling sad, sad, more sad, more sad, very sad, almost too sad, more sad than you can imagine, reaching that height and then beginning to ease off, and at the end of it there is a tremendous amount of change.

You can see the change. It sort of floats up and manifests on the physical and mental and emotional and subtle body levels; so when you look at people, they look different. And what they report is that physically the sensations are different, mentally their thoughts are different, emotionally they feel different. In fact, usually the experience will turn into its opposite—sadness will turn into joy, anger turns into peace. It's alchemical. Lead is turned into gold.

The Benefits of Riding the Wave

When your energy is allowed to move in the way it's trying to move, you get lots of benefits. For one, you learn to feel safe with energy moving in your body. You're no longer afraid of it, which is to say you're no longer afraid of a fundamental part of yourself. That's a huge benefit. So you no longer need to hold it back, and that leads to a lot of creativity and a lot of life. I think a lot of disease comes from energy being blocked, not being allowed to move through the body as it's trying to move, as it's meant to move.

A few of my clients are chiropractors, and one told me recently that the founder of one form of chiropractic, Daniel Palmer, said that 10 percent of all disease in the body is chemically based, and another 10 percent is from some kind of physical trauma, for example, if you broke a bone. And then he said the other 80 percent of disease originates from what he called "above atlas," in layman's terms, from mental and emotional causes.

There is no way to give an exact percentage, of course, but when you see a lot of people, you can make some sort of educated guess. It seems to me that a good 80 percent of what manifests as disease in the physical body is mentally and emotionally based. So when you work with the wave, you address all these bodies: the mental, the emotional, the physical, as well as the more subtle bodies—the astral body, the pranic body, the causal body.

When clients come in for a session, if they have a knee injury, that injury in the physical body will come up at some point in their work. If not in this session, then another. It presents itself at the right time. When it does, the clients will all of a sudden, out of the blue, begin to be aware of and feel their knees. That's because the energy is working there. It's healing the injury.

There is actual healing happening right then because, as the energy is streaming there, they are allowing it and being there with it. Not trying to *do* anything, but just being there with it, allowing the amount of healing that needs to be done at that time to occur. It works with injuries in the mental and emotional body in the exact same way.

It seems that two things are needed from us in order to heal. One, we need to allow what's there to be there, not trying to change it in some way; two, we need to be present with it, not split off from it. When we're there and not doing anything to change it, it has what it needs to change itself and can deliver to us what it's trying to give to us—its gift for the evolution of our consciousness. It's ironic, really. We keep trying to make something happen that's already happening, right under our noses. What we want is already there. We just don't recognize it.

It's very important to pay attention to whatever is there in any of the bodies. Some clients will work more in one body than another. Others will have equal access to all of them. Everyone works differently. Some see colors, or pictures, or symbols, or they'll just feel energy in their body. Some feel like they're floating or swinging. These are energy experiences taking place in the subtle bodies. Each experience has a purpose and is healing and transforming us in a very specific way, even though we may not understand it in the moment. In The Wave Work, we try to allow the system to present exactly what it is presenting, in exactly the way it's presenting it.

Sometimes we may be more aware of one body than the others. Take the example of the knee hurting. That's primarily in the physical body, but the other bodies are actually part of that experience, too. There are mental, emotional, and subtle body components to it as well—we may just not be aware of them at the time.

But, as the client is present with the sensation in the knee, it's very likely that a thought or a feeling may also emerge. Maybe a memory from the past, like hurting the knee in a football game, or a feeling that is somehow part of or merely triggered by the sensation in the knee. So from the physical comes the mental and the emotional. One tumbles out from the other.

I just tell clients to keep watching and keep telling me what is happening, keep reporting out. So they may say something like, "My knee hurts." My coaching to them is to see if they can let it hurt and just be there with it. Trust that this is what is here, that it's the right thing. I encourage them to see if they can just hang out there and feel how that feels. To just allow it.

As they're there with it, in it, they might say, "I just remembered how I got this, how I hurt my knee." So their mental body is kicking in, memory is coming in. And then I'll say to them, "It's okay to remember that. Now notice how you feel as you remember that. Notice if there are any feelings with that." When they get in touch with how they feel, I just encourage them to give that room and to let it integrate. This is how the work unfolds, one thing leading into another.

Identifying the Voices

All children know how to do this, know how to be with whatever is present and let it move through their body. That's what crying is all about. Most of us marvel at two-year-olds. They will fight and then, in a moment, they are friends again. And we say, "How did that happen?"

We're so amazed at this, and all it means is that these children know how to be present and know how to integrate. They are not suppressing their natural way of being. Somehow, over the centuries, we have learned to distrust the natural, organic Self. We feel the body is bad, the body isn't pure, the body is something to be distrusted. All of those cultural beliefs are in our psyche and when those natural functions start to come up, the voices start firing off.

We've all gotten so many messages—I call them voices in this work—that say "Don't trust what is happening inside you. Trust me, let me tell you what to do here." These are the voices of our parents, our teachers, our rabbis, our priests, our ministers, our girl scout leaders, our boy scout leaders, our professors, even some of our gurus, our spiritual teachers, our therapists.

And these voices are completely disempowering. They separate people from their own body, from their own knowledge, their own internal wisdom. So another important piece of this work is about identifying those messages, those voices, when they come in.

As a coach, I watch for voices, and train clients to watch as well, for those voices that say sadness is wrong or anger is wrong. Suppose someone is doing a piece of work and some anger comes up. She makes space for her anger, and then she learns to be on the watch for these voices that say, "You shouldn't be angry…What's wrong with you?" Or "You're still doing this work? Aren't you over this yet?" Or for men it might be, "Men shouldn't cry…" or "You're a sissy."

When we were little, at some point we began to hear that the way we were wasn't right. We heard, "You shouldn't be crying…You shouldn't want your truck. You should share your things. You shouldn't want your dolly just for yourself…Be nice…anger isn't good…You should sit with your knees crossed…You shouldn't have your mouth open…" and on and on.

So in the work we first try to identify the voices as just that—as voices, as learned concepts. And they are just that: Concepts. Ideas. Worldviews. No more. So, if you're lying there and you start getting angry or irritated, often a voice will also come up right on the heels of that feeling, saying something like, "That's not right. You shouldn't be feeling this."

But, organically, you *are* feeling it. That is what is really so in the moment. The truth of the moment is that you are angry. You weren't trying to get angry. You were just lying there minding your own business, paying attention, breathing through your mouth—and all of a sudden this memory floats up. And with that memory, that thought, is the accompanying emotion of anger. Then comes the voice: "You shouldn't be angry."

It can be very helpful to identify where that voice came from, who it sounds like. Some people know right away. "That's my mother, my father…Oh yeah, that's society, that's my friend, that's my boyfriend, that's my wife…"

We're not identifying where the voice originated from in order to demonize that person or that group. It's not so we can blame them. It's more to recognize that these beliefs were taught to us, that they originated outside of us, and that they are, in fact, another person's worldview. We have taken them on. They are now running through our head. But they didn't come from our own original thoughts or perceptions or our experience for that matter. As we identify where they did come from, it can help us get some separation from them.

Often people will say, "Well, I think that, too. I think I shouldn't feel like that. Those are my thoughts...." Yes, they are our thoughts now. We take them on generally when we are really young. And we believe them because it could have been dangerous not to believe them. I mean, the adults are feeding us and clothing us and taking care of us and they have the ability to abandon us. So, under that kind of threat, and because we also love our caretakers, we take on their belief systems. But, nonetheless, the concept that we shouldn't be a certain way, when we are, isn't ours initially. It came from outside of us and it simply scared us into compliance.

You Get Your Life Back

As you do this work, you begin to identify learned concepts or ideas that run your life. As you start to get clear that they're really messages that you've taken in from various sources, you begin a process of disengaging from them, actually dis-identifying with them. You get some freedom from them and that opens up a space where you can hear your own thoughts, your own feelings.

You basically start to get your self back. You get your life back, your process back, your feelings back. You begin to hear your own inner voice and to trust it. You begin to trust in your own evolutionary process.

People ask if they can do the work at home, alone. Definitely. After all, these are just very fundamental life skills—skills that we had as two-year-olds, or whenever it was, before we heard that it wasn't okay to be the way we were. We're just going back there. But it's very helpful to have a coach in the beginning. Because there are so many messages that we've heard that keep making our process wrong, it's really helpful to have someone there pointing them out and pointing you back to your process.

Most people apply what they learn in their work to their everyday life. Say they're at work and they get angry and they hear that voice that says, "You shouldn't be angry..." Because they know the work, the self-coaching kicks in and they start to hear themselves say to themselves, "There is nothing wrong with my anger. It's absolutely fine. Just give yourself a little bit of space for it...." They don't necessarily go through a huge wave, but they do a piece of it. They know how to contain for themselves while they are at work, while they're with their kids, while they are driving. The work becomes part of their life. It's part of their consciousness. It becomes part of them.

If people do meditation or have a yoga practice and are used to feeling energy, then they may feel safe enough to lie down and do the process that way, more like we do it in a session. But it's not necessary. Others sit up. Some use an audio tape I've made. They say they keep it right next to their bed and play it every night.

One client does his work in his Lazy Boy recliner. Every morning after his yoga practice, he puts his coffee on, sits down in his chair, leans his head back, breathes through his mouth and just watches himself. For the six minutes or so that it takes for the coffee to be made, he is doing his work. Every morning. And he is changing. He is absolutely changing. It doesn't have to be a lot of work or a long period of time. The important thing is to practice it, to apply it to your life.

You Get to Have Boundaries

In the work, people learn to have their anger, have their joy, have their love, have their brilliance, their loudness, their shyness, their quietness, their everything. Anything that shows up in them, they learn that they can have that. It is absolutely fine when it's happening inside them. This is their realm, their domain, and they get to have it. Nobody has any right, really, to tell us who we are in there, to tell us about ourselves. All this telling other people who they are and labeling them is very disempowering. It crosses boundaries.

We need to ask if we may offer insights to one another. With my clients—even with my closest friends—I say, "May I offer something…" or "May I come in…," which is like saying, "May I come into your boundary, into your domain?"

And then I'll say to them, "Feel inside how you feel when I say this, because that will guide you as to whether what I'm saying is right for you or not. You can tell whether what I'm saying is accurate or appropriate for you by how you feel. If it doesn't feel good to you, then don't take it in. You're the boss. I will ask you when I want to come into your space and offer you something. And, even if I ask you, always check in with yourself, check in with your own source to see if this is appropriate for you or not."

So the work is hugely empowering to people. It gives them back themselves.

"I'm Here to Witness Evolution Happening…"

As a coach, I'm not trying to get people some place. I'm not directing their flow. What the clients are getting is the most important thing. I'm here to witness that,

to witness a miracle. I'm here to witness evolution happening, and to be graced by that, to keep them safe and to remind them of the technology. But what they are getting is up to them.

If I were placing myself in a role of leading clients, I might think, "Okay, I want to take them here...now they need to see this..." and then I would manipulate their process in some way in that direction. I could also add to the insights they are getting at the end of the session, convinced that it's important for them to get these extra points—points that their inner Self didn't really choose to bring to them yet.

While it may be true that under certain circumstances caution may be advised, and it may be our duty, in a sense, to provide that, most of the time the add-ons are simply unnecessary and disempowering.

There is the distinct possibility that they in fact don't need to know more in this moment, because if they did, perhaps they would have gotten it. Perhaps it's a question of the nervous system, or the mind, being ready or able to take in one piece—not more, not several. Perhaps that's all they can organically integrate into themselves. Maybe that one piece is the turnkey to a whole piece for them. How can we say? Only they and they alone live within themselves. And there may be a deeper and wiser design than what comes from our theoretical under-standing of things, even from our heart—one that is directed and paced by the Soul.

Of course this brings up huge questions for all of us in the helping professions—questions about help and what it is and what it's not, the timeliness of things, con-traindications, exceptions, etc., etc. And all of those questions are relevant and important. This isn't a black and white process. But I think that there is something here for us to look at or consider—i.e., to respect just the amount of what the soul has given and to refrain from adding on to that. The wisdom in that may only be able to be gleaned as we deepen in our own process, and, especially, in our own di-rect experience with the energy and with the Soul.

So I'm here to watch people closely to see if I can follow where they are. Sometimes I'm literally and physically inches away from them so I can sense on as many different levels as I can where they are and what's happening within them—so that I can appropriately and sufficiently contain for them.

If, for example, I see someone take a breath, I can say, "Yes, good, great...let that happen." Or if she says, "I'm really scared to do this...," I let myself get that, let her know that I'm right there with her, that I'm getting it, that I'm not leaving her in any way, and I keep coaching her that it's safe to be experiencing what she is experiencing then. But I am not guiding it.

All Experiences Are Spiritual Experiences

There can be a tremendous amount of change from working this way. One client of mine is what she calls "illegitimate." It's such a terrible word for the simple fact that her mother and father never married. The whole event had a huge impact on her. She felt that she didn't have any rights, whether it was to stand up for herself, to be angry, to have feelings, to ask for what she needed, and deep inside, even the right to exist.

But she's been changing. She used to be very quiet. She calls people on things now and has become quite outspoken, and not in an inappropriate way. She basically feels more deserving—that she deserves to be respected, to be informed about certain things, for example, things related to her job, things she would have let slip by in the past. But she doesn't let them slip by now, mainly because she feels so much more self-respect, self-love. And she is starting to contact her family. It's still in process, but she's come a long way.

Another client got rid of the fear of flying—mostly through doing the work alone, with a tape of mine. I think she saw me once and then basically practiced on her own. She was terrified of flying and now her fear of flying is gone. Some people have lost a lot of weight. I have seen depression lift and have seen people get clear about what they want to do with their lives. Most become much more comfortable with their feelings and more accepting and loving of themselves and others.

And they have more compassion. I have a client who is a physician and has used The Wave Work in the emergency room, helping patients integrate the fear that's present in trauma. She said they shifted within minutes. The work has so many applications. It's endless.

People have many experiences during the work. Sometimes they feel like they are floating or that energy is tingling throughout their whole body or that their arms are lifting when they are not physically moving. People regularly have what I know to be spiritual experiences or energetic experiences.

Quite frankly, I think all experiences are spiritual experiences. The pain in your knee is a spiritual experience. That's why I don't call the subtle bodies spiritual bodies. The fact that we can't see them doesn't make them any more spiritual than the physical body or the mental body or the emotional body. I think it's all a spiritual experience.

Once they clear on the human level, once they start clearing their pain, people often feel a deep peace, a deep stillness that they've been trying to get to in meditation. Not every time, but often clients will feel this deep peace or see colors, or feel like they are floating or this quietness. Sometimes they have a clear knowing or insight. And they become more comfortable with how it feels to have a lot of energy moving through their body. They learn that it's safe, that it's just another part of who they are.

The Difference Between Action and Inaction

One of the most important teachings of The Wave Work is that we can have all of our Self and all of our feelings and—if we actually feel them internally, without doing anything to them—they will integrate. They will digest and metabolize and evolve our consciousness.

That doesn't mean that if I'm angry I get to "dump" on people, that I can yell at them. It's not about that. That's what we see on the streets, that's what we see on television and in the news. And for many of us, that's what we've seen in our families. That's what I call being "off the wave." Violence comes from being off the wave.

Let's use anger as an example. When anger comes up, what we want to do is learn how to have the anger in us and let it move through us, inside our bodies. It's not about putting the anger out and hurting people, screaming at them, criticizing them, or speaking harshly. That action is against the first yogic tenet, which is nonviolence—and this work is about nonviolence. If we are not able to hold that line and not act, then we have to go back and do what I call the chitta work, the work that strengthens the will, our ability to choose our actions.

In the case where people have been, say, battering their child, husband, or wife, I would first determine whether they are able to not hit. If they are unable to stop that behavior, then they need to do the chitta piece, the work that strengthens their capacity to choose their action instead of being driven by it or being under its control.

Until they can do that, they can't do what I call the prana work, the energetic work. In this work it's chitta and prana, yin and yang. I don't want anyone to think that this work is just about feeling and acting out. You have to have chitta, the ability to think clearly and not hit, not act. You have to be able to really be very clear about that line in order to go in and feel your rage and not act on it.

So it's very important to have that distinction, to be able to integrate and also have a lot of will or discernment. You have to be grounded, not just expanded. Once people have that ability they are ready to do the non-willful work, where they can go in and presence their anger and let it integrate instead of acting on it.

Most of us need to learn this very important principle, especially if we're going to be in direct contact with our energy. We've all yelled at or hurt in some way our children, our animals, our mates, our friends, our parents, our loved ones. We've all done that. So we need to be clear about this distinction. That "acting out" or discharging the energy is "off the wave," and often leads to injury and creates karma.

Yogis teach about another kind of action. They refer to it as "action in inaction." What they are referring to is the action that is inherent within the non-willful, organic, energetic experience in the body. That activity is not from the will. It's happening on its own accord. Through that very natural process of energy moving through the body, much work gets done, much change happens.

It's important to get to the energetic piece, because of the tremendous amount of healing that happens through it. I believe we all need to get to that piece some time or another for complete healing. But if we need to slow down and do the willful work first, the chitta piece, that's fine. It's not a problem. The non-willful work will not be able to be done without it. That's just the way it works scientifically.

So you strengthen your will and learn how to ground, learn how to contain for yourself. And how you do that is through a concentration meditation practice. Actually, there are many ways, but they all basically involve learning to focus and concentrate the mind. The Buddhist practice of mindfulness is one example of such a practice. Sometimes, when there has been a lot of trouble with acting out or discharging, a stronger practice is needed—not necessarily a change in the outward form of the practice, but a stronger practicing of it.

We will not be harmed by being in direct contact with our energy if we learn to integrate. To integrate means to digest and metabolize, to make part of. If we integrate our food, for example, we take in the nutrients of the food and use it to build our organs and blood and body systems. We take in its life energy and make it part of us.

Life experiences work the same way and we can integrate them in the same way. We can integrate rape, and incest, and being robbed, being physically or verbally abused. We can integrate loss, we can integrate divorce, or getting a big raise or winning the lottery! It's not just what we call the "negative" things that need to be integrated. We can integrate all our life's experiences and have our consciousness be evolved through them. Those experiences are meant to further us and deepen us as human beings, not do us in and get stuck in our bodies.

What we get when we integrate our experience is a deeper and a fuller understanding of human-beingness. And the icing on the cake is that often forgiveness appears. We all try to forgive, but it's hard. It's not that easy to do, willfully.

Forgiveness does not lie in the domain of will. It happens automatically, organically, from integration. Then the experience transforms into one that "grows" us, one that has the capacity to move us along on our evolutionary journey.

The Purpose of Evolution

As our consciousness evolves, we deepen our understanding of why we're here in this body—and what life on this planet is all about. We begin to get answers to our core questions, such as "What is the meaning of my life? Do I belong? How am I a part of the greater whole? How are we part of each other? How is the human species part of other species and part of the earth, and this galaxy part of other galaxies?" All those questions, no matter how subliminal in our awareness, begin to get answered, internally.

We've been treating our planet this way only because we haven't gotten the interconnectedness of all things. We haven't evolved to that point where we know, without any shadow of a doubt, that the loss of any species, the loss of any part of the whole, is simultaneously a loss of ourselves.

Because as we do deep work, we get information not just from the mental body but from all the bodies—the physical, the emotional, and the subtle bodies as well as the mental body. Take insight, for example. Insight comes as a direct experience. I'm not sure we can say from where it comes, but it doesn't come from an analytical process, that seems clear. It comes from some place deeper than the logical, analytical mind.

I've had experiences where, all of a sudden, I would just see an image of a person and I would see him at such depth that I felt I saw what I would call his essence. And once I had that vision—or, more accurately—that experience, I never looked at him the same again. From that moment on, I felt I knew him, and I would add, loved him. It went so deeply into my being that I was changed by it. And it translated out into the way I related to him. It was wonderful.

As we do our inner work in a more energetic way, we get in touch with more levels of ourselves, and we begin to understand ourselves—and each other—more deeply. We reach that level of insight, that direct knowing place, where we can get how your pain is part of my pain, how your evolution is a part of mine—and the repercussions of that, for ourselves, for each other, for our society, and our planet, are endless.

Jason Shulman

A Society of Souls®, Morristown, New Jersey

The Kabbalah is a relational path.
It knows we are created in "the image
of our Creator," in total relationship
with all that is around us and in us.
This means that there is no such thing as
someone completely set apart from others,
no one who is completely without hope,
no one who cannot once again find his or
her connection with the Source of All Being.

We were initially led to Jason Shulman by our friend Kris, who had taken three or four of his courses in Boston and New York and undergone several Kabbalistic healings with practitioners trained in Jason's New Jersey-based school, A Society of Souls. Kris is a spiritual seeker who has studied a number of the world's religions and experimented with a wide range of healing practices, so we took her recommendation seriously and attended one of Jason's evening lectures. What we heard—more importantly, what we experienced in our hearts and souls that evening—motivated us to arrange a meeting with this man.

Before founding A Society of Souls, a three-year professional-level training program for healers in 1992, Jason Shulman was himself an internationally recognized healer and a senior teacher at the Barbara Brennan School of Healing. A student of the major world religions and a long-time practitioner of Zen Buddhism, Jason has based the deeply spiritual approach to healing taught by A Society of Souls on his personal understanding and work with the Kabbalah, the mystical books of Judaism.

Threading our way from Brooklyn to nearby New Jersey through dense Monday morning rush-hour traffic, we became confused about the signage on the turnpike. Had we just whizzed by our exit? We started to panic and were wondering if we should turn back to check the road signs when a truck roared by our car. "Jayson," said the large red letters painted on its side. "This way," it implied as it pulled ahead.

We decided to take the hint and stayed on the road. Twenty-plus miles later, we found the correct exit and arrived at Jason's home exactly on time for our interview.

We were impressed by the peacefulness and beauty of his surroundings, by the light that flooded the room in which we met, the room in which he teaches his students. Jason, we quickly learned, is an accomplished painter and musician as well as a healer and teacher.

The words Jason used to describe himself and his work were complex and often abstract, but his manner was kind as he sought to clearly explain concepts and experiences that were often difficult to put into words. We were impressed with the strength of his intellect, the depth of his knowledge, the warmth of his smile, and the passion he brings to his life and his work. He appeared to us to be a man of deep devotion.

Born in the Williamsburg section of Brooklyn, New York, Jason currently works and lives in rural New Jersey with his wife and daughter. In addition to working with the students at his school, Jason lectures and teaches workshops for the general public *at the New York Open Center in Manhattan, at the Omega Institute in Rhinebeck, New York, at Esalen Institute in Big Sur, California, and Naropa Institute in Boulder, Colorado.*

I f we look at the Shema, the great prayer-mantra of Judaism, it says "Hear, Oh Israel, the Lord our God, the Lord is One...." I translate that: "Listen, you who struggle—'Israel' means 'you who struggle'—Listen, you who struggle to figure out what Reality is, Reality is one."

That Oneness is a dynamic oneness. It does not segregate itself or fragment itself from anything. So, if you say you have a notion of what duality is, the Shema says, "Well, that's true...but it's also true that, in and of itself, duality is also Oneness. Duality is Reality."

This is an extremely powerful thing to say. It's saying that the ego, which we do all this work to heal, has within it a kernel of oneness, that healing is not just some transcendental state where we don't have egos and we don't have problems, that somehow—within separation—there is some wonderful gift to be had.

My Early Spiritual Teachers

I grew up Jewish, studying in Talmud-Torah, Jewish day school. I really loved the ideas and the stories but, when it came time in my life to pursue spiritual things, it wasn't Judaism that I turned to. It was Zen Buddhism.

I had read *Zen Mind, Beginners Mind* in my teens and gone out to California to find Suzuki Roshi. My pal and I went out there and walked into the middle of a sessin, which is usually a week-long period of intense meditation practice. I didn't know what a sessin was, so I simply sat down. Suzuki Roshi came over and fixed my posture. Later he gave his daily lecture. I didn't understand a word he said. It was his accent; I couldn't understand a thing. But when he smiled, I felt the beams of the church that we were in at that time just bend, as if the whole church smiled along with his smile—so I knew something was going on.

One day I found a little store called the Little Library near Brooklyn College, where I was a student. The Little Library was a free lending library of all the world religions. It had a Jewish section, a Christian section, Islamic, and Buddhist sections, assorted spiritual psychic books, and so on. It had been started by Doris Carlson, the widow of Chester Carlson, the man who invented the Xerox process. He was into giving money to democratic institutions, and she set up a few of these free lending libraries of spiritual books from every tradition in various locations around the country.

I met a very interesting man there named Rick Hart, who was an ex-Marine Corps drill sergeant and a Zen practitioner. A group of young people formed around him and we began a very intense Zen practice. We meditated at least an hour in the morning and an hour and a half every night. Every month we had a full two-day sitting. And, since he had a lot of marines in his Zen, we did things like walk barefoot on the ice outside—slowly. Rick was my first big teacher.

I also studied yang style Tai Chi Chuan for several years at a very well-known school run by Master Cheng Man-Ch'ing, and tried to work on my psychological problems at that time—the difficulties of my childhood, the difficulties of intimacy, of being a person in the world—all very difficult for me. I got into a practice and community called the Pathwork, and stayed in that for many years as well. I was teaching yoga, I was practicing Zen, and I was having deep and powerful spiritual experiences.

I searched out everybody. I was reading Ramakrishna and he became one of my teachers. I found the Ramakrishna Center in Manhattan. I went to a Sunday meeting there and felt totally alienated from everybody in the room. "Who are these people," I thought. "Why are they here?"

Swami Nikhilananda was still alive then. He was about eighty-five at that time. I went over to him at the end of the meeting. People were shaking his hand and he just looked at me and looked right through me. I had never before had the experience of anybody looking through me. To feel as though someone can look at you and fully know something about you that you don't quite understand about yourself—because you don't know much of your interior—is a very powerful experience.

So I kept getting guided by having my ideas of what life was about blown apart. I was doing lots and lots of reading, but it was the personal contacts that made me understand. These experiences kept happening. And I kept going back to Judaism.

I found out that the mystical path—the direct path of Judaism that involved a personal contact with God, a personal realization and understanding of God—was called the Kabbalah. I would get Kabbalistic books and read them. They were extremely intellectual and erudite and abstract and conceptual and didn't make a lot of sense to me. I was very disappointed. I felt I could read Buddhist works and Hindu works and they spoke directly to the mystical experience. This Kabbalistic work seemed very abstruse to me, but I kept being drawn to it.

The Path Toward Healing

Meanwhile, my life was going in a very different direction. In 1979, I suddenly became ill. The illness lasted for seven years. I was practically bedridden for the first year, and my lifestyle was completely curtailed for the next six years. By "curtailed," I mean it would take me half an hour to walk a city block.

I was very sick. At the same time, my defenses were so softened by the illness that all the things I couldn't do before, I was now able to do. Gradually—my path was a gradual one—I was able to marry the woman that I had been with for years. I was able to start a business. I was able to have a child. All sorts of things that I couldn't do before on the human level, I was able to do now—mainly because I was so transformed by the illness.

I feared getting well because I knew that, as I got well, I'd have to deal with some deep-seated problems. But I was also determined to get well. So, during that time, I was involved in the Pathwork, I was practicing Buddhist meditation, and I was also seeing a psychic, a fellow named Vincent Ragone, may he rest in peace. Vincent was a pretty amazing guy, a medical intuitive.

I wanted to have someone help me figure out what was going on with this illness, but no one could figure it out. I wrote to Vincent for an appointment and I got a letter back from him saying, "Yes, you can have an appointment with me. It's three years from now." And I said, "Three years?" But, sure enough, three years later I was still sick and I went to see him. After that, I would see him once a year. This only lasted a few years.

Every once in a while, people who came to visit would say to me, "You know, a lot of people who are shamans and psychics get sick. Until they take on their mantle, so to speak, they stay sick." In retrospect, I realized that I was afraid of this stuff. Getting involved in psychic stuff made me feel like a marginal person. So, when people would say things like that to me, I would dismiss it.

I did have psychic experiences. In fact, my first Zen teacher was very psychic.

But my concept of Zen was that it didn't bother with these things and—since I believed enlightenment was around the corner—I shouldn't pay any attention to these things, either.

Near the end of the seventh year of my illness, three people in one week came to say such things to me. So I said, "This is something I have to look at!" and I devised a method to figure out if I was or was not psychic. I still teach this method to my students.

I went to Vincent with my notebooks and said to him, "Well, Vincent, I'm a psychic." And Vincent said, "No, you're not!"

You know the scene in the opera, *Don Giovanni*, where he falls through the floor into hell? Vincent said, "No, no. I am a psychic. You get psychic information because you are a healer."

You have to understand that I was not interested in healing anybody. I was doing an intense five-year Pathwork training program, the goal of which was to become a helper for other people—and I was one of the only people in the class who didn't have any aspirations to be a helper. I had no desire to heal anybody on any level except myself, so to hear this from Vincent was bad news.

But I had developed a very accurate channel at that point, so I went home and said, "What about this?" and it said, "Glad you asked!"

And it began to train me. It trained me for a year. At the end of that period of time it said, "You've done very well. Now go get a teacher."

I said, "Okay. I'll look up an old friend who has been into healing and whom I've never talked to about it since I was never interested." So I looked her up—that was Barbara Brennan—and Barbara became my teacher.

Over the next few years, I began to do healings on other people. As I began to do these healings, by the way, I got well. I suddenly found people who were able to help me. So—as I had the business, as I was getting married, as I was having a child, as I was healing—I was also becoming a healer and changing my practice from being a publisher to being a healer.

Establishing a Society of Souls

At the same time as I was teaching for Barbara Brennan, I was continuing my study of Kabbalah. There's nothing about healing in any of the books of Kabbalah but—since that was my passion—I looked at everything through the lens of healing. My thought was that if something is real, if a mystical tradition means anything, it should be able to be used to help people directly and not only as some interesting, but ultimately abstract, knowledge.

One night in a hotel room, studying Kabbalah, I got some help. That night a voice spoke to me. It said only one sentence, but that sentence was a revelation! I spent the next three years illuminating, expanding, deepening my understanding of that sentence. And I began to experiment with various healings that I started developing based on my continued reading of Kabbalah and the inspiration of that voice.

Based on that work, I started running small-group experiences to explore what I had developed. People started seeing that something profound was happening and asked me to teach them. I had no desire to teach them. Now, this is called low IQ! This is reluctance! When they said, "Teach us...," I said, "I don't know...I don't want to do this...."

Meanwhile, with the other part of my brain, I was writing a curriculum. I wrote about a thousand pages of curriculum, then I completely wrote it over about three to four times. I would sit every day at my computer and write for a few hours and then my wife would read what I wrote. She's one of my teachers, and a magnificent editor. She would go through this material and I'd go back and rewrite it to get the ideas clearer and clearer.

Finally, as people continued to ask me to teach, I decided to do a one-year program with a small number of people. That was the beginning of A Society of Souls.

It quickly became clear that the training needed to be a seven-year program, so (in my continued reluctance) I made it a three-year program. The revelation or the understanding of this work opened more and more and it became an extremely powerful, a very different paradigm for healing, one that integrated my understanding of depth psychology, and advaitic non-dualism, with my understanding and experience of Kabbalah. I called it Integrated Kabbalistic Healing.

Healing Happens in Relationship
My particular mission seems to be to bring this healing process to everybody who is willing to do the work.

The traditional Eastern European Judaic way of studying Kabbalah is very different. It's traditionally been an advanced study for men who were already a substantial part of the community—which was expressed as being married and over forty. Those criteria really were about the need for someone who was following the rules and the regulations of the religion, so they were stable, solid citizens who had a stable culture around them—because, when you get into this kind of work, it can destabilize you.

I teach Kabbalah in a different way. It's very intense and we do a lot of work to embody the material in a physical way. We spend the first year creating a container for this work, not even going into Kabbalistic work directly right away.

There's a cantor in the course now, and I correspond with several rabbis. Reb Zalman Schachter-Shalomi is a mentor and beloved friend. It takes a certain kind of person to be open to this kind of work. It's non-traditional, but it is not watered down. And it is extremely Judaic in its approach without being tied only to the path of Judaism.

My basic approach is that Kabbalah, although it has strong intellectual and conceptual components, is really about the total transformation of the individual so that a person has access to consciously living in the Divine Milieu.

One of the basic tenets of A Society of Souls is that Kabbalah teaches us that healing happens in relationship. That's what it's about—having a relationship with somebody. The deepening of relationship and the removal of the obstacles that are between people—between everything, even our relationship with ourselves—is what the training is about.

Consequently, to have a relationship—to meet Kabbalah as a living being, so to speak—is to take on the challenge of being transformed as a human being. So this is not a passive study, not the way I approach it, in any case. It's a dynamic study which transforms the practitioner, the healer.

This transformation extends to breaking down the barriers between self and other, but not in a merged, trance-like way. If John were go to Mary, a Kabbalistic healer, and in the middle of this deep work someone said, "John…," John would know who John was. And John would know who Mary was. But at the same time John and Mary would be in a state of deep rapport that was probably beyond anything they had ever experienced before.

The Value of Suffering

The profound thing about the Judaic path is that it is not about transcendence in the way we sometimes think about it, so it makes for a very different way of working with our difficulties.

For instance, we work very hard to see the value of suffering, because every human being suffers. Even if you are having a good day, the next day may be difficult. Even if you are having a good life, it's going to end. Even if you have a wonderful relationship with your lover or mate, your husband or wife, you are going to leave them someday—or they are going to leave you. Just the fact of how this world is set up causes suffering.

The first of the Buddha's Four Noble Truths is that life is suffering. People like to skip over that one and go to the resolution of suffering. But that's the first truth. Life *is* suffering—so what are you going to do with it? The suffering takes on a healing property when it is taken to the heart, when it's taken in and allowed to exist not as the secondary suffering that we all have—the everyday agony and anguish of not wanting to suffer at all—but the primary suffering, the existential suffering we have as human beings, that we all must go through.

So the way Integrated Kabbalistic Healing works with our humanity is different. We're really trying to be human beings among human beings. You cannot, as a healer, do things for others that you are not also doing for yourself. One of the basic tenets of Integrated Kabbalistic Healing is that we can only bring people to where we ourselves are willing to go.

In other words, if you are still separated from your own suffering, you are not going to be able to help somebody else with his or her suffering. You would counter-transferentially try to fix the other person's suffering because it is a threat to you. But if your own suffering is something that you cannot only live with but flourish with, then you could see people's suffering and help alleviate it—you could be there with them without having to separate yourself from their humanity. So this is a very different approach to healing—a non-dual approach—which is not masochistic in any way, but also not willing to separate out the parts of life we like from the parts we do not like. And here I'm not talking about the neurotic parts, but the basic ground of our being, which includes our suffering and includes God.

Healing with the Kabbalah

Most of the technical aspects of Integrated Kabbalistic Healing involve working with the healer, not working with the client. When we put our hands on someone, we are not transmitting energy. We don't work with energy at all. People may feel energy, but not because we are transmitting it. We are working with conditions of unity that are prior to energy and it's these conditions of unity that are causing the effects, such as the energy, that people feel.

This kind of healing is so experiential that talking about it is very difficult. It's also difficult to talk about because our language is subject-object oriented. There is always an actor and an acted upon, a doer and a done-to.

Judaism, of course, acknowledges duality. It might say, "Yes, of course that's true. I know who you are and you know who I am and we are different people. You can go your way and I will go my way." But on some essential level, it's also not true. And this is the level where we need metaphysical or mystical experience. Kabbalistic healing tries to exist in the interface between those two approaches to Reality.

First of all, if you have a broken bone, God forbid, you're not going to want to go to someone who is going to do auric or Kabbalistic work on you. You're going to want to go to a physician, a surgeon who will set the bone. You may then want to go a healer to help it heal more quickly, but surgeons are very good at setting bones and taking care of them. So it makes tremendous sense and has intelligence in it to go to the right place for what you need.

We want to always use our intelligence to go to the right person for the job at hand. If we want to grow tomatoes we need to talk to a gardener; if you want a type of healing that is best done by someone other than a Kabbalistic healer, then part of the Kabbalistic healer's approach and understanding, through the use of the diagnostic process of Integrated Kabbalistic Healing and the integrity of the Kabbalistic healer, will be to understand that the client needs another type of healing first. So from the point of view of Integrated Kabbalistic Healing, everything has its place—as long as you know what that place is.

To talk about this I have to talk about things in a very paradoxical way. Everything that I say, I have to then say the opposite in some manner that will hopefully make sense.

For instance, one of the first Kabbalistic healings was developed when I was working deeply with the Shema. During that period, I would put everything that I did up against the unalterable benchmark of the Shema: "Hear, Oh Israel, the Lord our God, the Lord is One..."

One day a woman came in with a quadriceps muscle that was injured and I decided I was going to put Divine energy into this quadriceps. Then I said, "Wait a minute! Where am I talking to God from? If the Shema is real—if God is truly everywhere—where do I think I can go to get God? How could I bring God to someplace that God is not already there?"

This was kind of a revolutionary thought because, instead of bringing God to this woman, I decided to receive the already present Divine Presence in this woman, to receive it as what we now call a "Healing of Immanence." This healing consists of letting go of the egoic feeling that one has to do something that is already done.

This is a completely different way of looking at healing. It's nondualistic. And the Healing of Immanence remains one I teach in weekend workshops because it's easy to explain. All the advanced healers use the Healing of Immanence, too, because while it's very safe, it's also infinitely deep. The deeper you go into receiving the already present existence of God, the more the healing gives you. And the process of learning about this healing—which is really the process of the healer surrendering to the Greater Self—seems to be endless.

Broadening the View, Deepening the Relationship

The diagnostic processes in most psychologies are things that narrow down a person. Someone comes into a session and you say—I'm just making up some silly things—"She is wearing bracelets and a ring, so this is a person who likes jewelry. The pieces all have a kind of Western appeal, so maybe there is a Western theme here...." And you keep narrowing down this person, limiting who she is for the sake of some form of understanding.

Let's say she came into the session saying, "I have dreams of horses all the time...." So now you are onto the dreams of horses and the jewelry and you keep narrowing down and cutting away until you have some sort of understanding of the person. Then you do your technique and you heal her of her constant dreams of horses.

The diagnostic process in Kabbalistic healing is exactly the opposite. There are about fifteen to fifty Kabbalistic healings, depending upon how you count. To arrive at the healing that is precisely right for that person at that moment, we enter into deeper and deeper relationship with her—which means we want to broaden our view of her rather than narrow it.

So the process of diagnosis in Integrated Kabbalistic Healing is different in that it brings us precisely to the right healing through a method that creates more and more intimacy. That intimacy buds like a tree into a fruit and that particular fruit, we say, is the specific healing we are going to do for this person at this time. It is a natural, though deeply sophisticated, process.

If, however, I came to that specific diagnosis and recommendation and then told someone else to actually do the healing, it wouldn't be the same. Although we might choose the same healing, because the relationship between the healer and client was different, the healing itself would be completely different.

All Kabbalistic healings are completely contextual. They are about relationship. They are always about the healer's relationship with the client, and the healer's relationship with himself or herself as well. You might say that Integrated Kabbalistic Healing works by inference, by resonance. Nothing is transmitted. Instead, people enter into a condition of experiencing Wholeness.

The Experience of Wholeness

When you are with someone who is in touch with Wholeness in some manner, you begin to feel more open and more in touch yourself. Why is that?

There is a spaciousness that happens, and that spaciousness—in and of itself—seems to be healing. You go to see the Dalai Lama, for instance. Many people go to see him and they have transference. They feel like, "He's above me..." Well, that's transference—he's a man.

But, at the same time, he's a man who has done remarkable work on himself. He is a being through whom some universal quality is moving, and you feel better just being around him. Some people can even simply think about him or look at a picture of him and feel better.

Why is that? He's not doing anything to you. It's not that something is imparted. It's not an energetic thing, even though it has energetic repercussions in you.

Being around him allows you to be more and more yourself because he's already done that for himself. His own internal experience is probably quite different. I'm sure he is simply practicing all the time. I think he's simply looking at people and saying, "Ohhh, who are you? Ohhh, who are you?"

One thing I've heard about him is that he really knows how to listen. Pretty neat! To listen on that depth, it's not mystical. It makes you feel heard and it creates the intimacy needed for true healing.

Were we heard as children? We were not heard as children. Were we safe as children? To some extent. We grew up sane. But we also grew up pained and insane because we were not seen clearly for who we were as children.

To meet someone who truly takes you in, who truly hears you, makes you feel different. Kabbalistic healing exists in that same process, along with the added aspect of the diagnostic process. The Integrated Kabbalistic Healing diagnostic process—which is really a form of flowing, active meditation—is a precise, yet broadening, process that the healer uses to know which of the specific Kabbalistic conditions is going to help with the root of the problem.

The Healing Effect of Kindness

How do you want to die? How do you want to be with someone who is dying? Wouldn't it be nice to die looking around the world and feeling kindness toward it? Saying, "This was a wonderful world, I really enjoyed this...." And wouldn't that be a kind thing for all the people who were around you, who loved you and were going to miss you?

This is an idealized picture, of course, because some people will die in accidents and some people will die in pain. But, as a hope, it's something we need to mention. Imagine looking around and saying, "You know, I'm so glad to have known you. It was great. You've been a good daughter. You've been a good wife. I'm going now...." And imagine not dying. Imagine just living that way. Imagine the healing possibilities of living that way.

Why is it that kindness has such a profound healing effect?

Because true kindness comes from the same spiritual level that is responsible for all of creation. Creation, according to Kabbalah, is filled with God's kindness. Even though we can't see it all the time, it exists because of the way Creation happened. We are separate beings, but—if we were truly separate—we could never return to God.

The world is filled with kindness, things that bring us back to God, which is part of the repair of this world. There are hints of this all over the place for us to find, things we can see and hear and touch. We're talking about profound, non-dual, unsentimental kindness now—we're not talking about niceness.

Profound kindness can be stern. Profound kindness can be rough. Profound kindness can be Jesus casting the moneychangers and shopkeepers out of the temple. That was kindness. Understand? It was a wake-up call for them.

Kindness is not sentimentality. Kindness, true kindness—which we could say is compassion—is a non-egoic emotion. It's not even an emotion. It transcends emotion. And it's non-egoic because it's not something that I have for you, but something I have for myself as well because I am simply another created being who needs this kindness as well.

To go back to the Dalai Lama: He doesn't bow to people and say, "Ohhh...You're so small. Ohhh...You've got so many problems. Thank God I don't have these things..." He doesn't do that. He looks at you and says, "Ohhh...Buddha! Ohhh...Another Buddha! Suffering humanity..."

The Dalai Lama doesn't exclude himself—he includes himself. When you include yourself, it's non-egoic. It's nondualistic.

Since that feeling of kindness comes from such a profound and essential level, Kabbalistically we would say it originates in the universe of Atzilut. Because this universe, though infinitely high, is simultaneously at the basis of all of our lives in duality. It ripples back though the emotional world and the physical world and the psychological world so that everything else falls into place around this central idea or law.

Can cruelty kill? Yes. Can kindness heal? People will sometimes say to me, "I feel better..." And people will say, "Well, it's not really, really going to fix an ulcer, is it? It's not really going to fix a cancer, is it?" But it can.

Kabbalistic healing is another way of approaching this issue of profound kindness. There is no question that if you work with a Kabbalistic healer and you go through the diagnostic process, you're going to find it to be extremely kind. But feeling that level of kindness is not something that just happens. It takes hard work and dedication and a desire to heal the self to the point at which the Real Self— which is our true connection with God—becomes manifest in the world.

When I talked about kindness before, you understood what I was talking about, right? You understood what I meant by that, whether you had achieved that level of kindness or not. Why is that?

The only reason that you could understand what I was saying about that level of kindness is because it is already in you, because it is a true thing, a true part of our humanity. Just as suffering is a part of all us, this greatness and this kindness, this true non-dual praise, this beauty, is already in us—so you recognize it when you see it or hear about it.

Often, something is touched in people who get Kabbalistic healings and, when they recognize it, they say, "You know something, I want more of this. This is what I want in my life. This is what I want to study, this is what I want to give." I hear that all the time, in much more dramatic words than I'm using.

"People's Souls Are Touched by This Work"

It feels too self-serving to tell stories about people who have been healed with this process. It feels like, "Here is another guy telling you another wonderful story about how the work he does changes the world." There's no dearth of these stories in A Society of Souls, but I'm not interested in glamorizing this work.

What I can say is that the people I have trained who have really taken to this work see it as their life's path. There are psychiatrists who have changed their practice and are doing this. There are healers in many modalities who are doing this work because Integrated Kabbalistic Healing always heals the healer as much as it heals the healee. So, in this way, its never about burnout or doing something for someone else. It's not about some small-minded notion of sacrifice, but about the Big Sacrifice: the casting away of the tyranny of the small parts of ourselves in favor of the larger idea of our Real Connection to the Divine. This work is like nectar when you touch it. And what are we touching? We're not touching Kabbalistic healing—we are touching the tender face of God.

Integrated Kabbalistic Healing is a method of healing which asks us to heal from the position of the awakened state. That's what it wants us to do. When we touch that in ourselves, even briefly—and most of us only touch it briefly—we can't even consider not doing this as our full-time occupation.

At that point, it's not about Kabbalistic healing—it's about God. It's about whatever we want to call God—the source of our lives, the moment of Creation, Reality. And once you touch Reality you don't necessarily want to go back and pretend to be only a small and separate being again.

So people's lives have been changed. Has every client been healed? Absolutely not. Can any modality claim that? No. But I can claim this: I would say that I believe that probably everybody's soul has been healed. Even if their bodies were not healed, everybody's soul has always been made more whole than it was before they had Kabbalistic healing. People's souls are always touched by this work.

Purifying My Teaching

I've always been a musician. Before I was into healing, I was writing commercials and doing rock 'n' roll. It was always a painful area for me because I frankly do not like being onstage. I wanted to get my music out, but I never ended up doing that, so I finally just laid it to rest. I still wrote songs, but no one would hear them.

Then, at a certain point, songs and chants very different from my earlier work started coming out, and I no longer cared about anything but sharing this work. Just sharing it. So I made a CD—*The Great Transparency: Songs to God*—and I now use some of those songs when I sing during workshops and trainings.

Some people respond very potently to this music. I have a lot of technical knowledge about Kabbalah, philosophical knowledge, interdisciplinary knowledge, psychological and biological knowledge and so on—I have a lot to teach—and yet sometimes people will come away from a workshop saying, "Yeah, I got a lot of that...But the singing, that really transported me...." That's because somehow the music goes right to an essential place, like the kindness that we talked about.

You see, good teaching, good singing, is not going to bring anything new to you—if it were new, we wouldn't recognize it. It is going to awaken something that is already in you—something that is, therefore, yours. So if you learn a chant or a song of mine and it touches you, you can take it and sing it at home and it's going to evoke something for you by yourself. You won't need me to do that.

It may be nice to hear my voice, it may be pleasant, but that's a different experience. The important experience is about you feeling this opening up, because it is essentially yours. It's essentially your openness, your spirituality, your spaciousness, your kindness toward yourself. The music is just the key.

I had to say to myself, "Wow! Maybe singing is a really important part of my teaching." So I took a chance and, when the New York Open Center called me about my 1999 lecture series, I said, "I'm going to do a concert along with a lecture." And, because I was willing to give this music in a new way, in a non-dual way, I got to experience the songs as if I had not written them and was not singing

them. I felt healed by remembering, along with the audience, my true nature and my connection with God.

The Kindness That Is Beyond Life and Death

In 1998, I finished a small book of poems I had worked on for about eighteen months. Each morning, as I prayed and put on tefillin—small leather boxes containing quotations from the Torah that are bound to the head and arm by long, black straps—I wrote these psalms as part of my personal spiritual work. Here is one of them:

> If I need to bear this pain
> let me fill it with water
> and float on it.
> If I need to sink in it,
> let my lungs be huge and
> my breath deep and long
> and let me dive to the bottom.

If I must drown in it,
Dear God, let me swallow
as much of it as I can
and sink to You quickly,
rapid as a heartbeat
in a bird sensing danger.
If nothing like this is to happen,
and I am making too much of it,
and I am to walk, step by step
toward You, may I see
the water and the breath and the bird
as my illusions, and the pain I
bear as my ticket home.

That's it. That's really it, isn't it? This is the kindness that's beyond life and death. It's a kindness we can carry through us. It's not about floating about in some ambrosial heaven filled with pink flowers, it's about humanity. Integrated Kabbalistic Healing is a method of working with this level of humanity—very specifically, very accurately, with great precision and great integrity.

We want to make better human beings. I hope people understand that when they read this.

Peggy Huddleston
Cambridge, Massachusetts

The third step of preparing for surgery
is asking all the people who love you
to surround you with a pink blanket of love as
you're lying on a gurney outside the operating room.
In the hospital, you feel that love.
As you go into surgery, love is just pouring
out of you, and you want to hug each person
on your surgical team. It shifts the vibration
of everyone in the operating room
to a deep peacefulness and serenity.

We would call Peggy Huddleston a "hands-off" healer. Although she clearly sees what may be going on for an individual physically, emotionally, and spiritually, she neither touches her clients nor offers them second-hand information. Instead, Peggy carefully guides her clients into their own bodies and souls so they can make the first-hand connections and discoveries that will facilitate their healing process.

Peggy brings an unusual blend of intellect and compassion to her work. Sitting with Peggy in her office, we each had the experience of talking with a part of our body and receiving highly individual information that we could use for self-healing. Peggy's ability to point each of us in different directions while clearly articulating what was happening with each of us made the experience powerful for all.

Additional experiences support the effectiveness of Peggy's approach to healing. Last winter, Sarah, a young friend of the family, tore a ligament in her knee while skiing in Utah. She had an MRI taken when she returned to New York and was advised to have surgery as soon as possible to repair the damage. Because of insurance problems, though, Sarah learned that she would have to postpone surgery for a month or so, until she could return home to France.

To help her manage her pain while she waiting, we sent Sarah Peggy's book and relaxation/healing tape. Sarah listened to the tape faithfully while she was waiting for her surgery. When an orthoscopy was finally performed, both Sarah and her doctor were amazed to find that the ligament had repaired itself.

Recently, Susan hit herself in the mouth with a two-by-four while she was adding onto her studio. The accident set off severe pain in a molar. Her dentist told Susan that she could wait for a few days to see if it calmed down on its own, but that she would probably need a root canal to take care of the problem.

When Susan shared this with us, we suggested she use Peggy's relaxation/healing tape to see what her tooth had to say to her. After using the tape three times a day for three days, Susan reported that her tooth had told that she was biting off more than she could chew and that she should just pay attention to what she already had on her plate. When she subsequently said, "No!" to a freelance assignment she was considering, the pain in her tooth disappeared.

Susan saw her dentist again to verify that all was well. He was so amazed at the change in her condition that he blurted out, "But you had no right getting better!"

As we were leaving Peggy Huddleston's office following our interview, we suddenly realized that some pattern in our lives had been completed. We had been traveling the *country for more than three years, searching for people with extraordinary healing abilities and now—as we were finishing the book—we found ourselves back in Cambridge, just blocks from where we had first met each other more than twenty-five years ago.*

Susan, who was born and raised in Maine, was also included in the circle: Peggy's paternal grandmother, Roselle Woodbridge Huddilston, figured prominently in Maine history and her grandfather, Professor John H. Huddilston, served as Chairman of the Department of Greek and Ancient History for more than forty years at the University of Maine at Orono, where Susan had gone to college.

A graduate of the Harvard Divinity School, Peggy Huddleston has taught self-healing workshops to thousands of people around the world. Her groundbreaking research on the ways the human spirit can enhance healing has been featured in numerous newspapers, magazines, and television broadcasts.

In her private practice as a psychotherapist, Peggy works with individuals, couples, and families—in person or over the phone—on a wide range of physical, emotional, or spiritual healing issues. As a Project Director at the Center for Psychology and Social Change, an affiliate of the Department of Psychiatry at The Cambridge Hospital, Peggy organizes a one-week "Camp for Young Healers" each summer. She also works with the parents of children who have paranormal experiences so that they can be supportive of their children and answer their questions. Because these parents and children usually feel isolated by their abilities, Peggy links them with others having the same experience.

Peggy helps individuals prepare for surgery and teaches a two-day training and certification workshop based on her book Prepare for Surgery, Heal Faster, so health care professionals can teach the program in their hospitals or private practices. She visits hospitals all over North America, lecturing and explaining the research behind the program to surgeons and anesthesiologists.

Peggy is also a principal investigator of "Patient-Centered Techniques to Enhance Surgical Outcomes," two research studies based at the Massachusetts General Hospital, Brigham and Women's Hospital, and New England Baptist Hospital, all Harvard Medical School teaching hospitals. Her research tracks and quantifies the experiences of patients who use the emotional and spiritual pre-surgical preparation techniques described in her book.

W hen I was writing my book, *Prepare for Surgery, Heal Faster*, my inner guidance said that although it looked on one level as if the purpose of the book was to prepare people for surgery—to help them heal faster by showing them how to feel profoundly peaceful—for many people that peace would become transformative.

Surgery can be that doorway of transformation. When people are scared about surgery, their defenses break down. They feel a letting go, and often they fall into their souls. And, as they land in their souls, they connect with a deep peace that they have never known. That deep peace is what many people stay connected to for the rest of their lives. That's really the opportunity of the surgery.

"Our Ability for Self-Healing Is Phenomenal"

I'm doing research at a Harvard Medical School teaching hospital, documenting how much people can speed their healing process by getting deeply relaxed and participating in their surgery. The preliminary results of randomized, controlled studies show that some people are using about 23 to 50 percent less pain medication and others are leaving the hospital a day sooner than those in the control group.

As a part of this program, we have people talk to the part of their body that is having the surgery so they can ask it what emotions are stored there and what comforting feeling that part of their body would like to be given. Then, as they put their hands on this part of their body, a lot of healing energy will flow into the area. A few people who have used this process have been healed and avoided surgery.

For example, a woman had a tooth so disintegrated that her dentist thought that maybe they had to yank it out and not do a root canal. The dentist showed her x-rays to five other dental surgeons to see what they thought. And they all said, "There's no way you're going to save that tooth, even with a root canal."

So she began using the *Preparing for Surgery, Heal Faster* relaxation tape and book. In the book, there are five steps: the first one is getting deeply relaxed; the second one is visualizing your healing process; the third is having your friends surround you in a pink blanket of love during the half-hour before surgery; the fourth is having some healing statements said as you go under the anesthesia; and the fifth is talking with the person who will be giving you the anesthesia—having a human relationship with the person to whom you will entrust your entire consciousness and being.

This woman was visualizing a healing light pouring into her tooth throughout the day. She did it several times a day for two weeks. When she went back for the surgery, the surgeon didn't have to do a root canal—all he did was a filling!

The tooth had reconstructed itself in two weeks, just with her imagining light pouring into it. Luckily, she had five dentists look at her x-ray, because without that kind of evidence, someone would say, "Oh, she's made that up...."

Our ability for self-healing is phenomenal. I once worked with a woman who was having chemotherapy. Her four-year-old son had heard from his friends that his mother might lose her hair, so he said, "Mom, I'm going to help you. I'm going to pat your head and give you love every evening to help you keep your hair."

Every night, when she would be lying on the couch feeling tired from the chemo, he would gently stroke her head. And he said, "This is going to make your hair stay." And it did! She didn't lose her hair—and she'd been told, absolutely, 100 percent, "You're going to lose it."

There was also a research study done with people who were given chemotherapy. Even though all they got was a sugar pill, the control group thought they got real chemo—and 30 percent of those people lost their hair. *The World Journal of Surgery* reported these findings in 1983. It's awesome what we can do!

Another woman called me from Nashua, New Hampshire, with excruciating back pain. She was planning to have back surgery here in Boston with the idea that the surgery would really fix her back. She had been in so much pain that she could only stand up for ten minutes a day. She couldn't cook meals, she couldn't do laundry, or take care of her two sons.

When her surgery was canceled for insurance reasons, she was desperate. So I said, "Well, I could show you how you could talk with the part of your back that needs healing..." And she said, "Oh, I couldn't do anything to heal my back. There are all these MRIs that show the damage...I couldn't possibly do that."

And I said, "Let me just show you how to talk to your back." She was a house painter and she said, "No one can talk to a part of their body. That's ridiculous."

But she was desperate enough with her pain and not being able to work for three months that she said, "All right, I'll see...But this is absurd!"

I asked her to focus on where it hurt. She said, "That's easy." Then I said, "Ask this part of your body what is it feeling." And she said, "Yeah, that's right. It's telling me that it's angry. I'm enraged and I just pump anger into my back all day long because I'm a house painter and I've got to carry heavy ladders and I can't do it."

I said, "Ask your back what comforting feeling it would like to be given?" She was quieter this time, and she didn't say "This is ridiculous."

She said, "It wants to be given love. But how do I do that?"

I asked her, "What was the time that you felt the most love?" She answered, "When each of my sons were born, when they were placed in my arms in the delivery room, I felt a love I had never felt before."

"Let your mind go back to the delivery room, feeling your son in your arms. Let the love that you're feeling go down your right arm to your hand and put your hand on your back." I said.

She said, "Ohhh..." and then she said, "My hand is getting hot and it's starting to pulse." After about three minutes, she murmured, "My pain is going away...," and I said, "Ask your back how many times a day it wants you to give it this love."

She was quiet and then said, "It wants it all the time...Well, there's nothing else I can do—I'm just lying here—so I'll just give it as much love as it wants."

I called her back in ten days and I got her answering machine. I wondered where she could be because she was always lying next to the phone. As it turned out, she had walked a mile and a half into Nashua with her son and she was fine.

I'm just floored by the extraordinary ability people have to facilitate their own healing!

Remembering My Purpose

I'd grown up outside of Philadelphia—my mother's family lived in Bryn Mawr. When I was around twenty-two or twenty-three years old, I had a strong sense that my life had a purpose—but I couldn't remember what it was.

I was very influenced by both my grandmothers, especially my father's mother, Roselle Woodbridge Huddilston. (My father changed the spelling of our last name.)

As a suffragette, my grandmother was always chaining herself to the gate of the White House in Washington to protest women's inability to vote.

Because of everything she had done, when they finally gave women the vote they held back the polls in Maine so that my grandmother could be the first woman to vote in America. She was also the first woman in Maine to run for the state legislature. In the '30s, '40s and '50s, she was very concerned about clean air and clean water. She was one of the founders of the American Lung Association and was always pitting herself against the Maine lumbering interests who were polluting the air and water.

When my father was growing up, my grandmother was out saving the world. We'd always laughed, saying that the farmhands raised him. But I was lucky enough to be her first grandchild and I always got tremendous love from her.

I spent many wonderful childhood summers on my grandparents' farm in Orono, Maine. I can still smell the molasses cookies my grandmother baked for me in the big, black, wood-burning cast-iron stove in the kitchen. She played with me for hours and loved to brush my blonde hair in the summer sun, beside her garden of hollyhocks. I thrived on this love from my grandmother. Looking back, I think I reminded her of her daughter, Rachel, who had died in her early twenties.

During these summers, when I was three, four, five, and six years old, my father instilled in me a belief that I could do anything. An avid hunter and outsdoorsman, he taught me to blaze trails in the woods beyond the barn and cow pastures and swim across the ponds. Spook, his white Irish setter, followed us through the woods as my father put me through the challenges of what must have been his "Outward Bound Camp for Kiddies."

Having had grandmothers who were dynamos and a number of other members of the family who had accomplished all kinds of historical "firsts"—our family tree included a signer of the Declaration of Independence, founders of both Harvard and Yale, a number of the Magna Carta barons, several medieval Christian saints, and Eleanor of Aquitaine, who was a twenty-first great-grandmother—I felt a burden, a responsibility as I was growing up. I couldn't just grow up and have fun—there was something that I was supposed to do!

After college, I went through all the usual Philadelphia things, but they just weren't me. At that time, nothing in my society supported the idea that you could be attuned to an inner voice telling you there was something you came to Earth to do.

To peel off the layer that was my family and get to the layer underneath that was me, I got a job on a ski ranch in Dillon, Colorado. I thought that if I had a job where I was cleaning bathrooms and serving breakfast, I'd have the rest of the day to ski, be in nature, and get attuned to remembering what I was supposed to be doing with my life.

I started having dreams that I was breaking my leg skiing. I was so naive that I didn't realize the implications—that I was really broken in taking my next step forward. I finally did break my leg skiing, and I was so relieved. Now I could finally stop asking myself what I was going to do with my life. For the next six months, I could just be in my ankle-to-hip cast and get well.

Back home in Philadelphia, I would go around the corner every day to visit a wonderful friend, a man who had been like a second father to me. All I wanted to do was read his books, but he wouldn't let me read anything. He said, "We're just going to talk, because there are things that you remember from other lifetimes. If you start reading the books, you'll think you got it out of the books, and I only want you to let your memories come back."

This man, Arthur M. Young, was the person who had invented the helicopter. When he went to Princeton and studied physics with Einstein, he learned how to take problems and figure them out with inventions. He took some of his inventions to the Patent Office and found that most of them had already been registered, but the helicopter hadn't—so he began building little models and flying them around.

At the time, he was also going through psychoanalysis, and he had to tell his dreams to his analyst. Every night he'd wake up and write down his dreams and, in the morning, there would be drawings, blueprints of the helicopter he was building. This guided him through the whole process of invention.

At one point, he had finally built the helicopter and was flying it when he crashed. The helicopter was lying on the ground and his body was lying on the ground but he was floating above it, looking at it. He was having an out-of-body experience and thinking, like a good scientist, "Spirit can't be separated from matter. So how can I be up here watching my body and the helicopter on the ground? That's not supposed to be possible!" Yet he knew it was happening.

He realized that there were a lot of things happening that science said weren't possible. After he sold his patent rights to Bell Helicopter, he spent the next twenty years developing a whole new theory that put his experiences into a scientific theory. This is the theory that many physicists and parapsychologists now use. It's all about the descent of light into matter.

I would sit and talk to Arthur and he would just help me remember. I did that for six months and I remembered a lot in that process. And then I knew that what I really wanted to do was to show people how to heal.

Honoring the Inner Knowing

I began studying a lot of things, but I was really reconnecting with an inner knowing that each of us has this extraordinary capacity for self-healing.

It's so simple—if we're shown how to talk to our body. If we ask our body if there is a problem, what's happening and why, it will tell us the healing process. All we have to do is listen and have the courage to follow what we've heard.

Most of us know what we should be doing. What we need is the courage to actually do it—especially if it flies in the face of something else we believe or some convenience or something that we just don't want to deal with. If you'll just honor that inner knowing, all the answers are inside.

I taught about six thousand people in Philadelphia how to get deeply relaxed and, when they were deeply relaxed, how to talk to the part of themselves that needed healing. Many people would have ulcers go away or have their tennis elbows healed. Some people would have eyeglasses and leave them behind in the workshop. I need glasses, so I was always jealous of people who leave theirs behind.

Seeing...

When I was ten years old, I could see that my mother was going to die when I was a teenager. I always had this happening as a child. It was great seeing some things; other things, I just didn't want to see. It was too much to cope with the feeling that someone I got so much love from was going to die. I didn't want to have to see that and know that, so I wound up becoming nearsighted—just enough so that I couldn't see into the future.

Now, when I'm working with clients and seeing things, I always make a point of not saying what I see. Instead, I guide them into seeing things for themselves, so that they get the information firsthand.

I've always found that if a healer says to someone, "Well, I see xyz…," the person believes it, just because the healer said so. But it's not his or her original experience.

It's so much more powerful when people are their own healers because when you hear things firsthand—from your own big toe or your face or your throat, for example—you can just keep asking your body questions and it will keep telling you whatever it is that you need to know. When you go to the source, you get original information without anyone interpreting it for you. And you get to feel it in your body rather than just getting it intellectually.

For example, I was working on the telephone with a man who lived in New York but happened to be on business in Tokyo. He called because he had a tremendous pain in his right shoulder. I had my eyes closed and I could see his father, whom I knew had died. I could see his father trying to give his love to his son, who was a forty-five-year-old man. I could see the son pushing away the love.

I asked the man on the phone to close his eyes, feel into the place where his shoulder hurt, and just ask it, "What's happening?"

He said, "Oh, my father's here and he's trying to give me love." Then he added, "But I'm pushing it away." It scared him that his father was there. "He's supposed to have died," he said. "How can he be here giving me love?" He was afraid it meant he was going to die if his father was around him.

I suggested that he ask why his father was there. So he asked and his father said, "I've always been here; I'm just trying to get through to you. This is a time you really need my love." My client burst into tears—he was going through a divorce and it was a time he really did need his father's love.

I asked him to feel what it's like to let in his father's love and he said, "The pain just stopped in my shoulder." The pain was his resistance to the love and pushing it away.

I said, "Well, ask your father how you can get comfortable feeling his love and letting it in." His father told him, "Don't be frightened by the fact I'm here. It doesn't mean you're dying. It just means I love you."

Help from the Other Side

I remember sitting right here on this couch talking with a young woman in her twenties who had cancer, an inoperable brain tumor. I kept feeling this presence on the other end of the couch. It was so palpable. And I knew it related to the young woman who was sitting here.

But I didn't say, "Oh, I can see something on the end of the couch—let me tell you what it is." Instead I asked this young woman—because I could feel that it was someone who had died who really loved this young woman and was here to help her—"Is there anyone you know who has died, who really loves you, who you sometimes feel around you?"

Without skipping a beat, she said, "Oh, yes...My mother's sister, my aunt. I always feel her around me." Then I asked her if she felt her here now.

She said, "Yes." I asked where she was. "Right there on the end of the couch," she replied, pointing to where I had sensed the presence.

"Well, what do you feel from her?" I asked. "I feel her love," she responded.

"Ask her why she's with you," I said. And she said, "Well, I've never talked to her. Is that all right?"

"Of course," I said. "Didn't you know you can?"

"No! Can I?" she said. "Yes. Just ask her why she is here." When she asked her, her aunt said, "I'm here to help you get well. You can make this tumor get smaller. I'm here to let you know it's possible. And I'm here holding your hand all the way."

A lot of people, as they are preparing for surgery, will feel the love of a mother or father who has died around them. Usually they get scared and think that means they are going to die. It doesn't mean they are going to die. Rather, it means their mother or father is surrounding them in love in their time of need.

Going into the Light

That reminds me of one of the most amazing experiences I've ever had. It was the privilege of having my mother's mother, Margaret Merwin Dickson, die in my arms. It was an ecstatic experience even though my beloved grandmother was dying. She was eighty-five and she was ready to die.

As I held her in my arms, an astonishing light radiated through her eyes and her whole being. The light just pours into people before they die because they're connected with this other dimension.

I said, "Aren't you afraid of dying?" and she said, "No. Everyone in our family dies in each other's arms." And she said, "I know how it feels and it's wonderful to die." And I said, "It is?" She answered, "Yes. My mother, my husband, and your mother all died in my arms."

She gave me that gift of dying in my arms, so I got to feel how ecstatic it is. About twenty minutes after she had died, I was sitting in a chair and an incredible energy was up on the ceiling, shining down on me like a spotlight. I was surrounded by more love than I've ever felt in my life. I just knew it was my grandmother on the ceiling, and that she wasn't going to leave until she knew that I knew she was fine...And then, voom! She was gone!

That experience took away my fear of dying.

I've subsequently shown many people how to use the process she taught me. There's a very simple way, when people are dying, to show them how to connect with the light so that they don't resist dying, don't go into the fear and get stuck. You can connect them with the light so that they're hooked up to it for hours or days before they die and they become luminous, radiant. When they go into the light, they die very beautifully.

"We All Have an Inner Knowing..."

Until recently I've remained hidden about my ability to see or sense or know. In Bryn Mawr, it wasn't okay to see these things. I was afraid I would be called crazy or weird, so I spent a lot of time trying to look normal.

I also think it's because I've remembered past lifetimes, in the Middle Ages, where I was killed for being a healer. I've images of being dragged through the streets, being tortured for being able to see and know things. So I was terrified that if I did anything, other than appear normal, my life would be at risk.

I think I've hidden behind my Harvard degree and my polite manners as a way to be safe in this culture. These were things that were honored and respected. And I think it's why I'm very careful to be doing my research at a Harvard Medical School teaching hospital, documenting the extraordinary ability people have for self-healing, for speeding their healing by preparing for surgery.

Going to Harvard Divinity School gave me a chance to plug some of the holes in my knowledge of physiological psychology and psychoneuroimmunology, but my whole work has been about hearing an inner voice. Words that would guide me would drop into my head. I would feel a light pour into me. Like a feeling of grace, this most delicious feeling would pour into me.

I was so used to it in my twenties that I would just keep doing whatever I was doing when it happened. Then I thought, "You silly thing...you fool...just sit down..." I promised myself that whenever I would feel this light pouring in, I'd stop whatever I was doing because nothing was more important than that. If I was walking upstairs, I'd stop and sit on that step and feel the light pouring in—I'd just feel it pouring in.

After all this, I put together a course on how to connect with your higher Self and feel that energy that's pouring into all of us, showing people how to let their body get used to that much higher vibration so that vibration could build and build in the body. The higher Self would have a voice and a person could ask it anything. Everyone comes to the course with a laundry list of things they want to know—I want to know this and I want to know that—and usually the questions are coming out of their minds.

The question that comes from a deeper place is: "What is the question I need to ask?" When you get that question answered, you can say, "What is the next question I need to ask?" As you do that, this amazing inner healer is revealed, an inner healer that can be used for physical healing, for emotional healing, for spiritual healing—or just for answering questions about what you need to do next in life.

We all have this inner knowing. People just need to be reminded to use it, the way you would use a hammer and a screwdriver. When my son was growing up, if he would lose a sock, I would say, "Just close your eyes and you'll see where it is." And he'd close his eyes and say, "Oh, yeah, I see it." And then he'd run and get the sock. It's so practical and helpful and matter of fact.

I've been finding there are a lot of psychotherapists who hear words being dropped in the top of their head. Of the nurses that I've trained in my "Prepare for Surgery, Heal Faster" workshops, at least three-quarters nod and say, "Yes," when I ask if they hear inner guidance.

And there was a great study done at Princeton that showed that the most successful executives and stockbrokers were those who used their intuition to make decisions in the boardroom. They went with their gut feeling but found facts to back it up so it looked rational.

Many of the people who are open to inner knowing just don't go around talking about it. I hope that my work is giving them more courage and support to trust and act on it.

A Camp for Young Healers

I've been working for about eight years with children who have what's called paranormal experiences—which is the scientific way of saying that they see angels, other beings, or people who have died. Some of these children sense the presence of God. Some see the human aura. A number of these kids remember where they came from and why they came to Earth. Most of them heal with their hands.

If they had been brought up in another culture, these children would all have been their village shamans. But there's nothing in our culture to help them be recognized, honored, and listened to. Luckily, a lot of these kids have great parents who home school them.

When they're younger, say three, four, and five, they just think all this is normal—which it probably is. As they grow older and discover that other kids don't have these same abilities, they become afraid that they won't fit in. Every adolescent wants to have friends, so these kids will often drop their abilities to fit in. Or, if they keep to the truth of their experience, they'll feel very lonely and left out of the mainstream. What these kids most need is other kids like themselves, kids with these same gifts.

Through the Center for Psychology and Social Change, an affiliate of the Department of Psychiatry at The Cambridge Hospital, I put together a "Camp for Young Healers" for a week each summer for these children. The purpose of the camp is to create a community where all these things can be talked about, because the counselors have the same paranormal abilities. The camp also has a Web site so that children from different parts of the world can have a chat room, a community of support wherever they are.

Although we'd said the age limit was sixteen, one girl called and said "Can I please come? I'm seventeen but I *need* to come." I asked why. She said, "I grew up on my parents' farm outside of Louisville, Kentucky. I've always had a guardian angel, but I don't see him anymore and I'm so lonely without him. I got so much love from him and guidance from him. I want to come to camp because I want to reconnect with my guardian angel." I said, "Yes...but I can't guarantee that you'll reconnect."

So she came to the camp and I worked with her the first afternoon for about an hour, sitting beside the lake, and she discovered that she had disconnected from her guardian angel because she didn't fit in having him. He popped back in and you could feel his love again.

Then I said, "Ask him what happened that made you feel like he went away." She asked him and he said, "I never left you; you left me. I've always been here." And she said, "That's right. But now that I feel what it's like without him, I will never let go of him again."

She's now a freshman in college in Florida and, when I talked to her recently, she said, "I will never let go of that connection to my guardian angel. It's too important. No matter how different I am, that's staying with me!"

This past summer, the kids did a healing on the cook the first night of the camp. The cook had terribly arthritic knees, but she didn't tell them what the problem was. They just went right to her knees and began doing a lot of healing. And the cook said that she would usually get more exhausted every day of a week-long program, but with this group, she felt better every day because the kids were doing healings on her. She was amazed.

And she said that what was so surprising was that when these kids were in her kitchen having milk and cookies they were just like normal, basic kids. But when she was having the healing done on her, a presence would come over them—there would be this whole inner knowing. They changed in front of her eyes as they started to do the healings.

There was one child at camp who could see beings who have died. Luckily, her father and her aunt could also see them. When she would be in a restaurant having dinner, she'd see a stranger across the room, and she would see the beings that loved this person around him or her. The beings knew she could see them and they'd all stream across the room to her, giving her messages to give the person having dinner. She was only fourteen, but sometimes she would go over and tell the person what was being said. It was a little hard, but she had gotten used to it because her father and her aunt could do this, too.

I got an e-mail from a psychologist in North Carolina that said, "Thank you for doing this work. I have clients who have been hospitalized because they said they saw angels, and they are perfectly healthy and fine. They are being given medication when they shouldn't be, and we can't get them out of the institution..."

For many children, it's perfectly normal to be seeing all these other dimensions and realities. I think there are many children coming to Earth now who have these extraordinary abilities...and they seem to have tremendous patience and wisdom about what they've come into. I know one of them would say, "Well, you know, I've come here to help save the Earth...Am I the only one? Is anyone else going to help me?"

Storing Emotions in the Body

I worked with a woman recently who had a large fibroid tumor. She had called me to prepare for surgery, and said, "Now I really want to shrink this thing; I don't want to lose my uterus." So we worked together on what emotions were stored there and how she needed to release them.

She began taking a healing time for herself every morning—really entering into sacred time and space—and imagined her fibroid shrinking and shrinking. And, in two weeks, it shrank so much she called her surgeon and said, "You'd better check this fibroid, because I think you're not going to want to do this hysterectomy." The surgeon checked her and said, "This thing has shrunk so much you don't need the operation anymore."

The woman was fine for about a year, and then her mother and father came to visit and one of her parents died suddenly. It set off a whole crisis and, as a result of that crisis, the fibroid started growing again. When they actually removed it, the fibroid weighed eight pounds—it was almost as big as a baby!

About a week before surgery, this woman did a beautiful thing. She was talking to that part of her body that was going to have surgery, and she asked three friends who were in different parts of the country to be on the phone and witness this experience. As she began to thank her uterus for what it had given her—feeling the emotions that were stored there and needed releasing—there was a lot of sobbing, a lot of crying, a lot of raging.

When she hung up, all the chronic pain she'd had in her abdomen for months had stopped. Releasing all the emotions made the pain stop. She had thought the pain was caused by the fibroid, but it wasn't. It was caused by the emotions that were stored in her abdomen.

Most of us have emotions stored in our bodies. There may have been times when we were feeling something as a child (or as an adult) and we couldn't express it—we had to hold it in. All those emotions get stored in our bodies.

Usually, we pick a certain area in which to store these feelings. When too much is stored there, it begins to block the natural flow of energy along our meridians, the body's energy pathways. As a result, health problems usually will develop where the emotions are stored.

If people can go into the area of the physical symptom and feel what emotions are there—there are usually two or three layers of emotion—as they begin feeling and releasing them, sometimes the physical problem will totally clear up and heal. At other times, the physical problem will decrease.

The Healing Power of Love

The things that I've been saying here are not things I would ever say when I've gone to the chief of orthopedic surgery to say I'd like to do a research study with you. Instead, I would come with a protocol that I had spent three months writing and all the research articles that I had dug out of the medical literature.

That's how I can be useful, helping to document—in terms that are used in mainstream medicine—the capacity we have to speed our healing. I want to document the capacity we have for healing so that it isn't an either/or choice between allopathic and complementary approaches. Within the best of mainstream medicine, I want to show how you can bring people connecting with the love of their souls into the process of preparing for surgery so that they can have a much faster healing process.

In my work, I link people up to different supports, whether those supports are their own higher Selves or other people having the same paranormal experiences. But I've always felt that my purpose was to bring love back into mainstream medicine, and to document the healing power of love. I've always felt that that's what I'm supposed to be doing.

Resources

Winter Robinson

Books

Intuitions: Seeing with the Heart. Tor Down Publishing (Saco, ME) 1988 (revised 1993).

Remembering: A Gentle Reminder of Who You Are. Tor Down Publishing (Saco, ME) 1994.

Audiotape

Discovering Intuition. Tor Down Publishing (Saco, ME) 1994.

To order Winter Robinson's books and tape, subscribe to her e-mail newsletter, "Morning Coffee," schedule an intuitive reading, or receive additional information about her training programs, seminars, and business consulting service, write to: Winter Robinson, Tor Down Publishing, P.O. Box 484, Bar Mills, ME 04004-0484; phone: (207) 929-6960; e-mail: winter@winterrobinson.com; or visit her Web site: www.winterrobinson.com.

Peter Roth

To learn more about the Heart River Healing School or to contact Peter Roth, write to: Heart River Center, Inc., 270 Riverside Drive, #1C, New York, NY 10025; call: (212) 222-7748; or visit the school's Web site: www.heartriver.com.

Carl Hewitt and Sidney Schwartz

You can reach Carl Hewitt and Sidney Schwartz at: The Gifts of the Spirit Church, 1595 Route 85, Chesterfield, CT 06370.

The first published book to come out of Sidney's dialogues with AWAN has been completed:

Schwartz, Sidney. *My First Encounter with an Angel: Revelations of Ancient Wisdom*. Medicine Bear Publishing (Blue Hill, ME) 1999.

KAY CORDELL WHITAKER

Books

The Reluctant Shaman: A Woman's First Encounter with the Unseen Spirits of the Earth. HarperSanFrancisco (San Francisco) 1991.

Sacred Link: Joining Forces with the Unknown. Journey Beyond Corporation, 1999.

CDs

Song Magic. Journey Beyond Corporation, 1999.

Dance of the Earth Fire Serpent. (Double CD) Journey Beyond Corporation, 1999.

Power Animal Journey. Journey Beyond Corporation, 1999.

Drumming to Journey By: A Continuous Drumming Atmosphere. Journey Beyond Corporation, 1999.

Private healing sessions, instruction, Bone-Throwings, and long-term apprenticeship are available. For more information about classes or to order Kay's books or CDs, write to: A World in Balance, 7 Avenida Grande #323, Santa Fe, NM 87505-9199; phone: (505) 466-3387; or visit their Web site: www.worldbalance.com.

DENISE LINN

Books

Sacred Space: Clearing and Enhancing the Energy of Your Home. Ballantine Books (New York) 1995.

The Secret Language of Signs: How to Interpret the Coincidences and Symbols in Your Life. Ballantine Books (New York) 1996.

Past Lives, Present Dreams. Ballantine Books (New York) 1997.

The Hidden Power of Dreams. Ballantine Books (New York) 1997.

Quest: Journey to the Center of Your Soul. Ballantine Books (New York) 1998.

Sacred Legacies: Healing the Past, Creating a Positive Future. Ballantine Books (New York) 1999.

Altars: Bringing Sacred Shrines into Everyday Life. Ballantine Books (New York) 1999.

For information about Denise Linn's seminars, video and audiotapes, her feng shui course on Interior Alignment™, or her hand-crafted ceremonial drums, write to: Denise Linn Seminars, P.O. Box 75657, Seattle, WA 98125-0657.

FRED WOODY

Fred Woody performs his healing ceremonies only for members of the Navajo tribe.

GRANDMOTHER CONNIE MIRABAL

To learn more about the "Spiritual Unity of the People" gatherings held in the United States and elsewhere, write to: Grandmother Connie Mirabal, Route 1 Box 117A, Santa Fe, NM 87501; or phone (505) 455-2979.

Among the people Grandmother Connie has adopted is a group called the PeaceWeavers. For more information about the annual Mother Earth Music and Arts Festival or other drug-free and alcohol-free gatherings hosted by the PeaceWeavers, write to: 8125 Crouse Road, Bath, NY 14810; phone: (607) 776-2026; or visit the group's Web site: www.peaceweavers.com.

Grandmother Connie has also given her support to a new non-profit organization, the Wisdom of the Grandmothers Foundation. For more information about the foundation, whose vision is "to heal the wounds and scars between the races by honoring one another's spirituality, traditions, and beauty while honoring the uniqueness of all cultures," write to: Neel and Nan Morton, P.O. Box 2247, Wimberley, TX 78676; phone: (512) 847-8914; or e-mail: wisdom@mmarch.com.

RON ROTH

Books

The Healing Path of Prayer. Three Rivers Press (New York) 1997.

Prayer and the Five Stages of Healing. Hay House, Inc. (Carlsbad, CA) 1999.

Audiotapes and CDs

The Dark Night of the Soul: A Sacred Journey to Joy and Enlightenment. Hay House, Inc. (Carlsbad, CA) 1999. (4-tape set)

Divine Dialogue: How to Heal Your Life with Living Prayer. Nightingale Conant (Niles, IL) 1999. (6-tape set)

Healing Prayers. Hay House, Inc. (Carlsbad, CA) 1999. (CD)

Holy Spirit: The Boundless Energy of God. Hay House, Inc. (Carlsbad, CA) 1998. (2-tape set)

The Lord's Prayer: Teachings on the "Our Father" from the Aramaic. Celebrating Life Resources (Peru, IL) 1995. (3-tape set)

Taking Control of Your Life's Direction: Holistic Spirituality for the 21st Century. Celebrating Life Resources (Peru, IL) 1995.

For information about any of the titles listed above; a full listing of Ron Roth's tapes, monographs, and books; a schedule of his workshops and retreats; information about his intensive training program; and/or how to add names to his prayer list, write to: Celebrating Life Resources, P.O. Box 428, Peru, IL 61354; phone: (815) 224-3377; fax: (815) 224-3395; e-mail: ronroth@the ramp.net; or visit Ron's Web site: www.ronroth.com.

MITCHELL MAY

For additional information about Mitchell May's workshops, his *Healing, Living, and Being* six-tape audio set, and superfood supplements, write to: The Synergy Company™ at HC 64 Box 2901, Castle Valley, UT 84532-9613; phone: (800) 723-0277 or (435) 259-5366; fax: (435) 259-2328; or visit their Web site: www.synergy-co.com.

JONATHAN GOLDMAN

Books

Healing Sounds: The Power of Harmonics. Element (Boston) 1996.

Shifting Frequencies. Light Technology (Sedona, AZ) 1998.

The Lost Chord. Spirit Music (Boulder, CO) 1999.

Audiotapes and CDs

Chakra Chants. Etherean Music.

Dolphin Dreams. Etherean Music.

Gateways: Drumming and Chanting. Etherean Music.

Healing Sounds Instructional Tape. Spirit Music.

Hermetic Harmonics. Spirit Music.

Trance Tara. Etherean Music.

For additional information about Jonathan Goldman's Healing Sounds Seminars, Healing Sound Intensives, Healing Sound Correspondence Course, the Sound Healers Association, or to order books, recordings, or other sonic tools from the Spirit Music catalog, contact Jonathan Goldman or Andi Hilgert at: Spirit Music, P.O. Box 2240, Boulder, CO 80306; phone: (303) 443-8181; fax: (303) 443-6023; e-mail: soundheals@aol.com; or visit Jonathan's Web site: www.healingsounds.com.

MARTY McGEE

Books

Llamas and Alpacas As a Metaphor for Life. Clay Press, Inc. (Herald, CA) 1996.

Llama Handling and Training: The TTEAM Approach with Linda Tellington-Jones, Zephyr Press (Dundee, NY) 1992.

Videos

Alpaca Training and Handling. Videosyncracies and Zephyr Farm, 1998.

Getting Started with TTEAM. Videosyncracies and Zephyr Farm, 1994.

Teaching Your Llama to Pack. Videosyncracies and Marty McGee, 1999.

To purchase Marty's books, videos, or to request a free catalogue, write to: Zephyr Farm, 4251 Pulver Road, Dundee, NY 14837; phone: (800) 570-5262; or e-mail: pzephyr@linkny.com.

For more information about any of Marty's lectures or training programs for llamas and alpacas, her "Doggy Different" workshops, or her "Learning From Llamas" programs for health professionals and teachers, write to Marty McGee

Bennett, 403 Apodaca Hill, Santa Fe, NM 87501; phone: (505) 983-0775 or (800) 883-2670; e-mail: HS@martymcgeebennett.com; or visit Marty's Web site: martymcgeebennett.com.

For more information about Linda Tellington-Jones and TTEAM, including a list of books and videos, write to: TTEAM, P.O. Box 3793, Santa Fe, NM 87501; or phone: (800) 854-8326.

DAYASHAKTI

Books, tapes, and videos about The Wave Work are forthcoming. If you are interested in receiving information when these materials are available, contact The Wave Work Institute for Integration at the address below.

For more information about private sessions or group programs, including Introduction to The Wave Work, The Wave Work Intensive, The Graduate Programs, or The Professional Training and Certification Program, write to: The Wave Work Institute for Integration, P.O. Box 23, Housatonic, MA 01236; phone: (413) 274-1404 or 1 (877) WAVEWORK (877-928-3967); fax: (413) 274-3871; e-mail: Dayashakti@aol.com; or visit their Web site: www.wavework.com.

JASON SHULMAN

Below are descriptions of Jason Shulman's books and recordings. To order any of these materials, or for additional information about Jason Shulman's evening talks, workshop schedule, or three-year training program, write to: A Society of Souls, 17 Witherspoon Court, Morristown, NJ 07960; phone: (973) 538-7689; e-mail: jan@kabbalah.org; or visit A Society of Souls' Web site: www.kabbalah.org.

Books

Finding Eden: Kabbalah, Healing and the Awakened State (Jason Aronson, spring 2001).

The Master of Hiddenness. This practical commentary on the prayer Adon Olam is designed to help readers return to their original connection with God. Contains meditations and exercises.

The Work of Briah [The Set of the World]. These philosophical essays describe the human search for Wholeness and the difficulties of the limited human view. They describe a Kabbalistic approach to the alchemy of being human.

Tefillin Psalms. These psalms/poetry of the Jewish spiritual quest are inspirational and accessible.

CDs

The Great Transparency: Songs to God. Intimate, heartfelt songs, chants and prayers written, arranged, and performed by Jason Shulman. Sung in English. Printed lyrics included.

Audiotapes

Kabbalah, Kavanah & The Awakened State: Making the Creator Sit on His Base. Kavanah, often translated as "intentionally," is really the state of Pure Presence. In this lecture, Jason Shulman describes how kavanah can be used to experience the Awakened State, the state of union with God. Includes meditations and exercises.

Integrated Kabbalistic Healing & the Five Universes: Everybody Has an Opinion. What do doctors, nurses, therapists, and energy workers have in common with Kabbalistic healers? This lecture describes how a Kabbalistic view of the Universe integrates all healing modalities in the search for Wholeness.

Kabbalah & Ecstasy: Omega 1999 Workshop & Concert. This completely new version of the well-known, evolving three-day workshop contains lectures, meditations, exercises, group chanting, and original songs sung by Jason Shulman. Topics include: Kabbalistic prayer, working with imperfection, and the origin and resolution of neurosis.

Kabbalah & Psychotherapy: The Process of Reincarnation into Our Own Lives. An important evening lecture at the Center for Spirituality and Psychotherapy of the National Institute for the Psychotherapies comparing the work of therapy and Integrated Kabbalistic Healing.

Newsletter

The Ray of Connection. Graduates and students of A Society of Souls offer their continually evolving insights and experiences as they incorporate Integrated Kabbalistic Healing into their healing practices.

Peggy Huddleston

Book

Prepare for Surgery, Heal Faster. Angel River Press (Cambridge, MA) 1996.

Audiotapes

Relaxation/Healing Audio Tape. Angel River Press (Cambridge, MA) 1996.

To learn more about Peggy Huddleston's "Prepare for Surgery, Heal Faster" training program for medical professionals, her workshops on connecting with your higher Self, her one-on-one counseling work, or to order the book and audio tape, write to: Angel River Press, Box 40-1038, Cambridge, MA 02140-0009; phone: (617) 497-9431; or fax: (617) 547-6970; or visit Peggy's Web site: www.healfaster.com.

To learn more about the Camp for Young Healers, call the Center for Psychology and Social Change in Cambridge, MA at: (617) 497-1553; e-mail: info@cpschange.org; or visit their Web site: www.cpschange.org.

We Know There Are More Great Healing Stories Out There!

We realize that this collection of interviews and photographs just scratches the surface. If you have a story about your own journey toward wholeness that you would like to share, or a healer you have worked with whom you would like to recommend, write to us!

Tracking Spirit© is a quarterly newsletter that will introduce new healers and share readers' stories of extraordinary physical, emotional, and spiritual healings. Its mission is to expand awareness of the amazing possibilities for health and holiness available to us all.

To submit a story or inquire about subscription rates, write to:

Tracking Spirit

P.O. Box 191

Bowdoinham, ME 04008

RELATED BOOKS BY THE CROSSING PRESS

All Women Are Healers: A Comprehensive Guide to Natural Healing

By Diane Stein

Stein's bestselling book on natural healing for women teaches women to take control of their bodies and lives and offers a wealth of information on various healing methods including Reiki, Reflexology, Polarity Balancing, and Homeopathy.

$14.95 • Paper • ISBN 0-89594-409-X

All Women Are Psychics

By Diane Stein

Women's intuition is no myth; women really are psychic. But your inborn psychic sense was probably suppressed when you were very young. This inspiring book will help you rediscover and reclaim your dormant psychic aptitude.

$16.95 • Paper • ISBN 0-89594-979-2

Essential Reiki: A Complete Guide to an Ancient Healing Art

By Diane Stein

This bestseller includes the history of Reiki, hand positions, giving treatments, and the initiations. While no book can replace directly received attunements, Essential Reiki provides everything else that the practitioner and teacher of this system needs, including all three degrees of Reiki, most of it in print for the first time.

$18.95 • Paper • ISBN 0-89594-736-6

The Healing Energy of Your Hands

By Michael Bradford

Bradford offers techniques so simple that anyone can work with healing energy quickly and easily.

$12.95 • Paper • ISBN 0-89594-781-1

Healing with Gemstones and Crystals

By Diane Stein

More than 200 gemstones and their healing properties are listed. Details on how to choose and use the Earth's precious gems are supplemented by explanations of the significance of this type of healing.

$14.95 • Paper • ISBN 0-89594-831-1

Healing with the Energy of the Chakras

By Ambika Wauters

Chakras are swirling wheels of light and color—vortices through which energy must pass in order to nourish and maintain physical, emotional, mental and spiritual life. Wauters presents a self-help program intended to give you guidelines and a framework within which to explore and understand more about how your energetic system responds to thoughts and expression.

$14.95 • Paper • ISBN 0-89594-906-7

LifeChanges with the Energy of the Chakras

By Ambika Wauters

When we face up to the reality of change, we learn to accept its challenges with grace and renewed grit. We can alter our old movies-our old patterns-and gain insights into our nature. We then can be released from the past and find new, healthy options for our lives.

$14.95 • Paper • ISBN 1-58091-020-3

Prophetic Visions of the Future

By Diane Stein

We all want to know what will happen to the earth and to those who come after us, our children and our grandchildren. Diane, seeking an answer, has gone to women visionaries and seers: women who channel the future and those who bring it to life in their writings: Sally Miller Gearhart, Sheri Tepper, and Marge Piercy.

$16.95 • Paper • ISBN 1-58091-046-7

We are the Angels:
Healing Your Past, Present, and Future with the Lords of Karma

By Diane Stein

Stein masterfully presents a detailed understanding of karma and the process of healing karmic patterns. She introduces the Lords of Karma, the supreme karmic record keepers able to grant requests for changed or released karma to those who ask for it.

$16.95 • Paper • ISBN 0-89594-878-8

A Woman's I Ching

By Diane Stein

A feminist interpretation of the popular ancient text for diving the character of events. Stein's version reclaims the feminine, or yin, content of the ancient work and removes all oppressive language and imagery.

$16.95 • Paper • ISBN 0-89594-857-5

To receive a current catalog from The Crossing Press
please call toll-free, 800-777-1048.
Visit our Web site: www. crossingpress.com

Welcome to Crossing Village

Home of the Crossing Press

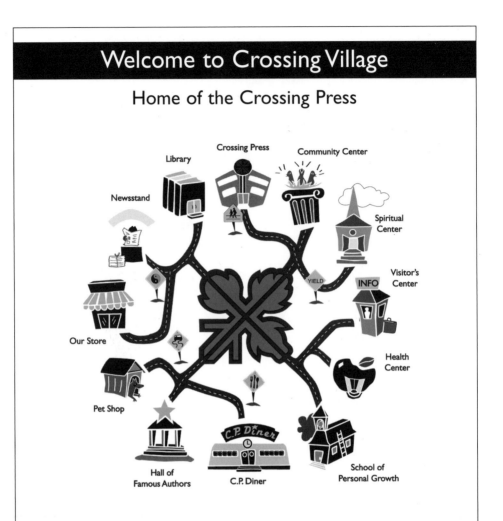

Visit the new and improved Crossing Press Web site for information you can't find anywhere else—interactive author chats, author calendars, reviews, special promotions, press kit materials, and our brand new store!

www.crossingpress.com